JWK

If You Don't Mind

ESSAYS ON MAN AND NATURE

JOSEPH WOOD

WILLIAM SLOANE ASSOCIATES

My Saying So . . .

KRUTCH

Foreword by JOHN K. HUTCHENS

NEW YORK   1964

To Marcelle

Contents

II

WRITERS AND WRITING

III

THEATER

IV

THE WORLD WE DIDN'T MAKE

By the same author

MORE LIVES THAN ONE

THE FORGOTTEN PENINSULA

HUMAN NATURE AND THE HUMAN CONDITION

GRAND CANYON

THE GREAT CHAIN OF LIFE

THE VOICE OF THE DESERT

MEASURE OF MAN

THE DESERT YEAR

MODERNISM IN MODERN DRAMA:
A Definition and an Estimate

THE BEST OF TWO WORLDS

THE TWELVE SEASONS

HENRY DAVID THOREAU

SAMUEL JOHNSON

AMERICAN DRAMA SINCE 1918:
An Informal History

WAS EUROPE A SUCCESS?

EXPERIENCE AND ART:
Some Aspects of the Esthetics of Literature

FIVE MASTERS:
A Study in the Mutation of the Novel

MODERN TEMPER:
A Study and a Confession

EDGAR ALLAN POE:
A Study in Genius

Foreword

Somewhere in the pages that follow, Joseph Wood Krutch speaks of himself—but without waving a battle flag, because that is not the Krutch style—as an "unregenerate humanist." That is to say, in this age which bows contentedly to the authority of science and the generally apathetic conformism of our society, a rebel. He would, I must imagine (for I never have met him except through the printed word), gently reject the label of rebel. What, he might quietly ask, is so very rebel-like about going one's own way, disdaining or rather disregarding fashionable factionalism, saying what one thinks, and reserving the right now and then to change one's mind? What else is a civilized man, the inheritor of a great humanist tradition, expected to do?

That a number of presumably civilized men in Mr. Krutch's lifetime have taken a quite different road, although the same great tradition was theirs for the following, only says the more about him. It chiefly says, I believe, that he has always had the strong if reticent self-assurance of one who is good both in mind and in heart but wastes no time in thinking about it. For one thing, apart from his innate modesty, he has had too many other things to think about.

No one could really doubt this who accompanied him through his spiritually and intellectually adventurous autobiography, published in 1962 and aptly entitled *More Lives Than One*—the Tennessee-born youngster who first envisaged himself as a mathematician, discovered at the University of Tennessee that literature was more important to him (indeed, all-important), and so, upon completing his graduate study at Columbia University, was on his way to joining those ready to take a vibrant part in the American cultural renascence of the 1920's. His own role in it was to be that of a literary and drama critic of the first order. Yet even then, while he was regularly on Broadway, he was not strictly of it, absorbing and exciting though it was, nor of the bustling literary market place of that (as it now seems) fruitful, golden day. He simply had too much else to do. Variously, then and in later years, he was surveying his own era with a rather dark pessimism in *The Modern Temper;* as Brander Matthews Professor of Dramatic Literature at Columbia he was concerned with stages far from Times Square; as biographer he was dwelling with Henry Thoreau in Concord and with Samuel Johnson in London. And then, at an age when most of his contemporaries would be willing to call it a day, he was entering upon yet another adventure, this time as a self-described amateur naturalist in the Arizona desert. Yes, most certainly there have been more lives than one in that of Joseph Wood Krutch.

Happily, there is something of each of them in this collection of sixty-odd essays, reflections, and conversational pieces which in sum are one man's credo, a sampling of what has held his interest in his seventy-one years. The range of that interest is amazing, from the genius of George Bernard Shaw to the stages in the life of the monarch butterfly, from a philosophical consideration of honor (as truthtelling) and morality (as expediency) to a sly demolition operation on the euphemisms by which we avert our gaze from reality.

But most inspiriting of all, as this incessantly curious mind reveals itself here, is the unpredictability of the uncommitted individualist, who is increasingly rare in our culture. Like one of his heroes, Dr. Johnson, he will have no part of cant; see his observations, in No. 6 of the selections from his "If You Don't Mind My Saying So . . ." department in *The American Scholar*, on the fallacy of pacifism and the adjuration to turn the other cheek. He is the idealist who nevertheless is chary of panaceas and utopianism, aware as he is that the Old Adam is ineradicable in human nature; see his "Confessions of a Demi-Bourgeois." He is the naturalist, with the scientific bent that even a non-professionally trained naturalist must have, who ridicules the claims of sociology and the behavioral sciences to measure the unmeasurable; see his "Through Happiness With Slide Rule and Caliper" and "Challenge to an Unknown Writer." He is the good citizen who does not recognize the notion that one must devote all of one's time and energy to public concerns; see his "Whom Do We Picket Tonight?"

With characteristic indifference to passing fashions in art and politics, and to the ups-and-downs of certain writers' and artists' reputations, he flatly declares that H. L. Mencken's prose was "the best . . . written in America in the twentieth century," defends Eugene O'Neill against those fussy latter-day detractors who miss the large essence of him, attacks the cocksureness of orthodox Darwinians, and at the risk of being called a sentimentalist, discerns in the animal kingdom aspects of joy, humor, and love denied by chilly specialists.

But is this not all by way of saying that here, in our age of automation, group thinking, and other manifestations of mass production, is a throwback to the old-fashioned individualist who spoke his mind as a matter of course and without looking over his shoulder in fear of disagreement? It is not by chance that Joseph Wood Krutch loves Johnson for his common sense and Thoreau for his unyielding, fierce integrity. We are luckier than one can say, just offhand, to have had him among us down the years and to have him still.

John K. Hutchens

I
MANNERS AND MORALS

If you don't mind my saying so . . . [I]

[1955]

Ours, so they say, is a world ready at last to "face the facts." Actually this has been the Age of Euphemism much longer than it has been the Age of Anxiety, and the softeners are still at work. Even in my childhood "graveyard" had already become "cemetery" and now cemetery has given way to "memorial park," because any euphemism ceases to be euphemistic after a time and the true meaning begins to show through. It's a losing game, but we keep on trying.

Highbrow prejudice notwithstanding, the Latins also have long played the game. What we call a "brassiere" (literally "shoulder strap") the French call *soutien-gorge* or "neck supporter." Then, having used up that innocent anatomical feature with French illogicality, they were compelled to call a neck cover a *cache-nez* or "nose hider." And haven't they, as well as we, tried to fall back upon foreign words only to discover that they don't remain obscure very long: as in the case of the once so elegant "water closet," which now sounds a bit crude even to them? Since we reciprocated by calling the same necessary piece of plumbing by their name for a lady's costume, it is not surprising that a departing French diplomat is said to have astounded reporters by telling them that the thing which had impressed him most in the United States was the ladies' toilets.

So far as I can see, we Anglo-Saxons have reversed the trend only in connection with the sexually significant features of anatomy. We were pretty proud of ourselves for getting back to "legs," and a little later we were equally proud of discarding "bosom" for "breast." If "rooster" still comes more naturally to most Americans than "cock," that is only because they are not sufficiently aware of the euphemism to get any kick out of changing back. But though we face the facts of sex we are more reluctant than ever to face the fact of death or the crueler facts of life, either biological or social. We feel that the poor will be happier if we refer to them as "people in the lower income brackets," and there are many worse examples.

Only this morning I read in a Tucson newspaper the headline: "Special Classes for Exceptional Children." "That," I said to myself, "is an encouraging development," and I had read well into the article before I realized that "exceptional" meant "exceptionally dumb." Or, if my phrase sounds too brutal, then "retarded," though that term was itself once a euphemism, since it suggests, contrary to fact, that the retarded usually catch up in time.

Most of these euphemisms, I will be told, are not prudish but merely kindly. And so they are. In all seriousness I believe that Americans are the kindliest people who ever lived. I believe, moreover, that they show their kindliness in many important ways. But I am compelled to add that sometimes we just don't seem to have much sense. Out of pure kindness of heart we butter our horses' hay. A story used to be told (in the days before dialect stories were frowned upon as transmitters of "offensive stereotypes") about a Negro youth who reads on a gravestone the legend: "I am not dead but sleeping." "Boy," he said to himself, "he ain't foolin' nobody but hisself." Whom, I wonder, are "memorial park" and "exceptional child" supposed to fool?

"The Rock of Ages" used to suggest God. Now a nationally

known manufacturer (vile phrase) uses it as the brand name for a highly touted tombstone, although the aged couple which is often shown contemplating it with something very like longing is never allowed to more than hint at what it is. There are a lot of delicate phrases about "eternal granite" and "not being forgotten," but no one comes right out and says what the huge block of polished stone is for. And here, as usual, commercial enterprise exploits squeamishness for profit. "Ye who went through life banishing B.O. and tattle-tale gray! Ye who showed off your furnaces, your linoleum, and your water closet bowl to envious neighbors! Ye who are numbered among the one out of five who shave every day and who demand the best! You wouldn't want to be buried under any old tombstone, would you? Go at last to some dignified funeral home. Let some well-known mortician superintend your last journey to a Memorial Park and rest under a Rock of Ages. Only one out of ten can afford it. Well may that one exclaim, 'O death! where is thy sting?' "

The present discourse started out to be a cheerful, inoffensive little piece. It is growing lugubrious; but we might as well risk going the whole way. Have you visited your undertaker recently? If you have not you would probably be surprised at how his vocabulary continues to grow and how dreadfully he oozes euphemisms. Also, at how much you can be expected to pay for all this delicacy. Middle-class establishments now keep in stock "caskets" (and what is a casket except a coffin ashamed to give its real name?) of a sort only gangsters used to fall for and which are priced as high as eight thousand dollars. For a mere ten or twelve hundred dollars you can get a wooden one elaborately fussed up with padded satin, and if you peep at the blue ribbon pinned on it you may read the legend: "Styled in Sun Valley"—presumably the ski resort. Meet Mr. Aloysius Throttlebottom, America's best loved casket styler. For a consideration he would probably whip up an original for you.

And don't think you can beat the racket by being cremated. Since cremation became respectable it has also become elaborate and expensive. In many states the undertakers' lobby has seen to it that you have to have a "casket" to be burned in. At the same middle-class establishment where the Sun Valley creations were exhibited you could get a flimsy box of kindling wood for as little as a hundred and fifty dollars, but it is not much to look at; and if you want to avoid the sneers of the mortician you cannot get off with less than six hundred. And do you know what the residuum to be put in a brass "urn" is now called? "The cremains." Dust to dust, ashes to ashes, and the cremains to a memorial park. All this is supposed to maintain the dignity of death. Or is it the dignity of undertakers? Nowadays we are not brave but vulgar in the infamy of our nature.

A few days ago I brought up the subject with my doctor. He smiled grimly and said that he had recently told an undertaker to go to hell when the latter had protested to him: "Your father was a man of some dignity in this community. It does not become you to haggle over the price of his casket." But the doctor was not very encouraging when I asked him what instructions I might leave to prevent the playing of any of these farces with my mortal remains. I was lucky, he said, to live in Arizona rather than California. Here the cremains may still be buried in your back yard. In California they have to be consigned to a memorial park. So far as he knew, the only people in Tucson exempt from the necessity of submitting to various indignities are the poor Papago Indians on the reservation near by. They can get a special license to bury their own dead if they do it quickly enough. I am thinking about applying for adoption into the tribe.

Logan Pearsall Smith once remarked that neither religion nor philosophy had ever made it easier for him to face the inevitability of death. The only thing which had ever done so was the splendor of the words which great writers have found when they discuss it. Though he had no hope, it was some compensation to share in a greatness. But if the morticians have their way, that consolation is not likely to be provided again. Gray could hardly have composed an "Elegy Wrote in a Memorial Park." Neither could Cleopatra have said, "The bright day is done and we are for the Funeral Home."

I am more ready to admit than I used to be that Rabbi Ben Ezra may have been half right. Still, aging does bring its own annoyances, and I have met one of them just now. Those of us who have to admit that old age is breathing down the backs of our necks can no longer mention death without self-con-sciousness. Even to talk about joining the Papagos makes me wonder if I am getting morbid. *A fortiori* I can't feel sorry about a friend who dies without asking myself if it is really he that I am sorry for. "What really troubles you," so I say to myself, "is the realization that it is for you the bell tolls." I can't even congratulate myself on my seeming good health without remembering that among all the famous last words none is better known than "I never felt better in my life."

So far I purge no amber gum and my hams are not too noticeably weaker. It is only these intimations of mortality that get me down. Not even looking into the mirror makes me *feel* old. And for the first time I recognize fully the signif-icance of a familiar observation: One's contemporaries don't seem older though the young seem younger. Forty looks thirty, thirty looks twenty, and I would hate to tell what twenty looks like. But the young are not fooled. They are struck dumb with astonishment when some fatuous elder happens to re-mark that he "feels young." "How," they ask themselves, "can he?" In another twenty or thirty years they will know. I only hope they will regret then that they called me "Sir" so con-temptuously.

Statisticians keep telling us that there are going to be more and more old gaffers and dames hanging loose on society.

Bright young "counselors" are talking more and more about how to keep us amused and "adjusted." "Gerontic" has become a fashionable word because it is a little less harsh than "senile," because, in fact, the analogy between it and "exceptional child" is uncomfortably close. But it is also, if anything, more lofty and condescending. Moreover, those who are planning our future seem to have especially in mind those of us who are able to find shuffleboard and bingo quite enough to live for. Perhaps that really does take care of the greater number. But not quite all. Shouldn't there be a textbook which might be called *Gerontology for the Intellectual?*

I don't mean merely a collection of platitudes about keeping up one's intellectual interests and sharing the problems of the young. I mean one which would, for example, discuss what kind of intellectual interests the aged really can keep up with and what attitudes, dubious perhaps in youth, are quite permissible to them.

Naturally I wouldn't have brought this subject up if I hadn't thought I had a contribution to make—and I have. Don't, say I, fight too hard against the growing conservatism which seems to come naturally. It's perfectly all right for the aged to believe in the good old days—social, moral, and artistic. Don't think it is smart to say that youth is always right. In the first place, youth isn't always right; and in the second place, it puts you in an awful hole to say so, especially since the young are so sure of it anyway. An occasional suspicion that somebody else may know better is very wholesome for them.

Don't try to assure anybody, not even yourself, that you are keeping up with the latest intellectual fashions and that you share the contempt of present-day youth for the gods of your own younger days. You ain't fooling nobody but yourself. The old fellow who tries too desperately to keep in the intellectual swim is almost as ridiculous as the one who tries to learn the latest steps, and is hardly more out of place in a night club than he is at an avant-garde concert. Our fathers waltzed while we did the fox trot. There is every reason why we should fox-trot while the young dance the mambo—or whatever has come along since.

So far as I am concerned I admit freely that I have less patience than I used to have with *Sturm und Drang,* with apocalyptic visions and descents into hell. Flowers of evil are less attractive, and the fact that a new book is described as "devastating" no longer makes me sure that I want to read it. I make no bones over the fact that I like Dickens better than Sartre, or *The Marriage of Figaro* better than *Wozzeck.* Melancholy, sickness, and despair have long been recognized as congenial to youth. It is cheered by such adjectives as "uncompromising," "grim," "revolutionary," "tortured," "decadent," and "decayed." Youth can stand it. Physically and spiritually. But the old need cheerfulness and health and hope. Even, perhaps, common sense. Without these, they are nothing. It may be, even, that they should admire the virtues.

When the truism begins to seem more important than the paradox we are getting old, which to the young means also fatuous and feeble. Perhaps if we were young our present convictions would be. Truisms are harder to understand and understanding them takes time. Perhaps the platitude really is false until it has been rediscovered. And perhaps when we return to it, it is not because we are senile but merely because we really have rediscovered it. A merely brilliant old man is a sad spectacle. Even the preternaturally young G.B.S. showed at last signs of becoming one. Some of his last attempts to be shocking were merely foolish. And they made one of his long-time admirers wish that he would say a few obviously true things before he died. Most of us can't help changing our opinions as we get older. Who knows? Sometimes we may even be righter than we were before.

Apropos of nothing, let me take advantage of a few remaining lines to pass on for the benefit of all husbands, young or gerontic, a remark made recently by a middle-aged individual. His wife had just returned from one of those forays across the border highly popular with Southwestern wives who return loaded down with Mexican knickknacks. This husband was looking sadly at his spouse's haul spread over all the tables and chairs of the living room. "It's amazing," he said, "the things women would rather have than money."

We need more than more facts

[1954]

Nearly everybody says nowadays that "what we need is more facts." Since I happen to be an essayist by habit, I have private reasons for doubting this statement and I admit them to begin with. An essayist deals with personal experiences, opinions, tastes, notions, and prejudices. For him, a fact is at best a peg to hang something on. But I don't believe that my doubts are purely professional. There are a lot of things we need more than we need still more facts.

Goodness only knows we have a lot of them already about a lot of different subjects—scientific, sociological, and especially statistical. No age before ours had one-tenth so many, or thought it did. People in other days frequently had firmer convictions but, by our standards, they were absurdly short on facts. They didn't know how much stress a two-by-four would stand or what is the relative frequency of color blindness among men and women. They didn't know to a decimal point the prevalence of illiteracy in every subdivision of every nation or just how many peanuts are produced in South Carolina.

Almost any popular article in a current magazine—about pearl fishing in Florida or the rise of juvenile delinquency in Detroit—gives more factual information on its subject than could have been given a century and a half ago about any subject whatsoever. And we love this kind of information. Even the semi-literate public dotes on facts—the batting averages of ball players, the number of TV sets sold last Christmas, how many movie theaters have closed their doors since the war. It may not remember any of them except the batting averages, but it loves the sense of having had "the facts" laid before it.

The theory is, of course, that once "the facts are all in" there will be no more room for difference of opinion and all men will agree on what ought to be done. So, over a limited field, it does work out. We do not come to blows over the question of how big the steel girders in a bridge ought to be. But does it work out that way in matters political, economic, social, or moral? Does the capitalist have any facts not available to the socialist? Does the proponent of birth control have any factual information denied to its opponents? Do the avowed Communist leaders sent to jail know any less about Russia than Senator McCarthy does? Would any of them change his opinion if a new super-factual study were published tomorrow? Facts are decisive when the question is one of means. They are not when ends are involved.

In most of the fields where facts are sufficient, we have been getting on very well. We know just how to build bridges, make aircraft fly faster, and make bombs more destructive. But we don't agree at all on the question of just who, if anybody, ought to be blown up by them. More facts are not going to settle that or any other "ought" question. And it seems to be the ought questions which are causing a great deal of the trouble. Unless we agree upon some of them pretty soon, there may not be much left to argue over or, for that matter, many people to argue. Even a wrong answer, if only there were general agreement upon it, might have less catastrophic results than violent disagreement.

Unfortunately, there is no simple term which will define what it is that we need more than we need "more facts." It isn't, indeed, one thing. But "wisdom," "conviction," "standards," even "general ideas," are all terms which suggest some part of it. So, of course, does "good will." At least they all indicate things for the lack of which we cannot agree where agreement is most vital. And the disagreements will continue to exist no matter how many new facts are made available.

Ignorance of "the facts" would certainly not remedy the situation. Probably nothing will ever dispose completely of the problem. But it cannot even be lived with successfully as long as we put our faith in "more facts" when they are not going to help. We might even do well to stop looking for them if that would release energy to be expended in examining those convictions, those standards, and those general ideas which more facts are not going to change.

What does change them is thinking rather than fact-finding, discussion about general principles rather than about "the facts," and, in the end, Moral Discourse. When men come to an agreement about what ought to be done, it is usually because some have been persuaded, not because they have been given new facts. And it is the use, the respectability even, of persuasion in which a fact-worshiping age has lost all faith.

Yet even a familiar essay may sometimes persuade.

Value judgments cannot be based on facts alone—and that's a fact

[1954]

Some of my friends—not to mention my enemies—have taken me to task for what I wrote in these pages a few weeks ago. They still think that "more facts" are what we need most, and that, if we only had and acknowledged them, we could answer at least all the questions concerning public policy, which are the only ones it is really necessary to answer. Bear with me for one more page, and I'll promise never to mention the subject again.

Let's take a specific public question which, in its implications, is not as minor as it looks—the proposal to build a storage dam in Colorado which would flood the Dinosaur National Monument. Quite a storm has raged around it. Not only certain private interests but, in general, all the enthusiasts for reclamation, public works, and so on are all for it. Quite as inevitably, most conservationists, believers in the importance of preserving some wild areas, students of natural history, etc. are bitterly against it. Congress didn't get around to a vote at the session just past, but the issue is pretty certain to be raised again.

"Fine," say the positivists. "Let's use the time to get the facts; once the facts are all in, no two reasonable men will disagree. How much does the Southwest need that project? Is there any other area equally suitable? Will the usefulness of the National Monument be destroyed? Answer these questions and a few more, and the problem has been solved."

Actually, answers to all of them have already been given—

at least to the satisfaction of the givers. You can find "the facts" in the two reports issued by the House and Senate. Of course, there is, and probably always will be, some disagreement as to what "the facts" really are. But that is not the point. Let us suppose for the sake of our argument that, insofar as ascertainable facts go, there is no dispute. Let's assume that the answers are (1) that the dam would be genuinely useful, (2) that there is no other site quite so good, and (3) that the character of the Monument will be changed from that of a moderately inaccessible wilderness into an easily accessible parklike area threaded by broad highways through which a much-increased number of visitors will zip along. And "fact" Number 3 is, by the way, pretty generally admitted on both sides.

Yet, even on the assumption that all three answers are accepted, does that mean that all will agree that the dam should or should not be built? Not at all. Does it mean, then, that one side or the other is irrational, unscientific or unwilling to "let the facts decide"? Again, not at all. The real issue does not involve facts but certain value judgments which mere facts cannot support or demolish. Among the most important of the real questions are these: How important is it that some sections of the great wilderness which all of America once was should be preserved? Does the existence of such areas contribute something important to the spiritual health of the comparatively few who visit—or, indeed, read about—these remaining wildernesses? Since there are already many parks admirably suited to zipping through, is it less desirable that one more should be added to their number than it is that one of the few remaining wildernesses should be preserved for the benefit of those who will take the trouble to get to them? These are not questions which any ascertainable facts can answer. They are, as is said, "matters of opinion"; or, as for the sake of clarity it ought to be said, "matters involving value judgments which facts cannot establish."

Even that old stand-by criterion, "The greatest good of the greatest number," here reveals itself as the fraud it so often is. If it were simply "the good of the greatest number," why, then, "the greatest number" might be measured. But "the *greatest* good" introduces an unmeasurable factor. How do you decide which good is greater than which other, or how many people have to benefit from a lesser good to make it preferable to a greater good for a smaller number?

That value judgments are important but not to be established on the basis of facts is itself a fact. A pity, perhaps, but a fact nevertheless. And, as such, it is also one not to be overlooked when "facing facts" is urged upon us. We don't face facts as often as we think we do. What we usually do when we find one is just run away and look for another, which is, perhaps, just one more form of "escape"—in this case, escape from the duty of doing something much more difficult than finding a fact.

Confessions of a Demi-Bourgeois

[1951]

For thirty years I have contributed to a leftish magazine, but I am still, so some people tell me, only a bourgeois at heart. Never, so they say, have I got beyond a muddled amiability and never have I understood the aims, the aspirations, or the values of those who look forward to a radically new society. I can't, for instance, get it into my head that the politically enlightened worker doesn't give a hang about Freedom or Culture as I define them, and I worry about the possible loss of this or that thing dear to the bourgeois heart when I ought to be saying "Good riddance." It is true, of course, that quite a number of those who used to reproach me in such terms as these have now moved so far to the right that I understand what they say today even less than I understood what they were saying yesterday. But the reproach continues from younger men with newer enthusiasms.

Sometimes I wonder if perhaps they are right. The prospect of a clean sweep of everything which the past twenty-five hundred years has thought good and desirable still fills me with horror. I don't believe that the *only* trouble with the poor is poverty; or even that all the evil in the world is rooted in economic injustice. I don't believe that the dignity of man is somehow enhanced by the doctrine that he is never anything but a "product of forces"; or even that concern for the common man means that mediocrity is, in itself, better than excellence. I do believe that if the time should ever come when the vast majority of men are able to live a good life, that life would be good by standards most of which are older than even the beginnings of the democratic movement. And if all that is bourgeois idealism, then bourgeois is what I certainly am.

Moreover, if it is thus that I seem to most of the more thoroughgoing radicals of my acquaintance, they, so it seems to me, are willing to settle for far too little, for something a good deal less desirable than what the few once had. They will accept indoctrination instead of education, propaganda instead of art, slogans instead of thinking, and conditioning instead of culture—if only you will assure them that everybody will get it. And they do not improve the situation when they insist that the second-rate substitutes are the only realities anyway.

In America nearly everybody goes to school and nearly everybody goes to the movies. A very impressive number also own radios and television sets. If that really meant that the people were educated and that the world of art was accessible to them, then the Chambers of Commerce would have a watertight case: ours would be the best civilization that ever existed and Utopia would be clearly in sight. The swindle is, to be sure, less obvious and gross than it is in the Communist "democracies," but it is a swindle nevertheless and a swindle for which most of the yet untried blueprints also seem to provide abundant opportunity. It is that fact which generates the skepticism at the head of the list of my bourgeois traits.

Never, I think, will I be able to join wholeheartedly the proponents of any program or panacea until they promise something really good enough and also demonstrate in advance an adequate awareness of the pitfalls into which they run the risk of falling. In Communism I never for a moment believed even during those days of the early thirties when most of the most cautious intellectuals went at least so far as to call it "an interesting experiment." Of specific proposals by the socialists I have often approved, but I have never called myself a socialist, never been one in socialism's own terms, because even Fabians (see Pearson's *G.B.S. A Postscript*, pp. 81-82, for example) always seemed to me dangerously uncritical of their doctrines and ready to accept as articles of faith propositions which I thought dubious at best.

Competition—so far as it affects my private life—I have always found so unpleasant a thing that I never enjoyed even competitive games. Great wealth, even the luxury of the very well-to-do, makes me uncomfortable when I am invited to share it. Disinterestedness, the desire to do something for its own sake, has always seemed to me one of the most admirable of human traits. And yet no scheme for the establishment of a noncompetitive society, in which no one could get rich and all men should do what ought to be done for the sheer love of doing it, has ever seemed to me to take proper account of the fact that evil is a protean artist terribly clever at discovering new roles to play when it has been deprived of an old one.

When men cannot compete for wealth they compete for

position, for authority, for influence in the right places. When they cannot own a palace, four automobiles, and ten servants, they manage to get themselves appointed to jobs in connection with which these things are assigned them. More dreadfully still, when these same men find themselves no longer required to pay the common man to do their work for them, they quickly discover that when the profit motive has been abolished the fear motive affords a very handy substitute. Instead of saying, "Do this and you will get a raise," they say, "Do this or you will go to jail," and thus he who was once a wage-slave now finds himself a slave indeed.

Part of the reason why such things can happen is simple enough. Because in an industrial society wealth is the instrument by means of which power is most easily exercised, it is an understandable, if naïve, mistake to confuse the instrument of evil with the evil itself and to forget that it can assume even more naked forms. But can power itself be abolished and, if not, can it ever be anything other than more or less corrupt? Is there, in the world, enough disinterested virtue to do the necessary work of the world, or must we still, for a long time and perhaps forever, have either to bribe with promises of gain or threaten with promises of punishment if men are to do the things which must be done?

In America today, there are a certain number of public servants who forgo the opportunity of making large sums in order to perform important tasks for small pay. My cynicism stops short of believing that in all such cases secret ambition or love of display is the real motive. But how many such men are there, and is such virtue common enough to do all the world's work for it? It is common enough, I think, to run the TVA and the Atomic Energy Commission. But are there enough such men to staff also even the executive offices of the steel mills and the automobile factories? I am not unfamiliar with the contention that in a noncompetitive society their number would multiply in a healthy atmosphere. That is an attractive hypothesis and it does credit to those who hold it. But does anyone know whether it is true or not? The state, so the Communists used to tell me, would wither away, but it does not seem to be withering very fast.

In the end, I suppose, it all comes down to the question whether or not man really is merely the product of his social institutions; whether, if you want to put it this way, the capitalist system as it exists in practice created greedy men, or whether men created that system because they were greedy. And I am afraid it is because the second assumption seems to me as true as the first that I have my doubts about the success of any scheme which depends upon the virtue to be created when the scheme is put into effect. Man is perhaps perfectible, but original sin is at least as self-evident as perfectibility.

Wells and Shaw, the two most influential English Utopians of the twentieth century, ended with precisely the same conclusion put into almost the same words. The first had begun by believing that technology would solve all problems and the second by believing that the abolition of poverty would do the same. Each, before he died, announced his conclusion that the trouble was far more fundamental: Man, each said, is not good enough to create Utopia—quite possibly not good enough even to survive much longer.

To make him better is not going to be easy. Perhaps education will do it and perhaps education has already, in the course of two thousand years, done something. But it will have to be real education, something perhaps even better than the best of the past, not the cheap and easy, jerry-built substitutes for it upon which not merely the totalitarians but even the mildest of American liberals seem content to depend. It will have to be something better than melodramatic movies about race prejudice, radio dramatizations of current problems, and lessons in economics presented in comic-book form. Nobody knows exactly what ought to be handed down to the people and, even if anybody did, the handing down would not be enough. If the best men are not good enough, the average man is certainly not going to be made so by bringing everything down to the average man's level. It is a good deal harder, of course, to bring him up. But it is the only thing worth doing.

"Whom do we picket tonight?"

[1950]

I do not know who first said that "Being a good citizen is a full-time job." In any event it is a current cliché and a rather staggering one at that. Very few, I suppose, ever live up to a literal interpretation of it but many seem to agree that everyone should. Moreover, it is a matter of sober fact that argument, speculation, and chitchat about social or political matters has pretty well monopolized what is called our leisure time. An overwhelmingly large proportion of contemporary books, magazine articles, novels, plays, lectures, and social conversations are concerned with such matters. So is nearly every "serious" movie or radio program. Indeed it has been almost forgotten that one can be serious on any other subject.

To object to citizenship as "a full-time job" on the ground that one has private business of one's own is not quite the thing. Dr. Samuel Johnson, it is true, once protested that "a man has a right to some time of his own" and Thoreau asked scornfully whether God had "sent him into the world without any pocket money." But Johnson and Thoreau were eccentrics and they died a long time ago. It is also true that Mozart wrote *Don Giovanni* just as the French Revolution was about to break and that Jane Austen published *Pride and Prejudice* the year before Waterloo. But no doubt both might have been better employed and the world have had more cause to remember them if they had considered the political responsibilities of their age a full-time job.

I am aware that our time is an extraordinarily difficult one; that the right to participate in the solution of public problems is one of the privileges won by the democratic revolution; and that an enlightened electorate is a *sine qua non* for success in our kind of government. But just where does the thing stop? A good deal has been said about the rising costs of government, about how much of the citizen's money that government spends. But how heavy a tax can it put upon his time—upon his very life, that is—without becoming an intolerable tyranny?

The machine was supposed to free us from the necessity of spending all our life making a living. It was said to be producing leisure for the cultivation of the arts, the sciences, and the philosophies. But if the end result is going to be a world in which everyone is as busy with the duties of citizenship as he used to be with the chores, the gain is not as obvious as it might be. Never before were political, economic, and social questions the nearly exclusive topic of even after-dinner conversation among cultivated people, and what one hears from them is as essentially the shop-talk of the citizen as talk about crops is shop-talk for the farmer and talk about the stock market is shop-talk for brokers. Moreover, most really responsible people find little time for even shop-talk of this sociable sort. If they are not attending meetings or dinners in favor of or against something or other, they are at least doing their part at the parent-teachers association— for being a parent is a second full-time job.

All this would not be so profoundly dispiriting to some of

us if it were recognized as a phenomenon of a world in crisis and obviously an evil in itself. We would still mutter an occasional, "Oh cursed spite, that ever *I* was born to set it right"; would still wish, now and then, that we had been born in some more peaceful time. But we would try to console ourselves with the conviction that things can't go on this way much longer. Either the world will have to settle down or go to pieces with a definite bang. But most of the liberal "blueprints" seem to assume that in Utopia the passion for political activity will be even greater and even more nearly universal than it is now. The very seers who pay at least lip disservice to "regimentation" and other evils, real or supposed, of the new world never seem to consider the cost of government measured in terms of its demand upon a citizen's time and cost at all.

In this respect the Communists have at least one small point in their favor. Often forgotten but officially a part of their dogma is the assurance that in some remote by-and-by when the state has withered away government will look after itself. But your liberal makes no such promise. The better the state of the world, the more ardently everyone will be kept busy, not only keeping it good, but improving it still further.

> As though society were intended
> For nothing else but to be mended.

Already it is getting so that even the most active attender of meetings and signer of protests is beginning to seem a bit Laodicean, and pretty soon anyone who does not want to be called slacker will set aside at least one evening a week for the picket line. Time was when this method of protest was pretty largely confined to the disputes of a trade union with an employer, but anyone can get in on it now; and the process of walking round and round with a placard is not only—and understandably—a recognized paid profession by which certain men earn a living but is getting to be also an avocation for many whose fathers probably marched with a plumed hat and sword in the parades of the Knights of Pythias, though the sons now regard that as merely quaint.

Any good full-time citizen who thinks, for instance, that some pianist's performance is tinged by alleged pro-Nazi sentiments will not merely stay at home or attend some other recital. Indeed he will refrain especially from doing that since mere music certainly comes under the head of escapism unless, at least, the executants have known political affiliations. Instead, he will hie him to Carnegie Hall, march back and forth, and, if no policeman happens to be looking at the moment, hurl insults at those who happen to differ with him over the rather difficult question of the exact limits to which art and politics may be dissociated.

Until rather recently employers did not commonly picket unionists, but there is nothing one-sided about the opportunities at present offered. If you don't want to picket Gieseking, then, unless you basely decide to remain above the conflict, you certainly ought to picket Paul Robeson. Not infrequently one set of pickets is re- or cross-picketed by another and you certainly owe it to society to be in the one line or the other. In a state where every citizen was as socially alive as he ought to be there would be few times when he was not either picketing or being picketed, and there would be many when, in connection with two burning issues, he was both marching and being marched against.

The fact that a quite considerable number of people do seem to find "social problems" their recreation and their hobby as well as their exacting responsibility is cited by some as the one sign of health in our sick world, but why on earth this should be so I cannot see. A healthy individual does not spend most of his life examining treatments and regimens. When a man does do that we say that he is either a hypochondriac or an invalid—not that he is leading the good life for which man was obviously intended. In fact we usually wonder why he finds it worth while to keep alive and, for that matter, so, often, does he. Why should the case of the body politic be so different? Wouldn't a really healthy citizen in a really healthy country be as unaware of the government as a healthy man is unaware of his physiology? The healthy citizen might get an annual check-up, but he would not consider comparative blood pressures and the latest remedies for constipation the only subjects which a serious man considered worth talking about. And however sick society may be it seems to me that we ought at least not lose sight of what health would be like. We ought not have as our ideal the state of universal hypochondria.

Even in the life of a chronic invalid there often comes a time when he says: "I shall never be well, and in all probability I shall not live long. But I might as well use, in so far as I can, whatever life may be left me. I shall not spend all my time in eating, drinking, and being merry, for there are other things which seem worth doing. But in the end 'Carpe diem' and 'Work for the night is coming' amount to much the same thing. And either one is better than refusing to use life because it may be short. Who knows? It is just possible that I may make a surprise recovery. If I do not I shall have at least made some use of my few last days. Not to do so is to be dead already."

Sometimes, at least, I am glad that everyone did not have in past days as much social consciousness as everyone is supposed to have today. Mozart might have been more effective in certain respects if he had organized a union of composers instead of quarreling sporadically and unsuccessfully with the patrons who treated him so scurvily. But in that case, of course, he might not have been able to find the time to compose a G Minor Symphony. And how about Shakespeare? If he had lived in the twentieth century he might have felt compelled to spend so much time helping young playwrights and speaking at meetings for good causes that he would never have got around to writing *Hamlet*.

Sometimes I even wonder whether the modern artist, at least, is really being as self-sacrificing as he seems and no doubt thinks himself. In the old days when a man could not quite make it in any trade, or profession, or art he took to drink as the most convenient way of covering up his incompetence. "Ah," said his pitying friends, "what a lawyer, what a doctor, or what a poet he would have been, if only he were not cursed with that unfortunate weakness." Today he can save his health as well as his pride by proclaiming that in such a world as this no one can and no one should function successfully. Thus social consciousness can become merely the brandy of the damned. Your aspiring playwright can go to a rally instead of on a toot when he wants to conceal from himself as well as from others that he cannot write his *Hamlet*.

At least there are more forms of escapism than those who bandy that word about are always aware of. An artist, for instance, may escape from the problems of his art—which are hard to solve—into a consideration of the problems of society which he sometimes seems to think require of him only that he complain about them. Even the ordinary citizen is not always guiltless of similar techniques and it is, for example, sometimes easier to head an institute for the study of child guidance than it is to turn one brat into a decent human being. All such I nevertheless forgive more easily than I do those who insist that they are setting an example of self-sacrificing good citizenship when they are merely riding hard what happens to be their hobby. Your doctor often finds nothing more intellectually interesting or more aesthetically satisfying than a good ulcer beautifully illustrating the typical features of its malignancy. When he meets socially with other doctors he may find it the natural and rewarding subject of conversation. But he does not assume that everyone's chief interest should be the same or that people who discuss topics having nothing to do with disease are necessarily shallow, ignorant, callous, or wicked. But an analogous attitude is exactly what most of your professional and amateur students of social pathology do take. Rubbing their hands as they contemplate the latest ucler on the body politic, they assume that any reluctance to spend the rest of the evening gloating over it is proof that one is indifferent to health.

I wish that I thought the unremitting devotion of the hobbyists was more likely than I think it is to restore the world to what I should call health. Meanwhile, I find myself looking backward with a certain sense of nostalgia into all those ages of Western civilization when no one supposed that being a good citizen was more than a part-time job. And I do not think, as correspondents will declare, that this means that I am secretly longing for a dictator. Dictators also, I notice, have a way of taking up a good deal of a citizen's time.

The European visitor and the good American

[1957]

The European visitor and the good American were engaged in their endless argument about American "materialism." As usual they were getting nowhere and certainly they were not saying anything new. Both got more heated as time went on just because it was so evident that neither was making the slightest impression on the other.

The European said we didn't care about anything except money. He even revived the phrase "almighty dollar" which I hadn't heard since 1929. The American replied with our schools, our libraries, our hospitals, and, of course, with European aid and Point Four. Both seemed so right and so wrong. But how could they be? Were they perhaps not talking about the same thing at all? If they were, how could one sane man see as white what to another sane man was as obviously black? There can't be that much to be said on both sides of the same question.

The American had facts and figures to demonstrate the generosity of his fellow countryman. Actually, figures are not necessary. It is obvious enough that no nation in all history ever before gave away so much in money or goods. More than a century ago de Tocqueville noted with amazement how the American private citizen got together spontaneously with his fellows for the purpose of righting some wrong or relieving some need. He thought the phenomenon unique, and he was probably right. Moreover, it has not only persisted but entered a new international phase. We are almost as distressed by suffering and want in distant places as we are by distress and want at home. And almost as determined to do something about it. Point Four is philanthropy on a global scale. Charity, we say, may begin at home but it doesn't end there. We are determined to do good all over the globe.

The European visitor shrugs. He hints that we probably have low, ulterior motives. Materialists wouldn't be that generous, and since we are by premise materialists there must be a catch somewhere in all this generosity. Actually, however, he does not seem too convinced by his own argument. Though he doesn't quite admit the fact, he is more puzzled than anything else. Both European virtues and European vices are different from ours and he can't make us out.

What really troubles him (and what might well trouble us too) is something he was not able to put into words and something the typical American has never felt any particular need to put into words because it does not strike him as a paradox. What that something is is simply this: Materialism and stinginess, thinks the European, inevitably go together —and in his experience they usually have. Actually, generosity and materialism are not at all incompatible—as the whole panorama of the American temperament abundantly demonstrates. We are not materialists in the sense that we love money for its own sake. We are not misers. Instead we are spendthrifts who lavish wealth on ourselves, on our families, on our fellow citizens, and, nowadays, on the inhabitants of the four quarters of the globe. But we are materialists— generous materialists—in the very simple sense that we believe everything worth having can be had if only we are willing to spend enough money to get it.

Nearly everything which makes American life both richer and poorer, both better and worse, than life in any other civilized community has ever been before goes back to the virtues and the limitations of our generous materialism. We believe, for example, in education—more passionately and more uncritically than any nation ever believed in it before. We believe in it so thoroughly that we are willing to spend on it prodigious amounts of public funds. In nearly every American community citizens vote to tax themselves at higher and higher rates to pay for the education of other people's children. But there are few to whom it ever occurs that putting more money into schools is not a sure way of getting more education or that any deficiencies which happen to become manifest will not be remedied by putting more money into school buildings. Being convinced that you cannot have what you refuse to pay for makes him generous; believing that you will get what you pay for or, at least, that if you don't there is no other way of getting it constitutes him a materialist.

Your true American never misses an opportunity to make

money. He assumes that no one else does either, or should be expected to overlook an opportunity. Perhaps, therefore, we actually are more devoted to the pursuit of the dollar than most other nations are to the pound or the franc or the mark. But we are not particularly anxious to hold on to it when we catch it. Acquisitiveness, not miserliness, is our vice. We are very ready to forgive a man for doing whatever is necessary to make a profit. We are quite resigned, to take small examples, to having the symphony concert interrupted by a commercial or the highway disfigured by billboards. You can hardly expect anyone to forgo a profit even if making it involves annoying everybody else. But you will expect him to give generously to charity and to vote for public improvements which will cost him much more than he will ever get out of them.

This same true American is not being hypocritical when he tells you that he is frantically making money because he wants his children to "have all the advantages." He really does; and he will spend freely the money he made to buy these same advantages. He is not a materialist in the sense that he is one who says education, travel, fun, even "culture" are foolish frills. But he is a materialist in the sense that he is quite sure no child can have "advantages" without having money to pay for them and almost as sure that if he does have money to pay he will have the "advantages." Thoreau thought money not required to buy one necessary of the soul. The typical American believes that no necessity of the soul is free and that there are precious few, if any, which cannot be bought.

None of this is consciously cynical. If it were, our civilization would not be the world's wonder that it is: materially richer than any that ever existed before and providing a larger proportion of the population with a considerable share of that material richness than any other rich civilization ever did. In fact our attitude is so far from being consciously cynical that not one American in ten can be made to recognize any inadequacy in generous materialism as a philosophy, a religion, or a way of life. He will call it merely realistic and practical; nothing more nor less than benevolence without humbug. He will sincerely suspect that anyone who does so much as hint at a limitation is merely seeking an excuse for denying the common people their proper share of material things. Tell him that man does not live by bread alone and he will accuse you of trying to find an excuse for denying bread to somebody. Only during the past hundred years have moral and social philosophers squarely faced the fact that it is at least easier to be law-abiding, well educated, and responsive to "the finer things of life" if you are not hungry or cold. Material welfare, they decided, is a *sine qua non* for welfare of any other kind. But most Americans have taken a further step which does not logically follow; and despite the fact that Europeans still blame us they and the rest of the world are following us as well as they can. We have forgot that a *sine qua non* is not always the "one thing necessary."

We take it for granted that when a people is well housed, well clothed, and well fed then it will inevitably add unto itself all other desirable things—that is if there really are any others of importance. But in actual fact it just isn't turning out that way. The vast majority of our well-fed, well-housed, and well-clothed population has not turned toward intellectual or artistic pursuits but simply taken a greater and greater interest in even more food, better houses, and more expensive clothes. The more abundant its material riches have become the more thoroughly it has come to believe that only material riches count.

Take for example that question of the "standard of living" with which we are so greatly and no doubt properly concerned. If we are to use it—and we do so use it—as an adequate measure of what used to be called "the good life," then the "standard" should take account of all the factors which contribute to make a life good. Most people seem to assume that in actual practice that is just what it does do. But does it? Does anyone who uses the phrase ever mean anything which is not purely material?

Unfortunately, of course, no one ever says just what "the standard of living" includes. When we talk of that "cost of living" to which the "standard of living" is related we know exactly how it is measured. Government statisticians will tell us just what items are included in their tabulations, and just how each is weighted. But we say "the standard of living is steadily rising" without ever stating just what we mean. And we are satisfied with such imprecision because, for all practical purposes, we are assumed to be in perfect agreement. "Standard of living," we assume, means "real wages" and the amount of material necessities, conveniences, diversions, and luxuries they will buy. Would our standard of living seem so high or be so steadily rising if the standard involved any one of a number of other things which used to be considered a part of the good life? We know that our standard of material living is high. Ought we be so indifferent to everything else? That we do tend to be largely indifferent is the real justification for the European's charge that we are more "materialistic" than Europeans have yet got around to being.

A large brewery has just recently been spending a lot of money on advertisements proudly informing the general public that the government statisticians have recently added beer to the list of commodities whose retail price is to be taken into consideration when the cost of living index is computed. Beer, in other words, has been recognized as a staple requirement in a satisfactory life, and with that fact I have no quarrel. But suppose that to our official index of the standard of living we were to add a few items which have at least as much right to be called factors in the good life as beer has to be considered a factor in a satisfactory physical life. Suppose we included, for example, the reading of books and made the modest assumption that people who read books do have to that extent a somewhat higher standard of living than those who don't. How would we stand?

The answer is, apparently, that we would not stand so very well and that so far as that one factor is concerned our standard of living is a good deal lower than that of certain European populations which we pity. According to the results of a survey recently published by the American Institute of Public Opinion, 61 per cent of those interviewed had not read a book during the past year. Comparison with a similar study made two years ago in other English-speaking countries produces these figures: in England 55 per cent of the population reads books; in Australia 34 per cent; in Canada 31 per cent; in the United States 17. And this is despite the fact that the average Englishman has had far less schooling and far less money spent on a so-called education.

Just how "reading" should be weighted in compiling our standard of living I do not know. Therefore I do not know just how far the Englishman's greater ability to find satisfaction in books would cancel out the much larger per capita supply of automobiles, television sets, and bathtubs in the United States. But ability to read should count for *something* and it is certainly not true that in all respects the "standard of living" is higher here than it is anywhere else.

What other items might be included—besides, of course, the other obvious intellectual and artistic aspects of contemporary life? The interest and satisfaction taken in the work by which a living is made? Freedom from financial worries—which depends upon the management of income as well as upon "real wages"? Opportunity to escape overcrowding? The extent of those inner resources which make leisure something more than a blank which only diversion can fill? The late Aldo Leopold once spoke of a minority for whom "the opportunity to see geese is more important than television, and the chance to see a pasqueflower is a right as inalienable as free speech." Perhaps that minority is too small to demand recognition in an index. But there are quite a few things which are important to the happiness of a considerable number of people but which are not commonly thought of as part of the standard of living.

Is it too much to hope that some statistical sociologist will take up the suggestion here offered? There are a lot of less important things for which indexes and "methods of evaluation" have been publicly proposed and even defective ones, if they state definitely what it is that is being measured, are valuable at least to the extent that they call attention to what is being taken into consideration and what is left out. If we are going to assume that a high standard of living is the *summum bonum,* then we oughtn't be as vague as we always are when it comes to letting it be known what we mean by a "standard of living." We ought to know in what direction we are going and just how rapidly we are moving. We might decide that where we are going is not precisely where we would like to go. We might even decide that two chickens in every pot, two cars in every garage, and no book in any living room does not suggest a standard of living as high as one of each would indicate.

If you don't mind my saying so . . . [II]

[1962]

Not many of our contemporaries would admit to taking either Rousseau or Augustine very literally or very seriously as a guide. Yet the question they raise is still (however differently we may phrase it) as critical, both practically and theoretically, as it ever was. Are we naturally good or naturally evil?

Most contemporary sociology and most contemporary education is based upon Rousseau's assumption. Whenever we defend permissive education or argue that crime is the result of some defect in our political or social system, we are Rousseauists whether we admit it or not. "The reality of evil" is a phrase now seldom used except by theologians and that considerable number of imaginative writers whom theology has influenced. No politician, psychologist, counselor, or sociologist admits it. Even the Roman Catholics "Boys Town" brandishes the slogan, "There is no such thing as a bad boy," and it is an indication of the prevalence of Rousseauism even in unexpected places that this heresy has never been officially rebuked. (Unless I completely misunderstand Catholic doctrine, it insists that all boys, like all men, are naturally "bad.")

Perhaps Irving Babbitt was right in his seemingly fanatical insistence that Rousseau was the dominant influence upon modern literature, modern society, and modern life—whether Babbitt was right or wrong in lamenting the fact. The very phrase "juvenile delinquent," not "juvenile criminal," is another evidence of the same conviction that wrongdoing must be learned. A teen-ager, we feel, hasn't lived long enough yet to have been so thoroughly corrupted as to merit the term "criminal." He must still be trailing clouds of glory from heaven which is his home.

A year or two ago I confessed in one of these pages that "I am a reality-of-evil man myself," and I suppose that the remark was misinterpreted by some to mean that I accepted Augustinianism in an orthodox Christian sense; perhaps even that I blamed everything on Eve and her perverted taste in fruit. Such is hardly the case. But there is indeed something disastrously wrong in the assumption that since all evil deeds can be explained as merely misguided they should never be punished, always understood and treated.

Those who take this attitude—and they constitute, I believe, the vast majority of the enlightened and liberal-minded —seem to see no way out of a dilemma. Since human nature must be either good or bad, they must choose between permissiveness on the one hand and repression on the other. You must, they think, either "break the child's will" as the Victorians put it, or you must give him "uncritical love," no matter how he behaves. Similarly you must either return to the brutality of the eighteenth-century criminal law or take it for granted that there are no bad boys—or bad men either —and that, therefore, both the delinquent and the criminal should be understood, helped, treated, and re-educated, but never punished.

Neither system seems to have worked very well. The humane are fond of pointing out that the most ferocious laws did not abolish crime. They are less ready to admit that "modern methods" haven't either. If the first do not really deter, the second, if you may credit statistics, do not cure. There seems no doubt that adult crime and, even more strikingly, juvenile delinquency have been increasing during the very period when both law and the social system are growing continuously more enlightened. *Post hoc* is not necessarily *propter hoc*. Most liberals will insist merely that we are not enlightened enough; that what is called for is even more complete commitment to the theory that the criminal must be simply a sick man, and that the society which made him sick should bear the responsibility for the fact.

When faced with a dilemma of this kind the most characteristic technique of recent thinking—I don't know who first used it—is to say that we are asking the wrong question or asking it in terms that do not fit the situation. This seems to me obviously the case here. "Are men naturally bad?"

suggests "sin," and that is a word with connotations highly distasteful to the modern mind. If we were to ask instead whether men are naturally "civilized," it seems to me that the answer would be immediately obvious. They are not. And, to me at least, that answer suggests a more sensible attitude than any usually taken toward the delinquent and the criminal. They are not necessarily sick, or the victims of something aggressively corrupting in their society. The wrong that society has done them is a negative one. It has failed to civilize them.

To be as orderly and as regardful of the rights of others as civilized life requires is not "natural." Whatever tendencies in such directions we may have inherited from our animal ancestors are simply not adequate to a way of life so very new as even the most primitive civilizations are. In that sense men are not born "good" and they will not become "good" if merely uncorrupted. So far as my observation goes, neither the child, the adolescent, nor the adult is likely to become a good or civilized man unless positive pressures (sometimes including deliberate punishment) are put upon him. To say that all men are born good is a seductively pleasing idea. To say that all men are born civilized is obviously preposterous.

When I first began to practice literary journalism in the twenties, one of the great debates was between the "realists" or "naturalists" and the members of the school of Irving Babbitt, Paul Elmer More, and Stuart Sherman, all of whom accused the naturalists of reducing the analysis of human motive to a mere "theory of animal behavior." To do anything of the sort, I agree, is to libel human nature. But when a question arises concerning that human nature and what it consists of, it is certainly wrong not to consider what light can be thrown by asking whether some tendency we are tempted to describe as either a purely human virtue or a late corruption and perversion is not actually part of the subhuman inheritance. If, for example, Proudhon was right and "property is theft," then thievery must be pretty deeply rooted in our animal nature. Modern study has made it clear that a "defense of territory" is one of the major keys to the understanding of animal behavior and a defense of territory is the most primitive expression of a sense of property rights. That alone should be sufficient to give pause to those who found their Utopias upon the assumption that the desire to own, being merely the product of a corrupt social system, could easily be got rid of. Even the Communists seem to have recognized promptly that this desire to own is not easily destroyed and that the despised incentives of capitalism do continue to be useful.

When I asked a somewhat cynical friend what he thought of Robert Ardrey's *African Genesis,* he replied: "When in college I was taught that man's remotest ancestor was an unusually intelligent ape I never quite believed it. Ardrey seems to prove that this ancestor was actually a singularly unpleasant one. And you know that makes the whole thing seem a lot more probable."

Perhaps that is too desperately simple both as a summary of and as a response to a brilliant book solidly founded upon the best and most recent information that science has been able to gather. But it is by no means entirely beside the point. Although Mr. Ardrey never says in just the words I chose that man is by nature "uncivilized" rather than either "good" or "bad," this is one way of stating what his thesis comes down to. The missing link (or at least the latest candidate for that dubious distinction) came to dominate his environment not because he was especially intelligent, but because, unlike the other apes, he was a predator and therefore aggressive. His earliest invention was a weapon, and to this day weapons of one kind or another tend to be the most passionately sought product of human technology.

This basic fact which, seemingly, is forced upon us by recent anthropology is something with which we must reckon. So also are certain other basic facts that are emerging from studies of animal behavior. One of them is that sex (which we like to think evolved into love) is not, as Darwin supposed, the most fundamental dynamism in the living organism. The impulse to defend territory (that is, the desire to own, privately and exclusively) plays an equal if not greater role. And the desire to own is rather more resistant than even sex to sublimation.

The other basic fact is that society is not, as Vico announced centuries ago and as sociologists sometimes like to assume, a purely human invention since its beginnings also can be traced far back in evolutionary history. If that sounds encouraging it is not as completely so as at first sight appears. It means that man cannot, as he has often dreamed of doing, invent a workable society on a basis that to him is purely rational and human. He must reckon not only with the instincts of the animal but also with those features of society which are so ancient that they too are nearly instinctive.

None of this is radically new. The facts upon which the interpretation is based have been increasingly recognized by anthropologists and students of animal behavior. But the implications are too novel and too disturbing always to have been faced clearly. Mr. Ardrey's thesis does not imply a necessary return to the simplicity of the social Darwinism of the late nineteenth century. No competent student of evolution today believes that the evolutionary process itself was so simple as early Darwinism made it. The struggle for survival does not explain everything. The living organism "wanted" (dreadful word) to become "higher" (although no one is quite sure what that means) as well as "more fit to survive." Hence a society exclusively and ruthlessly based upon the devil-take-the-hindmost principle is not actually analogous to the evolutionary process.

Nevertheless, to accept the theory that man is born uncivilized although not evil, and that he must reckon with
his inheritance, does mean to remember that he is not as
readily plastic as we sometimes like to believe. Human nature is (for both good and ill) a reality. It is something far
less easy to deal with than the theoretical blank slate upon
which conditioning writes what other more healthful conditions can erase whenever it seems desirable.

None of this is, and none of it is made to seem in Mr.
Ardrey's book, an invitation to hopelessness. But it does seem
to mean that utopianism is even more unrealistic than it
used to appear, and that the road even to amelioration is not
quite the one that either the naïve permissionists or the
proponents of social engineering propose.

Mr. Ardrey's conclusion, to which he admits a somewhat
tenuous hope, seems to me the weakest part of his thesis—
not because it is hopeful, but because his determination to
avoid facile solutions makes him draw rather darker than
need be the picture of what our African Genesis implies.
That "conscience," which man seems somewhat mysteri-
ously to have developed and upon which we sometimes build
the hope that he may eventually become a pleasanter creature, Mr. Ardrey dismisses as a delusion and more of a
threat than a promise. It has been appealed to, he points out,
in order to justify the greatest of crimes in both private conduct and public policy. It is less often something we follow
than something we invent to justify the acts our animal
nature inspires us to perform. At best, so the relativist will
add, it merely approves or disapproves in accord with what
a particular culture has come to accept or reject.

In place of this untrustworthy conscience Mr. Ardrey attempts to put something that may actually be the same thing
under a different name but is even more difficult to define. He calls it a sense of, or a desire for, order; and he dis-
covers it, far back in time, already modifying to some extent

the purely aggressive impulses long before our immediate ancestor the predatory ape learned how to make aggressiveness more effective than it had ever been before. Mr. Ardrey does not seem to dismiss Reason quite so summarily as he does Conscience, but the case for and against one or the other seems to me much the same. Too often, perhaps usually, Reason also is only rationalization. We convince ourselves of what we would like to believe. As Nietzsche said, if you wish to understand a philosopher do not ask what he says; find out what he wants. But if, as it seems to me, Reason can be, and at least occasionally is, more than rationalization, then I do not see why conscience may not also sometimes be a genuine guide. Just where two such remarkable things as Reason and Conscience may have come from, I do not know. Perhaps they emerge from feeble hints of some such independent powers in the lower animals. But in some individuals they do occasionally put in an astonishing appearance. As Pope said, they afford "at least a glimmering light."

A few of the animals far below the anthropoids (some wasps, for example, and one species of finch) use tools although they do not make them. The evidence suggests that our singularly unpleasant great-grandfather broke skulls with a stone. Perhaps when he had practiced this effective technique, it may sometimes have occurred to him dimly that to kill more than he intended to eat was not quite nice.

One of Swift's *obiter dicta* occurs to me so often that I have probably cited it before in these pages, but it comes in here very pat. "I never wonder to see men wicked, but I often wonder to see them not ashamed." That they are, nevertheless, sometimes ashamed may be the last best hope of mankind.

The search for a rule of life

[1956]

When some developments in nineteenth-century science aroused the apprehensions of Charles Kingsley he communicated them to Thomas Henry Huxley, and Huxley struck an attitude: "Sit down before fact as a little child . . . follow humbly and to whatever abyss nature leads or you will learn nothing."

Even today it would hardly do to reverse this injunction. We can't always refuse to face a fact before we know where it is going to lead or whether we want to go there. But so many abysses, physical and moral, have been opening since Huxley's time that we can't quite share his Victorian confidence and we might well add a *caveat* more often than we do: "Be quite sure that it really is a fact before you follow it too blindly and too far." Even science revises its facts from time to time, and sometimes it happens that we fall into an abyss between the time when a "fact" is announced and the time when it is discovered to be an error. Science is not so nearly infallible that the warnings of instinct can always be disregarded.

Just how blindly and just how far should we follow what, for instance, we can read as a fact in a textbook called *Psychology and Life*? This bulky work by a professor of psychology at the University of Southern California is described as "intended to meet the needs of students without sacrificing scientific rigor." Of its more than six hundred pages little more than one is devoted to "morals," and here is the definition propounded: "Morality is the quality of behaving

in the way that society approves. . . . When a person obeys
the rules and laws of his society we say that he is moral or
good."

If this is a fact, then obviously "moral" and "immoral"
have no meaning except in the context of a particular society,
and it must be meaningless to say either that one society is
morally better than another or, what is probably more important, that any individual is morally superior to the society
in which he lives. Moral *excellence* is a phantom, because
you cannot exceed the standard. In Nazi Germany, for instance, the torture and murder of Jews and of political opponents constituted "moral" conduct because it accorded
with "the rules and laws" of that particular society. Any
individual German who refused to take part in such activities was judged to be immoral by the other members of
his community, and therefore he *was* immoral according to
our California professor.

Is this conclusion an inevitable consequence of a "scientific
rigor" which we should follow "no matter to what abyss it
may lead"? Or is it merely a reckless opinion to be distrusted just because it has already led Nazi Germany and
other societies into what many men regard as a very black
abyss indeed? The question is of considerable importance in
view of the fact that what *Psychology and Life* states with unusual clarity is what has been widely taught by many sociologists and anthropologists as well as by psychologists, none of
whom calls it "moral anarchy" (which is what it is) but "cultural and moral relativism" (which sounds not only innocu-
ous but laudably broad-minded and tolerant).

As an esoteric doctrine "cultural relativism" can well
serve the purposes of the rulers of a totalitarian state raising
up a generation of mass-men fanatically devoted to "ideals"
which the rulers alone know to be neither good nor bad except in relation to secret power aims. But what will the effect
be in a democracy like our own, committed to popular edu-

cation and to the widest possible dissemination of "the truth"? What line of conduct will a thoughtful man in possession of such a method follow? How will he order his own life in the light of such facts as "scientific rigor" compels him to accept? And to what abysses will he follow these facts?

These questions I have recently been asking myself, and it seems to me that there are only two logical life-plans between which I could choose. The first and most obvious is a Machiavellian egotism. Since what is called "right" is merely the law or the custom of my community, I need have no concern with anything except what the community knows about. I will be careful to retain its good opinion while secretly taking advantage of every possible opportunity to violate law and custom with impunity. As Machiavelli said, the wise man will by no means always tell the truth but will take care to preserve his reputation for truth-telling because he can't take advantage of others unless they trust him. If, for example, you have a chance to take candy from a baby ask only how likely it is that you will be found out. Conscience will then become nothing but what Mr. Mencken once called it: "That still small voice which whispers, 'Somebody may be looking.' "

The only other possible rule of life consistent with an acceptance of the supposed fact is less sensational but will also lead in the long run to consequences less than desirable. Should I be so timid or—by heredity or conditioning—so "group minded" that I cannot face even in the secrecy of my own heart the knowledge that I am violating the mores of my community then, for me, virtue will have to consist in the completest possible conformity to those dominant opinions which, for that community, define the meaning of "good." I can never aspire to be better than the average except insofar as I am better because I deviate less than most of my fellows from the norm. I can never hope to raise the standard of my society, because "raising the standard" is a meaningless phrase if the highest possible standard is, by definition, that generally accepted at the moment. Only an absolute conformist on the one hand and an anarchistic individualist on the other can be said to "follow the facts."

Is there no *tertium quid?* I have searched without finding one. Any society which actually accepts and acts upon what "scientific rigor" is said to compel us to believe will presently be composed of a certain number of absolute conformists plus a certain number of unscrupulous "men of *virtu*." And there are, of course, those who say that it is precisely toward such a society that the Western world as well as the world behind the Iron Curtain is tending.

If we have not quite got there yet, it is because we have not yet followed Huxley's advice with resolute consistency. But we are on our way. As soon as enlightenment has overcome the effectiveness of residual prejudices, in favor of various traditional notions, we will get there. *Psychology and Life* says that philosophy and literature have long concerned themselves with morality but that only recently has science taken over. And it is no doubt because of literature that, for the present, most of us act sometimes as though we believed that "vice" is somehow recognizably a creature of hideous mien no matter how persistently custom or laws may describe it as divinely fair.

As Pope himself knew, his couplet is not always a safe guide. Vice does not always strike us as hideous because, so the next two lines warn us, the customs of a civilization do sometimes make us callously familiar with her face. But the abysses to which too confident a reliance on the moral instinct have led mankind are neither so numerous nor so deep as those toward which the moral anarchists (pardon me, the cultural relativists) invite us to plunge. And there is one striking cultural phenomenon they seem never to have noticed.

The most antithetical standards of value can, they are fond of telling us, serve equally successful societies. One flourishing race may believe that taking human heads is the most laudable act that any man can perform. Another, like the American Hopis, may live by peace. Competition may be the very breath of life in one place and so frowned upon in another that any sort of personal distinction is almost a disgrace. As Lecky said, there is no possible line of conduct that has not been condemned as a sin at one time and place, enjoined as a virtue at some other. But there is at least one doctrine which no successful culture seems ever to have accepted. And that is cultural and moral relativism!

No matter how outlandish the ways of some may seem, if there is anything to be learned from anthropology it would appear to be that the only really deadly social philosophy is that which holds that one way is as good as another. At the present moment we are hardly more sure than we were a generation ago where to look for a valid "ought." But we are growing notably less sure that we can get along without one.

Cant, candor, and the class war

[1949]

Some months ago I read in the New York *Herald Tribune* a statement attributed to a very successful playwright with political interests. Its vertiginous implications have troubled me ever since, and I have lost some sleep trying to think my way through them. The tentative conclusions I now put up to *Nation* readers, for the problem is important. A good deal of what people like this playwright call "the confusions of our time" is certainly exposed.

The occasion was a dinner in honor of the Reverend Howard William Mellish, and the subject was our proper attitude toward Russia. The speaker was denouncing those liberals who criticize the alleged defects of the Soviet system and he said, still according to the *Herald Tribune,* that "the concept of intellectual honesty does not apply when peace is at stake." Now this is at least refreshingly frank, and it struck me first because contempt for intellectual honesty is more often exhibited than openly defended as a principle. Even more striking, however, is the implication that the more crucial a problem becomes, the more reprehensible honest consideration of it is.

A good many different roads to peace have been widely advocated. Some believe that it is possible only when supported by overwhelming military might, and some only when law is universally respected. There are those who put their faith in world government and others who hope for the gradual spread of the Christian principle of nonviolence. But never before have I seen it suggested that intellectual honesty is the great impediment and that what is needed is neither armaments nor love but simply a rigorous determination not to look facts in the face.

Why, I wonder, should we confine the benefits of the new method to Russia? Since we want to live in peace with all the world, a universal "Dishonest Neighbor policy" would seem to be called for. Nor do I, for that matter, see why the benefits of the method should be confined to international affairs. We have domestic problems too and some of them are quite pressing.

It is here that the vertigo begins. Once international peace has been solidly founded on intellectual dishonesty, we pass to the labor front and begin to be thoroughly dishonest about industrial monopolies as well as about union racketeering. Unless it be insisted that in relatively trivial matters intellectual honesty should be maintained as some sort of curiosity we might then get rid of it in our private lives. For all

I know, it may be not only a threat to international peace but also one of the principal causes of divorce and the real secret of the housing shortage. Perhaps what all these problems need is some good, hard crooked thinking of the sort which promises such admirable results in our relations with Russia.

We may, I think, take it for granted that intellectual dishonesty, like most other virtues, becomes easier and easier to attain the more we practice it and that we should soon learn to shut our eyes almost automatically. If, as I have been told, there is no difference between morality and *mores*, then the truth about anything would soon come to seem genuinely shocking, and once people were thoroughly ashamed of it in connection with anything at all we should be in sight of our goal. Utopia would be complete as the last shred of intellectual honesty had been rooted out of the humblest citizen. Peace, plenty, and universal happiness would be realized in a classless society where all men were liars but where no one knew that he was—because no one would ever think the truth even in the depths of his soul.

At present this Utopia is only in the dimly foreseeable future. Meanwhile, we live in a world not only complicated by abnormally acute differences of honest opinion but infested at the same time by people who practice dishonesty as a deliberate method. They invite us to battle over fictitious issues and pretend to defend hotly principles for which they have the utmost contempt. There seems only one thing which those of us who belong to the past can do—attempt to recognize them as promptly as possible and treat them in some appropriate fashion. But what is the appropriate fashion?

As a drama critic I shall probably be called upon to review future plays by the dramatist whose incautious confession furnished the text for this discourse. Shall I, in that case, feel compelled to ask myself first of all how important he seems to consider the subject of the particular play, and then, if it appears to be intended merely as a trivial amusement, give him the benefit of the doubt by assuming that he means what he says? And if I am right in understanding him to maintain that there is a certain critical point at which a subject becomes important enough to make sincerity a vice, shall I therefore conclude that his most serious plays will be intellectually dishonest? Shall I have to ask what ulterior purpose has persuaded him to avoid the truth as he sees it, and what it is that he is trying to achieve by pretending to believe the things he is saying?

Naturally, I should prefer to deal with the work of a man who professed to believe that sincerity is a virtue even when a good deal is at stake. But my problem is minor by comparison with that of those whose business it is to deal with action in the political and social fields. The only hope I can offer them is the hope that intellectual dishonesty is ultimately self-destructive. Those who practice it usually end by deceiving themselves, and they generally begin to deceive one another even sooner. It was Plato who pointed out that even thieves cannot succeed unless they behave honorably toward one another. And usually they don't—for long.

If you don't mind my saying so . . . [III]

[1960]

We often say of a person that he "looks young for his age" or "old for his age." Yet even in the more extreme of such cases we seldom go very far astray in guessing what his age actually is. And this means, I suppose, that almost invariably age reveals itself by easily recognizable signs engraved on both the body and the mind. "Young for his age" means only the presence of some minor characteristic not quite usual. Stigmata quite sufficient for diagnosis are nevertheless there. An assumption of youth, or the presence of a few youthful characteristics, deceives no more successfully than rouge or dyed hair. "Looking young for your age" means "for your age" and it means no more.

A mind expressing itself in words may reveal itself a little less obviously as old or young. Its surface loses its bloom and submits to its wrinkles in ways less immediately obvious than the body does. Youth may be, and often is, skeptical, cynical, or despairing; age may be idealistic, believing, and much given to professions of optimism. But there is, nevertheless, always a subtle difference in the way in which supposedly similar opinions are held. The pessimism of the young is defiant, anxious to confess or even exaggerate its ostensible gloom, and so exuberant as to reveal the fact that it regards its ability to face up to the awful truth as more than enough to compensate for the awfulness of that truth. Similarly the optimism of age protests too much. If it proclaims that the best is yet to be, it always arouses, at least in the young, either a suspicious question or perhaps the exclamation of the Negro youth who saw on a tombstone the inscription, "I am not dead but sleeping." "Boy, he ain't foolin' nobody but hisself."

We may say of some unfortunates that they were never young. We cannot truthfully say of anyone who has succeeded in entering deep into his sixties that he was never old. Those famous lines of the Greek Anthology with which a fading beauty dedicates her mirror at the shrine of a goddess reveal a wise attitude:

Venus, take my votive glass,
Since I am not what I was,

What from this day I shall be,
Venus, let me never see.

No good can come of contemplating the sad, inevitable
fact that once youth has passed "a worse and worse time still
succeeds the former." But there are at least two reasons for
contemplating one's *mind* in even a cracked mirror. One is
that there sometimes are real although inadequate compensa-
tions in growing old. Serenity, if one is fortunate enough
to achieve it, is not so good as joy, but it is something. Even to
be "from hope and fear set free" is at least better than to
have lost the first without having got rid of the second. The
other reason (and the one with which I am here concerned)
is that one thus becomes inclined to inquire of any opinion,
or change of opinion, whether it represents the wisdom of
experience or is only the result of the difference between
youth and age which is as inevitable as the all too obvious
physical differences. One may be exasperatingly aware that
if the answer is favorable it will be judged such only by
those of one's own age. But at least the question has been
raised. Many readers of this department no doubt discount
certain of my opinions for the simple reason that they can
guess pretty accurately, even if they have never actually been
told, what my age is. At least I should like them to know
that I know these discounts are being made.

Let me then (and in public) glance into the mirror. I
have known some men and women who said that the selves
they are told about or even remember seem utter strangers
to them now; that their remote past is as discontinuous with
their present selves, as lacking in any conscious likeness to
their mature personality, as the self of a butterfly may be
imagined discontinuous with that of the caterpillar it once
was. For my part I find it difficult to conceive such a state of
affairs. I have changed and I have reversed opinions; but
I am so aware of an uninterrupted continuity of the per-

sona or ego that I see only as absurd the tendency of some psychologists from Heraclitus to Pirandello and Proust to regard consciousness as no more than a flux amid which nothing remains unchanged. So far as I am concerned, the child is unmistakably father to the man, despite the obvious fact that child and father differ greatly—sometimes for the better and sometimes for the worse.

Fundamental values, temperament, and the way in which one approaches a conviction change less, of course, than specific opinions. That fact is very clearly illustrated in the case of the many present-day intellectuals who were Communists or near-Communists in their youth and are now so extremely conservative (or reactionary, as many would say) that they can define no important political conviction that does not seem so far from even a centrist position as to make the distinction between Mr. Nixon and Mr. Khrushchev for them hardly worth noting. But in ways more fundamental than specific political opinions they are still what they always were: passionate, sure without a shadow of doubt of whatever it is that they are sure of, capable of seeing black and white only and, therefore, committed to the logical extreme of whatever it is they are temporarily committed to.

To those of my readers who find many of my opinions morally, or politically, or sociologically antiquated (and I have reason to know that there are some such), I would like to say what I have already hinted, namely, that some of my opinions may indeed be subject to some discount on the simple ground that I am no longer young and therefore incapable of being youthful of mind. But I will also remind them that I have always been inclined to skepticism, to a kind of Laodicean lack of commitment so far as public affairs are concerned; so that, although not as eager as I once was to be disapproved of, I can still resist prevailing opinions.

At about the age of twelve I became a Spencerian liberal, and I have always considered myself a liberal of some kind even though the definition has changed repeatedly since

Spencer became a reactionary. Several times in my youth I voted the socialist ticket, but less because I was a socialist than because I was not either a Republican or a Democrat, and I voted for Franklin Roosevelt every time he was a candidate. Yet during the years when I was on the staff of the *Nation,* I tried to the limit the patience of the editors on almost every occasion when I was permitted to write an editorial having a bearing on a political or social question.

Never once during the trying thirties did I come so close to succumbing to the private climate of opinion as to grant Russian Communism even that most weasel-worded of encomiums "an interesting experiment." There are few things of which I am prouder than of that unblemished record. Many of my friends at the time thought that I had received a well-deserved condemnation when Lincoln Steffens denounced me in a review of one of my books as a perfect example of the obsolete man who could understand and sympathize only with the dead past. But he, as I can now retort, was the man who could see so short a distance ahead that after a visit to Russia he gave voice to the famous exclamation: "I have seen the future and it works."

The favorite excuse of those who have now recanted their approval of Communism is that they did not know how things would develop. With this excuse I have never been much impressed. There was, it seems to me, enough in the openly declared principles and intentions of Russian leaders to alienate honorable men without their having to wait to see how it would turn out.

Once many years ago I sat at dinner next to Arthur Train, and the subject of the *Nation* came up. He asked me suddenly, "What are *your* political opinions?" "Well," I replied, "some of my colleagues on the paper regard me as a rank reactionary." After a moment's thought he replied, "That still leaves you a lot of latitude." And I suppose it did.

I never have been, and am not now, any kind of utopian.

When I first came across Samuel Johnson's pronouncement, "the remedy for the ills of life is palliative rather than radical," it seemed to me to sum up the profoundest of political and social truths. It will probably explain more of my attitudes toward society than any other phrase or principle could.

Why did I choose to fill these pages in this particular issue with this mixture of rather tenuous reflections and autobiography? The reason is, I think, my awareness that my remarks last quarter on pacifism may well have served to confirm the opinion of some that my tendency to skepticism and dissent gets us nowhere, and that I am simply too old to hope. I would, however, like to suggest that, wrong though I may be, the tendency to see dilemmas rather than solutions is one of which I have been a victim ever since I can remember, and therefore not merely a senile phenomenon. I know that one must act. But one need not always be sure that the action is either wise or conclusive.

Apropos of what some would call cynicism, I remember an anecdote the source of which I forget. It concerns a small-town minister who staged an impressive object lesson by confining a lion and a lamb together in the same cage outside his church door. Not only his parishioners, but the whole town and, ultimately, the whole county were enormously impressed by this object lesson. One day he was visited by a delegation of would-be imitators who wanted to know his secret. "How on earth do you manage it? What is the trick?" "Why," he replied, "it is perfectly simple; there is no trick involved. All you have to do is put in a fresh lamb from time to time." Cynical? Blasphemous? Not really, it seems to me. The promise that the lion and the lamb will lie down together was given in the future tense. It is not something that can be expected to happen now.

Without really changing the general subject, I take this opportunity to confess that I am troubled by doubts, not only about pacifism, but also when asked to join in the protest against a law that most of those who consider themselves humane and liberal seem to regard as obviously barbarous; namely, the law that prescribes the death penalty for murder when there seem to be no extenuating circumstances. It is not that I am unaware of the force of their strongest contention. Life, they say, should be regarded as sacred and, therefore, as something that neither an individual nor his society has a right to take away. In fact I cannot imagine myself condemning a man to the noose or the electric chair if I had to take, as an individual, the responsibility for his death. Just as I know I would make a bad soldier even though I cannot sincerely call myself a pacifist, so too I would not be either a hangman by profession or, if I could avoid it, even a member of a hanging jury. Despite these facts the question "Should no murderer ever be executed?" seems to me to create a dilemma not to be satisfactorily disposed of by a simple negative answer.

Punishment of the wrongdoer, so liberals are inclined to say, can have only three possible justifications: revenge, reformation, or deterrent example. The first of these, they go on, is barbarous; neither of the other two seems, on the basis of the evidence, actually to achieve the result hoped for. The criminal is not reformed, and the punishment meted out to him does not deter others from committing the same crime.

Grant, for the sake of argument, that all this is true. There remains a fourth, seldom mentioned but possible justification: the bandit cannot attack again during the period of his incarceration, and the murderer who has been hanged cannot murder again. Ought the latter be humanely given his second chance, or does the law-abiding citizen have an even greater right to protection?

Even those who, like myself, read newspapers only occasionally can hardly be unaware of the fact that an astonishing proportion of seriously criminal acts are committed by those who have a record, frequently a long one, of other offenses, usually of gradually increasing violence. This proves, it may be said, that punishment as now administered does not reform the criminal. But it is equally true that the bandit could not have managed another armed robbery if he had still been in prison, and the killer could not have killed again had he been sent to the electric chair. We spared his life, but in so doing we took another and perhaps an innocent life.

I have collected no large dossier, but I did some time ago make a note of two cases reported in the local paper within a period of a few weeks. One concerned the case of one Joseph Corbett convicted of the kidnap-murder of Adolph Coors. Corbett, said the AP dispatch, was "an escaped California murderer." About two weeks before the same newspaper reported the case of another man who had previously served a twenty-year sentence for manslaughter and had now killed two others before doing away with himself. Here, within a very short period of time, three men had lost their lives because two known killers had been again let loose upon society. Would it have been more barbarous to take their lives than it was to take, indirectly, the lives of three presumably innocent men? Who has the best right (if, as it seems, one must choose between them): a known killer or the still unknown person who may be his next victim? If the liberal humanitarian knew that he himself might be exposed to the attack of the murderer whom he had saved, would he still wish to save him?

If you don't mind my saying so . . . [IV]

[1963]

Many years ago I read a short piece by H. L. Mencken about honorable men (whom he admired) and moral men (whom he did not). It wasn't, I think, more than a paragraph and it didn't give him much room to maneuver. But if I have remembered it for so long he must have made it pretty clear what he meant by the distinction. Reduced to the simplest terms it was that an honorable man is one who keeps his word; a moral man one who insists that he always does "what is right under the circumstances."

From the first you at least know what to expect and you can count upon him. The second seems to cover a lot more ground and assumes a larger responsibility. He would do what is "right" even if it isn't (as is all too often the case) exactly what he said he would. He is strong for the spirit rather than the letter, for equity rather than legality, and he puts the greatest good of the greatest number above the promise of the contract. Though that sounds persuasive, one trouble is that equity and the greatest good so often turn out to be what is most convenient for him.

Now I realize of course that "honor" and "morality" are both concepts inadequate to cover so large and shifting a concept as those we try to indicate by them. But the distinction I follow, and Mencken is trying to make, is very important and it is easier to discuss when you are willing, for the moment, to adopt the two words as I define them. Moreover, it is evident that if you do accept them, then the relative importance which a civilization puts upon honor on the one hand and morality on the other has a great deal to do with the special quality of the civilization. To me, at least, it is equally evident that ours is so ready to give precedence to morality that honor is easily brushed aside when one seems to come into conflict with the other.

If this seems obscure let me give a simple example. I still remember my shocked realization of the seemingly irreconcilable conflict between honor and morality when Franklin Roosevelt (whom I never the less continued to admire and to vote for) announced the abandonment of the gold standard while I held in my hand a twenty-dollar certificate on which was beautifully engraved the statement that "the faith of the United States Government is pledged" to redeem this note in gold.

Please do not misunderstand me. I am not saying that we ought to have risked bankruptcy. Frankly I don't know whether we ought or ought not have done so. But if the action we did take was necessary and in the interest of the greater good, it still shocks me (and I think it should shock anyone who would like to believe that honor and morality are inseparable) that the pledged word of our government should have been so calmly broken.

I am well aware that when honor is placed above everything else it is likely to become no more than a personal and ruthless pride which can lead to such obviously immoral acts as killing your opponent in a duel or even arranging for his assassination for no reason except that personal dignity is offended; or even to such absurdities as the famous suicide of Louis XIV's cook when the fish failed to arrive on time—despite the fact that, at least in Mme. de Sévigné's version, he had been assured by the king himself that the contretemps need not be taken seriously. But if the concept of honor can grow malignantly wild like a cancer, the too easy disregard of it brings practical difficulties as well as moral shames.

When there is honor even among thieves (and there sometimes is) we at least know where we stand; when there is none among governors or nations we approach anarchy.

One of the relatively—but surely not trivial—side effects of justifying broken faith by invoking "the higher good" is the encouragement it gives to sophistical invasions and the blurring of actual facts. A generation before we found it necessary to break the pledged word of the United States Government in the matter of the gold certificates Woodrow Wilson announced conscription in preparation for World War I by proclaiming that "this is not conscription but a nation's volunteering as a whole." I am not opposed to conscription. Under the conditions of modern war to refuse to invoke it would probably be to accept inevitable defeat in advance. But is there in *1984* any more perfect example of "newsthink"? And should a government sink to the level of a Madison Avenue copywriter or the Soviet Politburo?

Newsthink, like everything good or bad, is of course not a new invention. In that line Tertullian's "It is true because it is impossible" has never been improved upon; and I sometimes think that the Miltonic conception of "true freedom" as consisting only in the freedom to do right, not in the freedom to do wrong, must regretfully be put in the same class as the Russian definition of a People's Democracy as one in which the people have nothing to say about what happens to them.

But if newsthink is not a modern invention it certainly is one we have learned how to exploit more exuberantly than ever before. (Incidentally it might be added that Anna Louise Strong once wrote an article in which she resolved the paradox of the People's Democracy by maintaining that though the Russian people probably would not have voted in favor of many of the regulations imposed upon them these regulations did nevertheless implement "their deepest desires.")

Once you accept the premises that any sort of misrepresentation is justifiable if it helps us to achieve a desirable end, and that befuddlement of the people in their own interest is moral if not entirely honorable, you run into another difficulty: just who has a right to befuddle and who has not?

Consider for example the case of our own government which attempts to restrain misrepresentation in the advertising of business enterprises but is less severe in regards to its own domestic propaganda. On the one hand the FTC recently filed a complaint against one of the large phonograph companies which had been advertising a special offer of "any six of these superb $3.98 to $6.98 long-playing 12-inch records for only $1.89." "In truth and in fact," said the FTC, "the amounts set out . . . were not and are not now the prices at which the merchandise referred to is usually and customarily sold at retail." In other words the advertisement disregarded the fact that most record shops are now "discount houses."

Is the record company's advertising any more misleading than that which the government itself sponsors for Savings Bonds? Does anyone responsible for them really believe that if you start now buying bonds to pay for the future education of your infant child on the basis of what education now costs, you will actually be able to finance it twenty years hence out of the accumulated funds? Isn't it nearly as sure as death or taxes that the value of the dollar must continue to decline, that, in fact, our ability to deal with an expanding public debt depends in part upon the assumption that we will pay it off in a depreciated currency? Also that, therefore, either the investor in Savings Bonds will be left holding the bag or the nation will go bankrupt? It may be a patriotic duty to buy Savings Bonds. But to do so is not to insure your children's future.

Such consequences of newsthink and the habit of putting morality (i.e., expedience) ahead of honor (or truth-telling) are relatively minor by comparison with the great fact that nations have come all but openly to recognize that solemn covenants are solemn frauds. Word-breaking by nations is of course also no new thing; but at least it used to be called "treachery" not "realism" and the famous World War I pronouncement that a certain treaty was merely "a scrap of paper" came as a genuine surprise as well as a shock. It remained for a younger generation to come very near to accepting the assumption that all treaties are no more. The most inclusive generalization is that attributed to Lenin: "There is no such thing as morality in politics," though "honor" might be a more accurate word than "morality."

Chamberlain justified the sacrifice of Czechoslovakia on the ground that it would serve the greater good of the greater number by assuring the peace of Europe. But as is so often the case it turned out that dishonor didn't actually create the greater good and, even had it done so in this case, it would still have remained true that the basis of international agreements upon which, in the long run, peace must depend had been destroyed. Shortly thereafter the French began to shout "don't die for Danzig," and now in our own country it is "better red than dead." No doubt I shall be told that I am idealizing the past; that individuals and nations are as honorable as they ever were; and that the only change lies in the fact that we now more frankly admit that pledges are seldom kept if they work seriously to the disadvantage of those who make them. But there certainly is less honor among individual soldiers. When we read in history about this or that captured officer who "gave his parole" and was released to go home, does not that seem merely quaint? Who would be given such a privilege today, and who, if he were given it, would not consider that violating the parole was serving the higher morality if it enabled him to render more probable the ultimate achievement of that general good for which his country was fighting?

Just before the First World War broke out, the *New York Times* printed a now famous editorial in which it regretted what it recognized as the probability of large European conflict but expressed also the comforting conviction that a war between great powers was certain to be fought with due regard to the laws and protocols of existing international agreements. Probably most people accepted the optimistic assumption of the *Times* that honor was something which nations were still anxious to preserve and that necessity, the tyrant's plea, would not be accepted as sufficient excuse for any amount of treaty breaking.

Does everything which I have been saying seem priggish and self-righteous, or, as we are more likely to say nowadays, "unrealistic"? Perhaps it will seem less so if I admit that I do not know how to resolve the problems I have been trying to face. I wish I could believe that there never is a genuine rather than a merely hypocritical conflict between the honorable and the moral. But that such a conflict can exist is exactly the most troublesome aspect of the whole subject. I am—to return to one of the simplest examples I have given— not by any means ready to say that Roosevelt was wrong in taking us off the gold standard or even that Wilson was not justified, if, at a time of crisis, he helped unify the nation by his willingness to employ that outrageous bit of newsthink about "a nation's volunteering as a whole."

The problem is even more thorny when it takes the form so usual today: "Shall I keep faith with an enemy who, I am quite sure, will not keep faith with me?" But it still remains true that of all the moral decisions a statesman has to make none is more difficult than that which seems to require him to sacrifice either honor or the general good. Even when the latter seems clearly of overriding importance there are always two dangers—the first inherent in the fact that human nature weighs the scale in favor of personal advantage; the second that you never know how much you are losing when you demonstrate the untrustworthiness of your word.

Machiavelli had a rule: "Get a reputation for truth-telling and promise-keeping by being scrupulous about both when there isn't much at stake: then, having established that reputation, you can take advantage of it when a really important piece of treachery is in the making." That solution, though eminently realistic (and seeming not sufficiently considered even for practical purposes by the Russians), can hardly be called either moral or honorable. The most I can say is only that if in certain other ages both individuals and sometimes governments too readily resolved the dilemma in favor of what they called honor, ours leans too strongly in the opposite direction and that we would all be better off today if the greatest good hadn't been so readily accepted. Lord Tennyson is responsible for the somewhat fusty Victorian paradox: "His honor rooted in dishonor stood, and faith unfaithful kept him falsely true." I only wish that some equally talented modern would describe as pointedly the opposite situation where a high morality and a greater good are rooted in faith-breaking.

I hold to the opinion that our own country has, on the whole, behaved more honorably in recent years than some of its allies as well as most of its enemies, though I am well aware that many intellectuals would hoot at this as a bourgeois prejudice. I am, on the other hand, less sure that we are any better than others when it comes to the individual's willingness to accept as a rule of private conduct that everybody does it so it must be all right.

Certainly the recent investigations of cheating in schools and colleges and the prevailing attitude toward it suggest as much, and I recently met with an extraordinarily complicated example, both of the practice and the attitude. The high school son of a Tuscon friend came to his father with a problem: pressure was being put upon him by a group of his fellows, all among the top students of the class, to join them in an elaborate scheme for falsifying the grades of some low-ranking members of the class. The conspirators would gain nothing scholastically—their grades were high already. But they would win the favor of those whom they benefited, many of the latter being among those "regular fellows" who, alas, have in the school society more status than the bookworms or the teacher's pets.

Accept honor as the decisive consideration and there is no problem; otherwise it is quite a thorny one. If you can both help the poor lame ducks along and at the same time make it easier for everybody to "adjust to the social situation," is that not achieving perhaps the greatest good for the greatest number? And isn't it therefore obvious that honor should be sacrificed to morality—that is, if honor be defined as it now so often is as no more than "that which is socially useful."

If you don't mind my saying so . . . [V]

[1955-6]

When I visited my native town in the spring of 1945, it was buzzing with rumor. At Oak Ridge, some fifty miles away, mysterious things were going on. Some said that they had to do with the disintegration of the atom, and when this guess was passed on I smiled a rather superior smile. "That," I said, "is a good many years away."

A few months later, on the morning of August sixth, my

wife broke my early morning sleep. "The radio has just announced that an atom bomb was exploded over Japan. What does *that* mean?" "It means," I said, "that I am scared to death." A bad prophet I had obviously been, but like a good many of my fellow citizens I could be wise after the event.

Usually the great crises of history have not been recognized at the moment. Few seventeenth-century Englishmen knew that an apple (the most fateful since Eve's) had fallen upon Newton's head. Decades later no Londoner exclaimed to another, "Watt has just invented the steam engine— and you know what *that* means." Only three Magi and a few shepherds knew that Jesus had been born. But we seem to have changed all that.

We may be wrong in our estimate, though it does not seem probable that we are, at least so far as the momentousness of the event is concerned. But it is less likely that we have assessed it with perfect accuracy, and ever since I recovered from the first shock I have wondered whether the most obvious meanings are the only or even the most important ones.

Everyone knows that what disintegrated along with some billions of plutonium atoms was the last small vestige of physical security for the civilian which TNT and the airplane had left us. So also, however, did various other things less immediately recognized. Even ten years later, optimists and pessimists are still concerned chiefly with the question of whether the new era is bright with the prospect of new powers and prosperity, or whether it is only a new era of destruction. But two fundamental premises vanished into thin air along with those certain material particles which ceased, in that instant, to be material at all. And the two premises were these: (1) that what we called our "control" over nature really is effective, and (2) that physical science had at last made the physical universe intelligible.

The first premise is no longer tenable because a force can hardly be said to be under control if it threatens to destroy all civilization and possibly all life. The second is not tenable because the physical universe has turned out to be so different from what was confidently assumed that some leading scientists are already expressing the opinion that it is radically unintelligible—that no image we can ever form of it will correspond to what actually is. Should we manage somehow to escape self-destruction, then it may quite possibly turn out that the abandonment of these two premises will affect the future of civilization quite as much as any new power the atom can be made to release.

That there was a catch somewhere in our boasted control was suspected by some from the time when we first began to boast of it. Those few always feared that, like Faust, we were selling our souls for powers which seemed unlimited but in fact were not. Like Faust we exclaimed:

Who would not be proficient in this art?
How pliant is this Mephistopheles,
Full of obedience and humility!
Such is the force of magic and my spells.

But like Faust again, we discovered that the Devil is controllable only so long as he consents to be, and that the more of his power we acquire, the more completely we become his victim. We controlled the steam in the piston and the electric current which circles the armature, but we neither controlled nor even foresaw the effects, good and bad, which the steam engine and the electric motor would have upon civilization.

To the few who pointed this out the reply was commonly either that the end would be somehow good or that, in any event, we must go where fate is taking us. But neither of these replies will any longer do. Mephistopheles is not to be trusted. Self-destruction is too high a price to pay for power or even for the disinterested pursuit of truth. We may be glad that we invented the Bomb first. But there are few who now doubt that it would have been better if its invention had been forever impossible to any human being whatsoever.

From the beginning, science promised us two things. Besides that ability to manipulate our physical environment which reached its ultimate when the atom was rent asunder, it promised something often called more important. Science would, it was said, do much more than make our lives more comfortable, more convenient, more safe, and more abundant. It would also give us a clear insight into The Nature of Things and replace with demonstrable Truth those fragmentary, illogical, and inconsistent notions about the structure and workings of the universe which poetry, metaphysics, and religion had foisted upon us.

The first promise has certainly been abundantly fulfilled if the word *manipulate* is insisted upon and not confused with the word *control*. But the once generally accepted belief that the second promise was also being kept turns out to be a delusion when even the less radically skeptical physicists admit that what used to be called "the scientific world view" is by no means clear or consistent and that, at a minimum, the universe is very unlike what it was supposed to be. The newest "scientific world view" dissolves nineteenth-century certainties into a mist of guesses and paradoxes at least as full of inconsistencies and incomprehensibilities as any mishmash of religion, mythology, metaphysics, and poetry ever was. "I believe because it is absurd" has come again to sum up the most advanced credo.

How many angels can stand on the point of a needle? That question, so I have been reliably informed, seems never to have been asked by any schoolman and was invented by some nineteenth-century rationalist who imagined that it was the sort of thing a schoolman would ask. Modern physics, on the other hand, does ask how many atoms could be placed on that point where angels might once have stood. Moreover, physics answers it—probably correctly enough. But it has no more idea what an atom is than it has what an angel would be like. It can count atoms and even disintegrate them. But it does not know what they are. The determination to manipulate the physical world has proved astonishingly successful while the determination to understand it seems to have failed completely.

Once we were told that if some results of technological advance were dubiously desirable we ought to be willing to accept them in exchange for that enlightenment of the understanding which accompanies the march of scientific achievement. But that understanding we now know has eluded us; and it will be a grim joke on the Hero as Scientist if the final result of his efforts is to be not merely that he will blow himself to bits, but that his last moments will be those during which he is less clear in his own mind than he ever was before concerning the real nature of the universe around him. May it be that the only things to survive Hiroshima are pure technology on the one hand and, on the other, philosophy, metaphysics, and even, as a remote possibility, religion? Did Science as Guide and Savior die there at the very moment when its claim to be a master of power was most abundantly vindicated? No poet, philosopher, or metaphysician has ever done his job one-tenth so well as the scientist did his— partly, perhaps, because the job of the scientist is easier. But no one except the poet, the philosopher, and the metaphysician has ever done the harder job at all.

Some few scientists still assure us that all they need is more time. The day will come, they say, when science will establish ethics and even aesthetics on a sound scientific basis. We shall then know what is Good and what is Beautiful as surely as we now know the formula for water. When that time comes we shall be sure at last of not only what is worth having, but how to get it; not only how to blow people up, but just who, and under what circumstances they should be disintegrated. Knowing, as then we shall, what good, wise (and of course "adjusted") men really are, we shall be able to produce them as surely as we now produce metals or plastics to fit the specifications drawn up in advance.

Perhaps. But time is running out. Can we afford to wait? Since August 6, 1945, it has seemed less likely that we can.

For as long, almost, as human thought has left a record, there have been those who insist that behind all the diverse manifestations of the universe there lies but one protean substance which reveals itself to our minds under aspects as diverse as what we call "matter" and what we call "energy," "thought," and even "spirit." Instead of saying that reality is "nothing but" one or another of these, they believed it to be something capable of being them all. At the very beginning of the scientific age, Giordano Bruno was one such. But during most of the three centuries which lie between him and us, the boldest, the most active, and the most successful investigators of nature assumed a premise directly antithetical to his. Matter and energy, for instance, were not one thing but two. What is called thought and emotion must be some form of energy if, indeed, they are to be assumed to exist at all as more than by-products of energy acting upon matter.

On the basis of this premise the great triumphs of physics and chemistry were achieved. When Einstein set forth his famous conversion formula he turned his back upon the working hypothesis which for more than three centuries had worked so well; and he took a long stride backward toward monism and Bruno. The mind-body problem did not, to be sure, concern him at the moment. He did not suggest that mind, or spirit, is the same as energy, just as energy is the same as matter. But the analogy is close and the speculative extension of the one proposition to include the other seems, at the very least, not fantastic.

Had Einstein's formula remained on paper where he himself might very well have left it, most of the world would have
been little impressed. Today, mathematics may carry more
weight than metaphysics does, but only to the new physicists, already deep in both, did a mere formula carry much
conviction. Most of us do not believe anything unless something happens when the belief is acted upon. And something did happen over Hiroshima. If a city is destroyed
because a small group of men were ready to proceed on the
assumption that $E=MC^2$, then we are willing to grant that
matter and energy really are convertible. A general public
which has never heard of monism begins to lean again in its
direction.

From news items I learn that several "teams" are still busy
officially investigating the various "side effects" of the first
bombs. But has anyone undertaken to investigate the ideological casualties, to determine not only to what concepts radia-
tion was fatal, but also what damage was suffered by those
which survived, and perhaps most important of all, what
gene mutations will reveal themselves in the next generation of concepts, philosophical as well as scientific?

Positivists are fond of assuring us that various current
terms are "meaningless." But they were hoist on their own
super-petard when its explosion rendered meaningless certain of their own favorite words, notably *material* and *materialistic*. If Einstein was as right as the bombs seem to have
proved him, then these terms have ceased to mean anything
at all.

To say "I am a materialist" is meaningful only if the concept *matter* can be defined in such a way as to distinguish
matter clearly from something else. Until a few years ago
such definition seemed easy. "Matter is that which occupies
space and has weight." This definition distinguished it as
clearly from *energy,* which occupies no space and has no
weight, as it did from *life* or *spirit* or *idea,* which, having

neither the characteristics of matter nor the characteristics of energy, were sometimes assumed not to exist at all. To say "I am a materialist" meant "I believe that the only fundamental reality is that which occupies space and which has weight."

But the matter which disintegrated privately over the American desert and then publicly over Japan ceased in those instants either to weigh anything or to occupy any space. At those instants, therefore, the meaning of the term *materialist* disappeared as completely as the disintegrated atoms themselves. When men fought in the streets of Byzantium over the terms *Homoöusian* and *Homoiousian,* some shadow of meaning may have remained in them. But between the man who says, "I am a materialist because everything is material," and the man who says, "I am not a materialist because nothing is ultimately material," no definable difference any longer exists. What is material at one moment may become, in an instant, not material at all.

On the basis of this seemingly demonstrated fact, many a scientific treatise will have to be revised if the now meaningless statements are to be eliminated from them. Almost at random I opened a recent book on one of the biological sciences. There the authority of a distinguished scientist is quoted to support the contention that the appearance of life on earth can be accounted for "without the intervention of the non-material." Does this statement, in the light of the most recent knowledge, mean anything at all?

On that morning ten years ago, my first reaction, formulated while I was still between sleep and waking, was proper enough. In fact I am rather proud of it. I had then—and we all still have—good reason to be scared. But I have wondered increasingly whether that phrase sums up everything we ought to feel. The metaphysical consequences, if we survive to enjoy them, may be salutary as well as immeasurable, and we may be waking at last from a long bad dream. It may seem a pity that blessings should come as thoroughly disguised as they sometimes do. Whoever arranged this one appears to have outdone himself—if he really did wrap up a boon in that package. But who knows? They say that God works in mysterious ways. Possibly they are sometimes even as mysterious as in this instance they seem to be.

If you don't mind my saying so . . . [VI]

[1961]

For obvious reasons there are probably more pacifists in the Western world today than there ever were before, but they are still divided into three familiar classes. Some are mystics, some call themselves rationally prudent, and some are merely muddled. I have often wished I could join one group or the other, and today it surely behooves every man to consider again the pacifist positions. But, although I have tried honestly to do so, I am still uncommitted.

The muddled are certainly the most numerous class, and they are exasperatingly noncommittal concerning what is to me a crucial question: Just what consequences do they expect to follow if one of the great powers—our own nation, for example—should accept their policy? Do they believe that the astonished aggressors would simply cease aggression, or that it is better to be a victim sure of his own righteousness than to win or lose in defense of one's life and one's place in the world? Is pacifism a wise, worldly policy or a saintly surrender?

To clarify that question, I go back to two of the hardest of many sayings in what Thoreau called an old book—the two, I mean, about turning the other cheek and about giving your cloak also. As injunctions they are unequivocal. That they should have been somehow explained away by the vast majority of those who profess to believe the Bible an absolute authority is almost enough to make one dismiss the human mind as a mere device for believing what one wants to believe. But, clear as these two injunctions are, they are also injunctions only. Like all but one of the Ten Commandments, they give not even the hint of a promise concerning the consequences so far, at least, as this life is concerned. You may infer either that the turned cheek will not be smitten, or that it is better to receive a blow on both than to resist or strike back.

Since primitive Christianity seems to have been primarily an otherworldly religion, I incline to the opinion that the second interpretation is the right one. But, just as most of those who profess to accept the authority of the New Testament have preferred to explain away the whole injunction, so most of those who have felt compelled to accept it urge it upon an easier ground. If you turn the other cheek, they seem to think, you will be rewarded, not with martyrdom, but with peace, prosperity, and a high standard of living.

Even Justice William O. Douglas, for whom it is impossible not to feel great respect in general, seems to take this position. In a recent book, *My Wilderness: The Pacific West,* he turns aside from an account of happy experiences in Alaska to comment on the fact that when two wolves threaten one another the less aggressive often turns his cheek. "This is not a signal to the other one to move in for the kill. The wolf who turns his cheek asks for a truce, and though the snarling continues, the truce is always granted. Turning the other cheek, the wolf teaches us, is not abject surrender but an honorable way to prevent a fight and save the species. As

Lorenz wrote in 'King Solomon's Ring,' a wolf has enlightened me: not so that your enemy may strike you again do you
turn the other cheek toward him, but to make him unable to
do it."

As what is sometimes contemptuously called a nature
lover, and as one who believes we should not only learn
about her but also learn *from* her, it might be assumed that
I would find this convincing. But are all men in every respect as admirable as a wolf? I am not sure that they are.
Does anyone believe that Hitler would have been unable to
strike a turned cheek? Or that Khrushchev would be? Non-
resistance may have triumphed in India, but that was because the English, whatever their crimes, were not completely ruthless. Did it work for the Jews in Germany?

The contention that only resistance creates aggression
seems to me as empty as the analogous argument of the old-
fashioned "Philosophical Anarchist" who maintained that
only law created crime. Those who contend that nonresist-
ance will actually work should be willing, I think, to demonstrate first that it will work in a single society before they
propose extending it to international relations. How many
of them if a man steal their coat will refuse to call in the police and, like the priest in *Les Misérables,* pursue him in
order to present their cloak also? How many would refuse
to ask the protection of the law if threatened by an assassin?

Ask such questions and there is usually a shifting of the
ground. "Oh, we really aren't anarchists, Christian or otherwise. We believe in the reign of law. We assume a world government and a police force under its control. Policemen
don't have to turn the other cheek, and it is only private ap-
peals to force by individuals or individual sovereignties to
which we object. Doesn't the history of the United States
show how federation is possible, and could not war be outlawed between nations as effectively as it has been outlawed
between our states?" But the appeal to our history is danger-

ous to their argument. One of the things that the experiment led to was the Civil War. We are told (truly enough, I'm afraid) that a third World War would be a catastrophe beside which the first would seem insignificant. But if you really insist upon the historical analogy with the United States of America, then a United States of the World would have to be confirmed on the most terrible of battlefields.

If the muddled still make up the largest group, the most rapidly growing is that for which Lord Russell has made himself spokesman. They do at least face squarely the necessity for a clear choice, and they rely little if at all upon any appeal to abstract righteousness. Prudence rather than virtue is the ground of their argument. Should it, they say, come down to nothing better than a choice of evils, then prudence requires that we should choose the lesser. The triumph of Communism, so Lord Russell said recently, would make the human race very miserable, perhaps for a very long time. But it would at least continue to exist and have in some distant era the chance of a new happiness. But armed resistance on any grand scale would extinguish it forever. If, as one of his supporters has added, there are those who prefer death to slavery, they could kill themselves when the invasion comes while those who would like to choose the other alternative would be powerless to do so if a policy of resistance were followed.

It is all very well to ridicule the rhetoric of Patrick Henry. But one wonders if those who do so would be willing to face the either/or and to accept as their own motto, "It is better to be a living dog than a dead lion," or "Who hath honor? He who died 'a Wednesday."

Actually, so it seems to me, they missed the real point which becomes plain enough if you go back to Patrick. When we say "give me liberty or give me death," we are not usually standing as he was on a gallows, and we are not usually taking it for granted that the choice is certain to present itself.

We say it because we believe that the best way to get liberty is to be willing to face death. Many of those who approved of what Patrick Henry said might very well, had the situation become hopeless, have preferred slavery to death. But had they said so at the moment, they might well have lost both. Surely our own situation is much the same. Even if Lord Russell is right that slavery is better than extinction, the fact remains that we have a far better chance of saving both life and liberty if we have the nerve to go to Patrick rather than Bertrand for our motto. Proclaim that you would rather lose liberty than life, and you are far more likely to lose the first and not improbably the second also.

From the standpoint of worldly wisdom, the English neutralists may be right so far as their own situation is concerned. It is indeed much what the situation of Ireland was during the Second World War. Participation would not have affected the outcome; England was compelled to give them all the protection that could be given; and they were exempt from direct attack. England today gets the advantage of whatever deterrent effect American arms may have, and so far as she is concerned to be unarmed would be perhaps safest. But we are either the first or the second great power (which may be unfortunate for us) and no one is capable of protecting us. England escapes the necessity of an either/or but we cannot; we must either assert our power or renounce it completely. To say, "I am not a consistent pacifist, but we should refuse to participate in an arms race" is to fall between two stools. To be inadequately armed is certainly (and from a purely prudential standpoint) worse than not to be armed at all—unless, as in the case of the weaker nations, someone else is strong enough to give the protection they cannot give themselves.

Thus I come back to my original contention that the only sound premise upon which pacifism can be defended is that taken by at least some Quakers and by the others who accept literally and without reservation the injunction, "resist not evil." This is something very different from and much more admirable than "better a living dog than a dead lion." It is somewhat different also from the Christian Anarchy sometimes expounded in, for instance, the *Catholic Worker,* which is, if I understand it rightly, the doctrine that since a community of saints could live without law and without property, such a community would spontaneously arise were law and property abolished. The purest pacifism is compatible with the belief that anarchy soon leads (as I believe it does) not to the community of saints but to the rule of the gangsters. It comes down ultimately to the belief that righteousness is more to be valued than security, prosperity, social order, and even life itself. All the more popular sorts of pacifism seek worldly ends by unworldly means. And that works no better than the policy of most organized Christianity which too often has been to rely upon the worldly as a means of achieving unworldly ends.

I am not by nature combative or even very competitive. I would make a very poor soldier, and I am not sure I would not be a cowardly one. I might even run away. But if I ever become a sincere pacifist, it will be not because I think it would save my skin (I do not think it would) but because I was convinced, as I believe the only logical pacifists are, that to be individually righteous is the first of all duties, come what may to one's self, to one's country, to society, and to civilization itself.

I am already half (or perhaps one-quarter would be more accurate) convinced that this is true. Why then do I reluctantly conclude, when all that can be said about the horrors of war, the insane folly of atomic weapons, and the very real threat of a horror such as the world has never known before has been said and proved, that I still side not with the pacifists but with those who say, "Let us, of course, explore every possibility for mutual (but not unilateral) disarmament and mutual (but not unilateral) guarantees against aggression. But until such desirable ends have been attained, let us recognize the fact that we must continue in the nearly but not quite insane race for arms." The answer to that "why" is, I suppose, partly that I am only one-half or one-quarter convinced that the highest and most desirable wisdom consists in not being wise at all in any worldly sense; that, to put it as directly as possible, the world is not worth having at the price one must sometimes pay to have it. The other part of the answer, if indeed it is not the same one, is simply that I am not saint enough actually to renounce a world that I may at some moments believe not worth having but which I have found at other more numerous moments something I would hate to give up. Thus perhaps I also, like the muddled pacifists I scorned, fall between two stools and may end as the most unhappy of victims, the martyr who finds little consolation in martyrdom.

Many years ago an astrologer cast my horoscope and predicted that I would live to a ripe old age but "die a public and spectacular death." I have often wondered what that might portend—the barricades, or perhaps a public execution? But surely no death could be more spectacular than that in the explosion of a hydrogen bomb.

That this is indeed to be my fate seems to have been made more probable by the fact that Tucson, Arizona, where I live, has been selected by the military authorities as one of the expendable cities to be ringed by Titan missile bases, and that these same authorities are frank to admit not only that it might well be wiped out by a direct hit, but also that due to the prevailing winds the fallout from even a near miss would blanket the city. We have been advised to build individual shelters and to stock them with food for several days, after which, we are told, it might be safe to emerge—assuming, of course, that a direct hit had not been scored. Until it is explained to me what I would want to come out either to or for, I plan no shelter. And I have been much interested in the attitude taken by the citizens when it was first announced that we had, as I put it before, been declared expendable.

There was to be sure a small minority protest from those who asked why the missile bases should not be placed away from the city rather than directly surrounding it. The reply from the authorities was that it would be too difficult and too expensive to construct them very far from the facilities that a city affords. This seemed a surprising statement to those who had supposed that the ultimate purpose of "defense" was not to save money, but to save lives. However, the argument apparently satisfied most Tucsonians and the protest got nowhere. On the other hand, the majority of the citizens and at least one of the newspapers rejoiced that our community was to be favored by a large construction project, and it warned the minority that unless they dropped their protest the army might decide in a huff to take its plans to some more cordial community. So far as I am aware, the plea for patriotism was never raised. No one said that we must be good soldiers, that some cities had to be expendable, and that if the choice fell upon us we must accept our fate. The talk was all of the money the bases would bring and the number, first of construction workers and then of military personnel, who would be added to our population. I have the consolation of believing that if my reasons for not being a pacifist are not entirely noble, they are at least not as ignoble as Tucson's reasons for welcoming a direct invitation to atomic attack.

One radio commentator did suggest that what we had won by our cordial welcome to the military authorities might best be described as "a disaster with fringe benefits." That sometimes seems to me a very good estimate of many technological triumphs. There is scarcely one of them—not even television—which does not afford at least fringe benefits. Many have made life easier and easier—temporarily at least. But what if they should end by making it not easier but impossible?

When cavemen were hitting one another over the head with stone clubs, it was not necessary to be either a pacifist or a glorifier of war. One could simply muddle through. We continued to do so as the bow, the cannon, the airplane, and the T.N.T. bomb came along one after another. But the time may have come when one must decide either to die as a saint or to survive as a gangster. And that leaves in a very awkward position those who, like me, do not want to be the second yet feel themselves not quite up to being the first.

Reflections on the Fifties

[1960]

To those (and they are many) who still have faith in American progress as we are accustomed to measure it, the fifties must have fulfilled expectations.

All the accepted indices continued to rise. Population increased at an accelerated rate; houses arose to shelter it; food continued to be produced in more than adequate amounts. Cities grew and roads were built as well as rebuilt. The national income and the average income rose. Production per man-hour increased and the work week shortened. The average (and less fortunately, perhaps, the above-average) man had more television sets and more free hours in which to watch them.

The only threat to prosperity seemed to be that our citizens could not be persuaded to spend enough and waste enough. At one point it threatened to falter, but the threat soon vanished and confirmed us in the belief that ours really is that New Era the twenties so firmly believed in. Prosperity, we now think, is not automatic (as the twenties believed) but is, nevertheless, "controllable" if you have the economic as well as the technological know-how.

No new technological development was quite so revolutionary as the preceding decade's great gift to mankind: atomic fission. Still, the bombs did get bigger and more destructive so rapidly that the little one which wiped out Hiroshima now seems as quaint as a Model T, and the sudden appearance of one Sputnik after another was proof enough that we are still in an age capable of accomplishing the impossible. Automation promised soon to make it unnecessary for men to work and electric brains promised to relieve them of the possibly more burdensome task of thinking.

Among the minor but nevertheless significant accomplishments of the decade should be mentioned the appearance of the first power-driven swizzle sticks (which were duly advertised in the class magazines) and, in the midst of a mechanized world, the touch of old-fashioned glamour provided by Miss Grace Kelly when she became the very first American ever to marry a ruling prince. International amity was increased not only by the visit of Khrushchev but also by the world-wide recognition of a new ideal of the eternally feminine as represented by Brigitte Bardot. Congressional investigation of quiz shows revealed that even scandals grow bigger and better. As for that campaign against prudery and puritanism of which many of us still living remember the earliest beginnings, it was by the end of the fifties so completely triumphant that the most recent work of our most talented playwright had a castration as its climax and one of our best-selling novels concerned the reciprocal seductions of an experienced satyr and a subadolescent nymphomaniac.

Thanks to the latter work "nymphet" became, along with "Sputnik" and "beatnik," the most significant additions to the vocabulary, and only a few noted that the Russian derivation of the two last might signal a shift of the center of cultural gravity from the West to the East.

A few scientists like the Messrs. Oppenheimer and Pauling suggested that it might be wise to ask where we are going rather than merely "How fast can we get there?" but they were in a minority. Eight other leading scientists (including two Nobel prize winners) agreed to celebrate the centenary of Seagram's whiskey by looking into the future. The event was not without significance just as an example of cooperation between science and commerce but it is even more revealing when one considers the nature of the blessings which the scientists promised to confer: vegetable steaks, mail delivery from satellites, recreational resorts on space platforms, and machines which will abolish all labor.

If we manage to survive we may really get all these boons; and, significantly, even among those of us who feel that the "if we survive" is a very large "if" indeed, a great many assume that such blessings are those which it would be most worth while to have, that they ought to be sufficient to make mankind say at last, "Life is good."

Nevertheless there is an aspect of the fifties which future historians (supposing that there are any) may judge quite as significant as either technological advance or the warnings of a minority among those who are helping (sometimes rather reluctantly) to promote it. It is this: the gap between those who find the spirit of the age congenial and those who do not seems to have grown wider and wider.

No doubt the philosopher, the social critic, and the poet often refuse to "go along" wholeheartedly with the ideals, dominant aims, and judgments of their society, but it is surely not usual for them to dig a gulf as wide as that which, during the fifties, separated art, literature, and abstract thought from what seemed to be the main stream of the age. If "progress" was still the key word and the key concept for the majority of Americans, "alienation" was widely accepted as the key word and the key concept for an increasing number of intellectuals and artists. While the one group hurried eagerly forward, the other rejected both what has been achieved and, often, all hope of anything which might be.

"Modern" poetry, "modern" art, and "modern" music no doubt won a larger audience than they had in the forties but they did not do so by moving any closer to the comprehension or concern of the majority, to whom they still remain a closed book. They got their larger audience by detaching an increased number of persons from that majority and thus increasing the tension rather than promoting harmony or even comprehension between the "adjusted" majority and the now more numerous "alienated." Poetry became, if anything, more "difficult" and esoteric; music less accessible except to aficionados; painting more "abstract." In literature the existentialist and the beatnik provoked the most discussion, but neither could be called anything but merely disruptive. During the twenties a Sinclair Lewis invited Main Street to mend its ways by berating it in terms which it could understand. But the modern novels most discussed in advanced circles during the fifties are nihilistic. They speak a language which those who now get their ideas from Madison Avenue rather than Main Street cannot understand and they preach despair rather than, as Lewis did, the benefits of a culture accessible to all who want it.

If we assume that the boasted alienation of the intellectual and the artist does not mean simply (as the alienated themselves seem sometimes to think) the end of everything, then it may foreshadow either of two opposite developments. It may mean that the artist and the philosopher are indeed on the way out as significant elements in the life of mankind and that what the fifties witnessed was simply their death agony and the final failure of an approach to life which will be completely forgotten in the purely rational, material, and scientific "culture" now evolving. Conceivably, on the other hand, it may mean just the opposite, namely that the world of science and engineering, of Madison Avenue and the usual ideas of progress, is coming to an end either by self-destruction or in response to the protest of an outraged humanity whose despair will vanish when the world ceases to violate it. The fifties have given no clear indication which outcome is the more likely to occur.

If the technician and the existentialist seem to have been living in worlds so completely discontinuous that no communication between them was possible, the less esoteric "social critics" did succeed in making some contact with those who directed the institutions under attack. Thus Madison Avenue took the critics of advertising seriously enough to answer them, and the dominant school of "educators" was, for the first time in a generation, compelled to defend rather than merely to take for granted the neglect of "basic education" in the interests of "life adjustment," "the normal child," etc. At the same time, criticism of "conformity" became so prevalent that nonconformists were, with some show of reason, accused of merely practicing a new conformity of their own.

Obviously, then, the accomplishments, the methods, and the ideals of those ruling our society did not go entirely unchallenged. The fifties was an ideological battleground. But the outcome is still dubious and the question whether or not the attacks will have any large permanent effect remains open. How deep will the proposed reforms in education go? Was the "hate Detroit" movement (as one automobile manufacturer called it) significant as at least a symbol of a real revolt against the whole insane tendency to regard "bigger" (also "faster," "costlier," etc.) as necessarily "better" or was it merely one of fashion's trivial shifts and no more significant than the rise and fall of hemlines and waists? Though Madison Avenue did deign to take notice of its critics it was not apparent that advertising either changed its methods or lost any of its power. Television was so little affected that it elaborated during the decade the most grandiose and unequivocal swindle ever perpetrated in the whole history of the medicine show—of which institution, rather than the theater, it is an extension. At the same time "popular culture" got so much (often favorable) attention from one section of the intelligentsia that it seemed as likely to convert the highbrow as to be reformed by him.

As juvenile delinquency continued to rise it was more and more discussed. Here and there individuals timidly raised the question whether the increasing lawlessness and violence of teen-agers did not cast some doubts upon the attempts to deal with it by "modern" methods based upon "understanding" and the assumption that since "society" was responsible, the individual could not justifiably be held to account. Juveniles themselves were prompt to proclaim themselves merely the product of their environment and even to remind law-enforcement officers that, as juveniles, they were specifically exempt from the normal legal penalties no matter how "adult" the crimes themselves seemed to be. But in the case of this particular problem also, it is still uncertain whether any fundamental change in the approach will actually be made or whether the majority will continue to agree that (as one of a band of teen-agers arrested for vandalizing a grave "just for kicks" recently complained): "Adults don't understand the problems of the juvenile."

Obviously (to put all this in another way) the decade of the fifties was aware of many unanswered questions, both detailed and more inclusive, but it gave no clear answer to any of them. Despite its almost obsessive concern with "security" it felt desperately insecure. The decade seemed to bring no nearer any new Age of Confidence like that to which it looked back incredulously, but which had seemed to those who lived in it before World War I the natural and permanent result of the answers—scientific, moral, and political—which the nineteenth century had given. Not a few of the most searching minds of the fifties were uncertain whether our world was, in fact, poised between two worlds, one dying and the other only temporarily powerless to be born, or whether it had reached an impasse beyond which no new civilization could even be hoped for. If the most notable achievements of the decade turn out to be merely bigger bombs and smaller automobiles, then history (again supposing that there is to be any) will not consider its contributions very great.

"Agonizing reappraisal," a phrase first applied to a specific situation, was found so generally apt that it became among intellectuals a cliché which by itself reveals a state of mind. But there are at least some who believe that if the fifties seem to have accomplished comparatively little it is because too few who believed that they were asking fundamental questions went on to ask others still more fundamental, but continued instead to accept premises which made searching inquiry impossible.

Most people supposed, for example, that they were raising an ultimate question when they debated Communism vs. liberal democracy as it exists in the United States. Yet, however important certain differences between the two systems may be and however preferable one may be to the other, the fact remains that the kinds of Good Life which each promises have a great deal in common. Both accept power, wealth, and the standard of living as the chief tangible evidences of success or failure and both accept much the same theories of human nature (the chief difference lying in the greater clarity and rigidity with which the Communists formulate them). Both tend, that is to say, to assume that man is the product of society, that his nature and his condition can both be improved only through the improvement of social conditions, and that, given material welfare, men will inevitably become more intelligent, more moral, and more cultured. The dispute between them tends to become merely a dispute over the question which system is most likely to produce the kind of society both aim at.

If you believe that there is something more than mere sentimentality in the charge that American life (indeed, the life in all "developed" countries) is materialistic, conformist, and increasingly barbaric in its indifference to any culture except that of TV, the movies, and jazz; if you believe that all the money spent on schools has not provided a good education and that juvenile delinquency is by no means confined to "the underprivileged"; if you believe all that, then you can hardly avoid asking, not only whether democracy or Communism will in the end be most successful in providing a high standard of living for all, but also whether the pursuit of a high standard of living is actually the chief end of man. Even if it is a *sine qua non* of the Good Life, it may not be the one thing necessary.

Perhaps the "agonizing reappraisal" so often recommended has not been profound enough, however agonizing it may have been. And perhaps it would be worth while to look at some of the most fundamental questions of our times, and see whether there is any sign that anyone began to ask them during the fifties.

The fundamental answers which we have on the whole made, and which we continue to accept, were first given in the seventeenth century by Francis Bacon, Thomas Hobbes, and René Descartes, and were later elaborated and modernized by Marx and the Darwinians. These basic tenets of our civilization (in chronological but not quite logical order) are: (1) the most important task to which the human mind may devote itself is the "control of nature" through technology (Bacon); (2) man may be completely understood if he is considered to be an animal, making predictable reactions to that desire for pleasure and power to which all his other desires may by analysis be reduced (Hobbes); (3) all animals (man excepted) are pure machines (Descartes); (4) man, Descartes notwithstanding, is also an animal and therefore also a machine (Darwin); (5) the human condition is not determined by philosophy, religion, or moral ideas because all of these are actually only by-products of social and technological developments which take place independent of man's will and uninfluenced by the "ideologies" which they generate (Marx).

Perhaps none of these answers to fundamental questions was given in quite so simple a form by the thinker to whom it is here attributed. Perhaps the assent given to them is more explicit and unqualified among Communists than among even left-wing liberals of the West. But at the very minimum they haunted the imagination and influenced the thinking even of those most disturbed by their implications.

To insist that these commonly accepted answers should be re-examined is not necessarily to deny that some of them served for a time as useful working principles. Marxism led to a recognition of the social factors which do indeed influence moral ideas and conduct. The assumption that all living creatures are machines did lead to a better understanding of the human mechanism. Darwinism did furnish the key to many secrets. Baconianism is responsible for all that is good as well as most that is evil in a technologically advanced civilization. But useful working principles outlive their usefulness. And just as the time came when a complete acceptance of Newtonian physics would have made further understanding of the physical world impossible, so a refusal to question Baconianism, Hobbism, Darwinism, and the rest makes it impossible to deal with the problems to which an uncritical acceptance of them has led.

Nevertheless a majority, even of the thoughtful, refuse to

recognize (to take specific examples) that still greater production will not guarantee a better life; that a refusal to recognize the moral responsibility of the individual cannot solve
the problem of juvenile delinquency; and, perhaps most important of all, that the invention of a device which may an-
nihilate the human race proves that our boasted "control of
nature" is so much an illusion that we have no idea how to
control a phenomenon far more dangerous than any previous
threats.

We have reached the end of an epoch because the accepted
answers to the most fundamental questions created a situation bristling with problems which cannot be solved in the
terms those answers prescribe. Unless we can to some extent
modify them the end of an epoch may also be the end of a
world.

To what extent, if any, did the decade of the fifties recognize the possibility of modifying the answers upon the basis
of which the good and bad of our world have been constructed? Paradoxically enough, the most radical revisions
were those that continued to be made by the physicists who
explicitly rejected the whole concept of a rigidly and mechanically predictable universe. While they were doing so,
sociologists, psychologists, and even biologists often seemed
unaware that by doing so the physicists had knocked the
props from under the now old-fashioned premises of the science of life and the science of man which had rested largely
upon the picture of the physical universe now abandoned by
those whose special field of competence it is.

The extent to which these latter were willing either to
draw conclusions outside the field of physics or even to admit
that such conclusions might legitimately be drawn varied
from individual to individual. But it is surely of great possible significance that during the closing year of the decade
Harvard's P. W. Bridgman, a Nobel prize winner and one of

the most distinguished of living physicists, should have published a long, closely reasoned, and difficult book (*The Way
Things Are*) in which he renounced his previous convictions
to declare that he no longer believed sociology, ethics, aesthetics, or even biology to be subjects which can be profitably
studied by the "positive" methods borrowed from the physical sciences. Thus he reaffirmed precisely what three centuries had tended increasingly to doubt—namely our mysterious, incommensurable humanness.

Though sociologists and psychologists may on the whole
have tended to cling most stubbornly to traditional attitudes,
not all of either did so and some biologists and anthropologists quite explicitly rejected century-old orthodoxies in such
popular books as *The Universe and You,* by McGill's geneti-
cist N. T. Berrill, and *The Immense Journey,* by Pennsyl-
vania's anthropologist Loren Eiseley.

Looking about for a single brief statement which would
illustrate what may possibly be the most significant tendency
of the fifties, I choose the following from Sir Julian Huxley,
partly because it opens a wide chink in the armor of the
mechanist, the positivist, and the determinist, partly because
no one questions the scientific competence of Sir Julian or
could accuse him of having been, in general, anything but
orthodox in his convictions. Writing a preface to a work by
the somewhat mystical French biologist de Chardin, he says:
"Some biologists, indeed, would claim that mind is generated
solely by the complexification of certain types of organization, namely brains. However, such logic appears to me narrow. The brain alone is not responsible for mind, even
though it is a necessary organ for its manifestation."

To anyone who will let those sentences and their implications sink in, it will be evident that once the independence
of the mind as separate from the brain is granted, once mind
is regarded as an independent creator, then every one of the

five basic assumptions upon which the modern world rests (or perhaps one should now say totters) is, happily, open to question.

Through happiness with slide rule and calipers

[1963]

From my own childhood I remember the story of a little boy whose chief delight was in his Sunday school—until a worldly uncle took him out to the ball game. That evening he announced that he was never going to Sunday school again. He had had some real fun for the first time.

Now the lesson to be learned from this story is that you can never evaluate an experience of your own without comparing it with something else and can't evaluate the experience of anyone else at all—because you can never really know what it was. When a man tells you that he enjoys Mickey Spillane and rock-'n'-roll as much as you do Tolstoy and Beethoven there is no way of knowing whether this is true or not. Maybe if he ever got from Tolstoy and Beethoven what you get, he would not waste time on his present favorites.

This is one of the many reasons why sociological measurements of contentment, or efforts to determine what people ought to have in the way of education, employment, and "standard of living" to make them happy, are very nearly meaningless. You can't tell how much contentment they expect or have ever known. This man's contentment may be what those who have been used to a richer life would call dissatisfaction or even misery. We can't even know whether or not it is true that most men lead lives of quiet desperation.

These ponderous reflections were inspired by a recent report from the National Opinion Research Center at the University of Chicago entitled *In Pursuit of Happiness—A Pilot Study of Behavior Related to Mental Health*. I presume that it is well done as such things go and that its "methodology" would be approved by other sociologists. But my own first reaction is simply this: the war between science and religion will be settled long before that between literature and sociology. The proponents of each were born under different stars and are equally incapable of seeing the same things as either significant or interesting.

To the sociologist it seems that the poet and the philosopher deal only in opinions and guesses for which they offer no substantiating proof and that they inhabit what I once heard a professor of sociology describe as "the never-never land of the humanities." To those who, for good or ill, exemplify what is called "the literary mind," the sociologist seems, on the other hand, to pretend to define the indefinable, to measure the unmeasurable, and then to come up with conclusions that are either not demonstrated at all or, quite as frequently, so obvious that they need no demonstration.

Before I go into more detail concerning any of the charges that I make so recklessly, let me give two specific examples of, first, the laboriously demonstrated obvious and, second, the measurement of the unmeasurable.

Example 1. On the basis of answers given to a questionnaire concerning things the questioned worry about, it is stated that only 4 per cent of those under fifty, as opposed to 21 per cent of those fifty or over, worry about growing old. Do we need any ghost come from the grave or any researcher from a National Research Center to tell us that? Without any investigation whatever I venture to state that only a fraction of 1 per cent of those under six worry at all about growing old—unless you count worrying because they are not growing old as fast as they would like.

Example 2. In an elaborate analysis of a set of figures dealing with (a) the degree to which a subject calls himself "happy" and (b) how much worrying he thinks he does, I read the following:

> Somewhat surprisingly, however, there is no relation between positive feelings and intensity of worry, 23% of both those with high and with low positive feelings and intensity of worry reporting that they worry a lot. We find also that men with high anxiety (34% as against 20% of the lows), those with high marital tension (26% as against 19% of the lows), and those with low job satisfaction (26% as against 18% of the highs) report worrying a lot. Intensity of worry is thus negatively related to well-being.

This is a real beaut. Note first the statistical proof of the obvious, namely the fact that those who are anxious and don't like their wives or their jobs worry more than those who are serene, happily married, and content with their jobs. Note second the gobbledygook. Instead of saying that those who say they worry a lot are not less likely than others to say that they are happy, you get "intensity of worry is thus negatively related to well-being." Note third that this supposed paradox is easily resolved on the basis of common-sense observation concerning the vagueness of the units of measurement and the subjective nature of the individual's estimate of his own condition. In the first place "a lot" is not a meaningful unit of measurement. In the second place, it seems obvious enough that when two individuals are asked whether or not they worry "a lot" the answer may depend upon how much worry each thinks is inevitable and how much he supposes most other people do. "A lot" may be very little to one, a great deal to another. Talk about the literary man's being merely subjective! There is no way of correlating external situations or even behavior patterns with the inner state that constitutes "happiness."

Ever since literature began it has had a good deal to say and even more to imply about happiness. Sociology is a much more recent enterprise and my impression is ("my impression"; there, says the sociologist, is the literary mind at work) that it was rather late in its own development before it took up happiness in addition to more tangible subjects. Presently I shall give some examples of the kind of thing literature on the one hand and sociology on the other have had to say on this subject, but first I must insist that it seems to me (there goes the literary mind again) that an important difference between the two is that sociology (unlike literature) professes to be a science and therefore has no right to talk about anything unless it can be clearly defined. Yet when the study under consideration attempts to define what it proposes to investigate it takes uneasy refuge by saying that "the underlying assumption of this research is that there is a dimension called variously mental health, subjective adjustment, happiness, or psychological well-being. . . . At present there is neither a generally agreed upon name for this dimension nor agreement as to the appropriate methods of deciding where a particular individual should be placed on such a dimension. . . . The pilot study reported here was undertaken in the belief that much of the disagreement stems from a basic lack of knowledge about the behavior of people leading normal lives."

Was there ever such a mare's nest of definitions in terms of things not themselves defined and equatings of the dubiously equatable? What is a normal life; or is it merely an average one? If "mental health" is synonymous with "happiness," if happiness is defined as "subjective well-being" and subjective well-being defined as "adjustment" and "adjustment" defined as "that which provides a normal life," which is to say "a happy life," how do we break out of this circular series of definitions? And of course there are also all the now-familiar questions concerning adjustment as an ideal.

Even more important is the fact that the whole of the ancient dispute about the contentment of a contented hog and the discontent of a discontented Socrates pops up. The present study seems to imply that the state of the contented (or shall we say "adjusted" and "normal") hog is to be preferred to that of the discontented Socrates, or at least may be compared with it. But Samuel Johnson (a man of letters) says something on the subject which a sociologist might ponder before he attempts to penetrate the secret of content and adjustment. Boswell is reporting:

> I mentioned Hume's notion that all who are happy are equally happy; a little miss with a new gown at a dancing school ball, a general at the head of a victorious army, and an orator, after having made an eloquent speech in a great assembly. *Johnson:* Sir, that all who are happy, are equally happy is not true. A peasant and a philosopher may be equally *satisfied* but not equally *happy*. . . . I remember this very question very happily illustrated in opposition to Hume, by the Reverend Mr. Robert Brown, at Utrect. "A small drinking glass and a large one, may be equally full; but the large one holds more than the small."

Questionnaires take the replies of any subject at face value; the questioner must assume that any man's reply is as reliable as that of any other. Hence he might find himself compelled to conclude that the well-fed hog wallowing in his sty was more content (therefore "happier," "better adjusted to a normal life," and in sounder "mental health") than the grumbling philosopher. There is no place in the present study where divine discontent may be recorded.

The person being questioned is occasionally asked such a question as "Did you feel on top of the world any time last week?" But "happy" seems often to mean "not unhappy" and the key terms—"mental health," "adjustment," and "normal"—are all rather negative, while happiness is or ought to be positive. Contrast the sociologist's few drab words, all of which are assumed to refer to approximately the same thing, with the rich vocabulary of literature that recognizes an extensive hierarchy, every level of which implies a discrimination instead of assuming a dubious identity. This hierarchy might run something like this: Contentment, amusement, fun, pleasure, happiness, delight, joy, ecstasy. It is true that literature does not attempt to define these terms and the sociologists will say that they are vague. But there is a complexity that the man of letters is aware of and the sociologist obscures.

At about the same time I began to read *In Pursuit of Happiness* I found in my newspaper a reporter's account of a check-up visit to a couple that had been married for seventeen years. He found them happy (the word is his) and got the opinion of a neighbor that the marriage had turned out better than most of those in the neighborhood, even though this "happy" couple lived in near destitution in a shack on a rutted dirt road in Kentucky.

Even this would not have made them newsworthy, but another fact did: Seventeen years ago, when the wedding took place, the husband was seventeen and the wife seventy-seven. I suppose that the sociologist would find them not "normal" (*i.e.,* average) but I don't see how he could escape the conclusion that they were, by his own definition, happy and well adjusted. Moreover, they enjoy a high degree of "job (or jobless) satisfaction" since they are content to live on the wife's relief payments.

Those of us who are blessed or cursed with the literary mind would not be greatly distressed by this happy couple's failure to be "normal" since we have no prejudice in favor of what we prefer to call, not the normal, but the average. We would, however, question the significance of the broad term "happy" and ask, "Where do they stand on the amusement, fun, pleasure, joy, and ecstasy scale?" Though both we and the sociologists will probably agree that the situation of this contented couple is not the most desirable one, literature would throw more light than sociology does on the question why most of us would not change places with either the ninety-four-year-old wife or the thirty-four-year-old husband. Neither would know how to make all men happy, but I still think that a familiarity with the best that has been thought and said by men of letters is more helpful than all the sociologists' statistics.

Misguided attempts to deal quantitatively with so complex a thing as happiness are the enemies of literature and perhaps of happiness itself because they encourage us to assume both that one kind of happiness is the same as another and that they are equally valuable. In fact nothing is more important, prudentially or morally, than the realization that whether or not the pursuit of happiness is a legitimate chief aim depends upon which of the many happinesses one chooses and upon the means used to pursue it. Taken seriously, statistical studies are all too likely to teach us only how to become dismally "adjusted." Is it safe to take seriously a study in which you put in the same category everyone who says that he frequently feels "on top of the world," even though feeling on top of the world may mean anything from the friskiness of a puppy to the joy celebrated in the Ninth Symphony?

Here, chosen almost at random, are some of the things that some of the best thinkers and sayers have had to say on the general subject of happiness—which Alexander Pope called "our being's end and aim." They are wildly diverse, sometimes flatly contradictory, and range upward from the profound pessimism with which my little anthology begins. But for all their inconclusiveness they tell us more about the experience of being human than all the sociologists' demonstrations that job satisfaction contributes to contentment and that older men worry more than young ones about growing old.

"The natural progress of the human mind is not from pleasure to pleasure but from hope to hope" (Johnson); "None would live past years again yet all hope pleasure from what yet remain" (Dryden); "Call that man happy and that man alone he who can call today his own" (Horace); "Pleasures are like poppys spread; you seize the flower the bloom is dead" (Burns); "We are never as lucky or as unlucky as we believe" (La Rochefoucauld); "Pleasure and beauty are byproducts: The direct pursuit of pleasure and beauty is folly" (Bernard Shaw); "Young men spend their time anticipating the future: Old men in remembering the past" (Anonymous); "Better a dinner of herbs where love is than a stalled ox with hate" (the Bible); "Rarely, rarely comest thou, spirit of delight" (Shelley); "Many green islands there must be/In the wide sea of misery" (Shelley); "That sad word joy" (Landor); "I have known such joys as might have inspired a Homer or a Shakespeare" (Thoreau); "God's in His heaven, all's right with the world" (Browning); "I have a lover's quarrel with life" (Robert Frost).

It is true that poets have more often written odes to dejection than exclaimed with Shelley "The world's great age begins anew" or with Donne "And now good morrow to our waking souls." But even in that fact there may lie the useful suggestion that to expect joy too often is to experience it less frequently; and literature, unlike sociology, offers consolation. Isn't Frost's lover's quarrel with life more fruitful than "adjustment"?

Since I would not like to deprive anyone of legitimate aid in reaching "our being's end and aim," I will pass on to those who may find them useful a few of the conclusions based on this "pilot study" of 2,006 persons, of whom 24 per cent said they were "very happy," 59 per cent "pretty happy," and 17 per cent "not too happy."

College graduates with incomes of $7,000 a year or more are happier than those who have had no formal education past grammar school and who make less than $3,000. But before you decide to make yourself happier by achieving some higher learning, consider a further fact: "When the income is the same, the better educated are less happy than their less cultivated counterparts. Single women are only slightly more unhappy than married women, but single men are twice as unhappy as married men." The conclusion for those who put their faith in statistics as a guide would seem to be, first, don't get too much education unless you think you are going to earn a considerable income and, second, if you are a man make every effort to find a wife, while, if you are a woman, leave marriage or single blessedness up to chance while you concentrate on goals like "job satisfaction" that are more likely to affect your happiness.

A more general conclusion is that the degree of happiness is influenced more by positive satisfactions than by dissatisfactions so that those who have many worries will nevertheless call themselves happy if they have many "positive feelings." "Happiness is a resultant of the relative strengths of positive and negative feelings rather than of the absolute amount of one or the other." These all-important positive feelings are said to be most likely to be dominant in those who are active participants in social gatherings. (This is a good place to point out that, however true this may be statistically, it doesn't mean that "togetherness" will necessarily produce results.) Thoreau—who, I suppose, was not "normal"—was one of the few men who have ever called themselves almost unqualifiedly happy. But I doubt that he would have been so if he had read a pilot study and decided to mend his ways. Statistics take no account of those who prefer to hear a different drummer.

Perhaps, indeed, the most important of all the limitations

of the sociological method is the result of its usual assumption that happiness or unhappiness is principally dependent upon some external conditions; that we are as content or malcontent as our situation ought to make us. Yet all human experience, as well as most literature, recognizes that such is very far from being the case. In his book on Dickens, Gilbert Chesterton points out that this extravagant optimist became such long before he had escaped from the misfortunes which persistently dogged his boyhood, and he adds other examples to support the paradox that personal experience does not make optimists or pessimists. Even more relevant perhaps are the lines Samuel Johnson added at the end of Goldsmith's "The Traveller":

> How small of all that human hearts
>   endure,
> That part which kings or laws can
>   cause or cure.
> Still to ourselves in every place
>   consign'd,
> Our own felicity we make or find.

Little things, even trivial things, often make us happy, while catastrophes are often surmounted. We go up or down for unreasonable reasons, finding the world alternately bright or dark because we are, as Pope said, "too soon dejected and too soon elate." All things considered, we can learn more about happiness as an inner and wayward state from *Happiness Is a Warm Puppy* than from the ambitious compilation of the answers to a sociologist's questionnaire.

To those who are already pretty normal and well adjusted but who would like to be even more so, such conclusions as this study offers may prove helpful, though the already normal should be warned that even among such one man's meat is sometimes another man's poison and that in the case of any thoughtful individual his own opinion of what would make him happy may be a safer guide than statistics. Even by strict mathematics he is at least one-fourth as likely to belong to the 25 per cent who react one way as to the 75 per cent who react another, and if he is the kind of man who turns to books for guidance he is much more likely than the percentage would suggest to be among the minority. Only those who have none of that self-knowledge that has sometimes been called the beginning of wisdom, and that literature endeavors to communicate, should play the game of life as though it were bridge (or even poker), where the odds are the same from one person to the next.

As for me, I shall continue to feel that for all the contradictions that literature exhibits, I get most enlightenment and most help in the conduct of my own life from those who dwell in what the sociologist called the never-never land of the humanities. And I have an uneasy conviction that the more legislators and educators come to rely on the sociologists' findings, the less the society they help to make will encourage the development of those "abnormal" and "maladjusted" individuals who have contributed so much to the civilization from which they dissent.

II
WRITERS AND WRITING

No essays, please!

[1951]

Every now and then someone regrets publicly the passing of the familiar essay. Perhaps such regretters are usually in possession of a recent rejection slip; in any event there are not enough of them to impress editors. The very word "essay" has fallen into such disfavor that it is avoided with horror, and anything which is not fiction is usually called either an "article," a "story," or just "a piece." When *The Atlantic Monthly,* once the last refuge of a dying tradition, now finds it advisable to go in for such "articles" as its recent "What Night Playing Has Done to Baseball" it is obvious that not merely the genteel tradition but a whole literary form is dead.

I am sure that the books on how to become a writer in ten easy lessons have been stressing this fact for a long time now. If *I* were writing such a book I certainly should, and I think that I could give some very practical advice. To begin with I should say something like the following:

Suppose that you have drawn a subject out of your mental box and you find that it is "Fish." Now if you were living in the time of Henry Van Dyke and Thomas Bailey Aldrich, your best lead would be: "Many of my friends are ardent disciples of Isaac Walton." That would have had the appropriate personal touch and the requisite not too recondite literary allusion. But today of course no live-wire editor would read any further, not because this sounds like a dull familiar essay but simply because it sounds like *a* familiar essay. But "Fish" is still a perfectly usable subject provided you remember that salable nonfiction "pieces" almost invariably fall into one of three categories: the factual, the polemic, and what we now call—though I don't know why we have to deviate into French—*reportage*.

If you decide to be factual a good beginning would be: "Four million trout flies were manufactured last year by the three leading sports-supply houses." That is the sort of thing which makes almost any editor sit up and take notice. But it is no better than certain other possible beginnings. The polemic article ought to start: "Despite all the efforts of our department of wild life conservation, the number of game fish in American lakes and streams continues to decline steadily." Probably this kind of beginning to this kind of article is best of all because it sounds alarming and because nowadays (and for understandable reasons) whatever sounds alarming is generally taken to be true. However, if you want to go in for the trickier *reportage* start off with a sentence something like this: " 'Cap' Bill Hanks, a lean, silent, wryly humorous down-Easterner, probably knows more about the strange habits of the American fisherman than any man alive."

Of course, no one will ever inquire where you got your statistics about the trout flies, whether the fish population really is declining, or whether "Cap" Bill Hanks really exists. In fact, one of the best and lengthiest "Profiles" *The New Yorker* ever ran turned out to be about a "character" at the Fulton Fishmarket who didn't. Whatever looks like official fact or on-the-spot reporting is taken at face value and will be widely quoted. The important thing is that the editor first and the reader afterward shall get the feeling that what he is being offered is not mere literature but the real low-down on something or other—whether that something or other is or is not anything he cares much about.

Fling your facts around, never qualify anything (qualifications arouse distrust), and adopt an air of jolly omniscience. Remember that "essays" are written by introverts, "articles" by extroverts, and that the reader is going to resent anything which comes between him and that low-down which it is your principal function to supply. "Personalities," the more eccentric the better, are fine subjects for *reportage*. Manufacture or get hold of a good one and you may be able to do a "profile." But no one wants any personality to show in the magazine writer, whose business it is to be all-knowing, shrewd, and detached almost to the point of nonexistence. This means, of course, that your style should have no quality which belongs to you, only the qualities appropriate to the magazine for which you are writing. The most successful of all the magazines functioning in America today seldom print anything which is not anonymous and apparently owe a considerable part of their success to the fact that nearly everything which appears in them achieves the manner of *Life*, *Time*, or *Fortune*, as the case may be, but never by any chance any characteristic which would enable the most sensitive analyst of style to discover who had written it.

The ideal is obviously a kind of writing which seems to have been produced not by a man but by some sort of electronic machine. Perhaps in time it will actually be produced that way, since such machines now solve differential equations and that is harder to do than to write the average magazine article. Probably if Vannevar Bush were to put his mind to the problem, he could replace the whole interminable list of editors, assistant editors, and research assistants employed by the Luce publications with a contraption less elaborate than that now used to calculate the trajectory of a rocket. Meanwhile the general effect of mechanical impersonality can be achieved by a system of collaboration in the course of which such personalities as the individual collaborators may have are made to cancel one another out.

This system works best when these collaborators are divided into two groups called respectively "researchers" and "writers"—or, in other words, those who know something but don't write and those who don't know anything but do. This assures at the very outset that the actual writers shall have no dangerous interest in or even relation to what they write and that any individuality of approach which might tend to manifest itself in one of them will be canceled out by the others. If you then pass the end-result through the hands of one or more senior editors for further regularization, you will obviously get finally something from which every trace of what might be called handwork has disappeared. One might suppose that the criticism of the arts would be a department in which some trace of individuality would still be considered desirable, but I am reliably informed that at least at one time (and for all I know still) it was the custom to send an "editor" along with the movie critic to see every film so that this editor could tell the critic whether or not the film should be reviewed. This disposed of the possibility that the review might in some way reflect the critic's taste.

Obviously, few publications can afford the elaborate machinery which the Luce organization has set up. However, a great many strive to achieve something of the same effect by simpler means, and they expect their contributors to cooperate by recognizing the ideal and by coming as close to the realization of it as is possible for an individual to come. The circulations achieved by these publications seem to indicate how wise from one point of view their policy is. Those which still permit or even encourage a certain amount of individuality in their writers—even those which still offer a certain amount of nonfiction which is to some extent personal and reflective as opposed to the factual and the bleakly expository—must content themselves with relatively small circulations. Moreover, since they also print a good deal of the other sort of thing they create the suspicion that they survive in spite of rather than because of their limited hospitality to the man-made as opposed to the machine-made article.

No doubt the kind of essay which *The Atlantic* and the old *Century* once went in for died of anemia. It came to represent the genteel tradition at its feeblest. No one need be surprised that it did not survive. But what is significant is the fact that, whereas the genteel novel was succeeded by novels of a different sort and genteel poetry by poetry in a different manner, the familiar essay died without issue, so that what disappeared was a once important literary form for which changed times found no use. And the result is that there disappeared with it the best opportunity to consider in an effective way an area of human interest.

Because the "article" is impersonal it can deal only with subjects which exist in an impersonal realm. If its subject is not ominous, usually it must be desperately trivial; and just as the best-selling books are likely to have for title either something like *The World in Crisis* or *My Grandmother Did a Strip Tease,* so the magazine articles which are not heavy are very likely to be inconsequential. I doubt that anyone was ever quite as eccentric as almost every subject of a *New Yorker* "Profile" is made to seem; but if a topic cannot be made "devastating" the next best thing is "fabulous."

Perhaps what disappeared with the familiar essay was not merely a form, not merely even an attitude, but a whole subject matter. For the familiar essay affords what is probably the best method of discussing those subjects which are neither obviously momentous nor merely silly. And, since no really good life is composed exclusively of problems and farce, either the reading of most people today does not actually concern itself with some of the most important aspects of their lives or those lives are impoverished to a degree which the members of any really civilized society would find it difficult to understand. Just as genuine conversation—by which I mean something distinguishable from disputation, lamentation, and joke-telling—has tended to disappear from social gatherings, so anything comparable to it has tended to disappear from the printed page. By no means all of the Most-of-My-Friends essays caught it. But the best of them caught something which nowadays hardly gets into print at all.

Somehow we have got into the habit of assuming that even the so-called "human problems" are best discussed in terms as inhuman as possible. Just how one can profitably consider dispassionately so passionate a creature as man I do not know, but that seems to be the enterprise to which we have committed ourselves. The magazines are full of articles dealing statistically with, for example, the alleged failure or success of marriage. Lawyers discuss the law, sociologists publish statistics, and psychologists discuss case histories. Those are the methods by which we deal with the behavior of animals since animals can't talk. But men can—or at least once could—communicate, and one man's "familiar essay" on love and marriage might get closer to some all-important realities than any number of "studies" could.

No one is, to take another example, naïve enough to suppose that all the current discussions of the welfare state are actually as "objective" as most of them pretend to be. Personal tastes, even simple self-interest, obviously influence most of them but only insofar as they introduce distortions between the lines. Everybody who writes for or against the competitive society tries to write as though he did not live in it, had had no personal experience of what living in it is like, and was dealing only with a question in which he had no personal interest. This is the way one talks about how to keep bees or raise Black Angus. It is not the way either the bees or the Black Angus would discuss the good life as it affected them, and it is a singularly unrealistic way of considering anything which would affect us. Even the objective studies would be better and more objective if their authors permitted themselves freely to express elsewhere their "familiar" reaction to conditions and prospects instead of working in these feelings disguised as logical argument or scientific deduction.

All the sciences which deal with man have a tendency to depersonalize him for the simple reason that they tend to disregard everything which a particular science cannot deal with. Just as medicine confessedly deals with the physical man and economics confessedly deals not with Man but with the simplification officially designated as The Economic Man, so psychiatry deals with a fictitious man of whom there would be nothing more to be said if he were "normal," and one branch of psychology deals with what might be called the I.Q. man whose only significant aspect is his ability to solve puzzles.

Literature is the only thing which deals with the whole complex phenomenon at once, and if all literature were to cease to exist the result would probably be that in the end whatever is not considered by one or another of the sciences would no longer be taken into account at all and would perhaps almost cease to exist. Then Man would no longer be— or at least no longer be observed to be—anything different from the mechanical sum of the Economic man, the I.Q. man, and the other partial men with whom the various partial sciences deal. Faced with that prospect, we may well look with dismay at the disappearance of any usable literary form and wonder whether or not we have now entered upon a stage during which man's lingering but still complex individuality finds itself more and more completely deprived of the opportunity not only to express itself in living but even to discover corresponding individualities revealing themselves in the spoken or the written word.

That the situation could be radically altered by the cultivation of the familiar essay I am hardly prepared to maintain. Its disappearance is only a minor symptom. Or perhaps it is just a little bit more than that. At least there are a number of subjects which might profitably be discussed by fewer experts and more human beings. They might achieve a different kind of understanding of certain problems and they might lead to more humanly acceptable conclusions. "Most of my friends seem to feel that . . ."

The creative muddle

[1936]

In a fit of irritation Mike Gold once denounced W. S. Gilbert as little better than a fascist ahead of his time. He may have been thinking of the anti-egalitarian sentiments expressed in *The Gondoliers* or perhaps of the irony implicit in the picture of a democratic navy as it is presented in *Pinafore*. But in either event he was, in a way, paying the librettist a compliment which he did not deserve, for the truth of the matter is that Gilbert hadn't the slightest idea what he was, and that, in all probability, he would have ceased to write with such sprightly perverseness if he had ever been able to find out.

It is true that he was, in politics, a nominal Conservative, but that appears to have been chiefly because he happened to be a member of a Conservative club, and it is hard to imagine how the various references to the hereditary aristocracy in *Iolanthe,* for example, could have gone down any better at the Carleton than the passages to which Mr. Gold objects would have gone down at the Reform Club. Unable to make up his own mind, Gilbert was constantly in that state of mild irritation which is a priceless boon to the professional satirist. Personally he would have been unpopular in any society, and he continually hit his audiences in unexpected places because he was continually getting hit himself in exactly the same ones.

Fortunately, moreover, it was not only on the subject of politics that he was completely muddled. His attitude toward questions affecting morals and manners were equally confused, and consequently he was driven to the refuge of wit, no matter what subject he chose to treat. Consider, for example, a fact recently pointed out—namely, that the rhyme he most frequently employed (fifteen times) was the rhyme of "beauty" with "duty." Here is material for a psychoanalytical field day that would not be wholly without justification. The sense of the antithesis and the inability to escape from the horns of the dilemma it presents were responsible not only for Gilbert the man, who could neither stop flirting nor be guilty of an indecorum, but also for Gilbert the humorist, who continually satirized Victorianism without for one moment ceasing to be a Victorian. He was not so pure as his collaborator, Sir Arthur, who solemnly expressed the opinion that one of the greatest glories of music was the (alleged) fact that it was incapable of suggesting an impropriety. If he had been, then he could hardly have been witty about the flesh. But he was never more than witty because it was only when impropriety was subtly veiled in wit that he would consent to be improper at all.

What a pity that he had no consistent point of view! So at least a thousand earnest souls have exclaimed when they seemed to discover in his nonsense a reformer *manqué*. If only the sturdy republicanism of "When Britain really ruled the waves" were not nullified by the Tory perversity of

"There lived a king so I've been told"; or if the promising misogyny of a dozen songs and situations were not taken back in an equal number of languishing Victorian ditties. But a Gilbert sufficiently integrated to be downright would in all probability have been a Gilbert who had no need to express himself through the ambiguities of wit. He might possibly have done more good, but I doubt whether his paradoxes would still be drawing crowded houses.

Bernard Shaw, I suspect, owes almost as much to those inconsistencies which become increasingly obvious and which are increasingly charged against him. Even Mark Twain— Van Wyck Brooks notwithstanding—seems to me to have been forced into being funny largely because he too was so imperfectly integrated a person, and before I can wish that he had been freer and better educated I should like to consider very seriously such a *mot* as the well-known "Wagner is not so bad as he sounds." Had Mr. Clemens been a thoroughgoing Philistine he would never have made a dutiful pilgrimage to Bayreuth in the first place. Had he been an ideally sensitive and ideally cultivated gentleman he would probably have written an essay in defense of Wagner—of which there are already in existence a sufficient number for all practical purposes. But because he didn't know well enough where he stood to commit himself unequivocally he evolved a pleasant quip which is safely open at both ends.

Someone, I don't know who, once defined wit as "the kiss given to common sense behind the back of respectability." Its charm lies in the quickness, the unexpectedness, the ambiguity, and the impropriety of the smack as well as in the adroitness of the technique with which the occasion is snatched. The bold rake is not funny and neither is the sex-reformer who dutifully busses the maid before his wife and assembled guest just to prove that freer manners are desirable for society. It must be done by someone who isn't sure whether he ought to do it or not, and Gilbert was in the perfectly delightful position of not knowing whether conformity or unconventionality was his lawful spouse. Fearfully he seized every occasion to kiss each behind the back of the other, and no matter which one he happened to be wooing at the moment he was always careful to explain to the spectators that he was only fooling, after all.

The result may have been a certain dissatisfaction with himself. He was apparently serious in the belief that his sentimental plays were much the best of his work, and once, toward the end of his life, when someone asked him if he were not proud to have made a fortune out of his brains, he replied that the fortune had been made not out of his brains but out of the folly of the British public. The fact remains, nevertheless, that it is not the business of a wit to be satisfied; it is his business to be amusing. And does anyone really prefer *The Mysterious Stranger* to *Innocents Abroad* or Gilbert's *Broken Hearts* to his *Iolanthe?*

Novelists know what philosophers don't

[1936]

In the issue of the *Commonweal* for August 21 there is an article called "Philosophy into Fiction" by Francis X. Connolly of Fordham University. I dare say that Professor Connolly and I would disagree about a number of things, including, perhaps, the ultimate implications of this very article, but I find here in an unexpected quarter a point of view which I should be glad to find more often in persons whose general convictions I am more inclined to share.

To begin with, Professor Connolly believes that today even

the average "intellectual" has been more pervasively influenced by art than by philosophy, that his intellect (I
should prefer to say his intellectual temper) has been
molded more by Proust than by Bergson, by James Joyce
than by William James, or, as he might have added even
more strikingly, by T. S. Eliot than by Jacques Maritain.
Even those who read stiffer and more formal works probably owe more to *Point Counter Point* and *Brave New World*
than they do to the works of futilitarian or anti-Utopian philosophers, and in most cases at least the admirers of Karl
Marx read him—if at all—long after they had read various
of the realistic novelists from Tolstoy to James Farrell. Nor
is it really necessary for Professor Connolly to limit himself to "today." The chances are that in so far as the average
Greek was imbued with the Greek Spirit he owed the fact
more to Aeschylus and Sophocles than to Plato and Aristotle.

Professor Connolly is pleased that all he says should be
so, and he finds it evidence of something more than a mere
childish desire on the part of the public to have its pill of
philosophy sugar-coated by fiction. He sees that the concrete-
ness which art requires holds the artist close to observed fact,
while the philosopher can readily escape into a world of
concepts much easier to manipulate. But I am not sure that
he would follow me all the way into a paradox which I am
tempted to risk—namely, that art is more convincing than
philosophy because it is, quite literally, truer; that, to take
cases, Proust is truer than Bergson and Mr. Farrell truer than
Marx.

The novelists are, to be sure, less clear and less precise.
But for that very reason they are truer. Every philosophy
and every "ideology" must sacrifice truth to clarity and precision just because we demand of a philosophy or an "ideology" greater clarity and precision and completeness than is
compatible with human knowledge or wisdom. What is most
true and most valuable in any philosophy is not the tight and

inclusive system which it presents but those glimpses and divinations and *aperçus* which the philosopher later formalized into his philosophical system. Most of us are not Platonists or Spinozans or Nietzscheans. We have accepted insight from each while rejecting the whole which each pretends to present. And it is just the philosophical superiority of art, not only that it suggests the complexity of life and human character, but also that it is everywhere closer to the most genuine and the most justifiable portions of man's thinking about life.

The realm of science on the one hand and the realms of logic and metaphysics on the other are separate from the realm of literature. The first deals with a physical world relatively so simple that systematic conclusions and usable laws may, temporarily at least, be formulated precisely. Logic and metaphysics, on the other hand, deal not with facts but with concepts, and their precision is analogous to the precision of geometry, where one is dealing not with complex and incompletely known nature but with premises of which one is sure because they are merely postulated. But philosophy in the more popular sense of the term, philosophy which consists in conclusions about human life in general, is often merely an inferior kind of art; art, that is to say, which has assumed a definiteness of statement which nothing can justify while it has lost the warmth, the vitality, and the eagerness of genuine art. Proust, one might contend, is truer than Bergson because Proust is communicating an experience to the meaning of which Bergson had attributed a specious definiteness and completeness. Mr. Farrell, one might go on, is truer than Marx because he is sharing with us those observations concerning the influence of economic factors on life which Marx attempted to reduce to laws and which his investigations of economic process were, at bottom, merely efforts to justify. And the larger part of the intellectual public is more familiar with Proust than with Bergson, more familiar with novelists like Farrell than with Marx, because, even when unaware of its reasons for doing so, it rebels against the ambitious falsity of philosophy while accepting the human persuasiveness as well as the human elusiveness of art.

I shall press the paradox no farther. Already it has carried me a bit farther than in sober earnest I should care to go, but the element of truth that is in it ought at least to make plain the error of those who insist that a novel or a play should have not only a meaning but a doctrine as well. The best as well as the most effective works of art may sometimes be those in which the author is in pursuit of a truth, but the only reason for composing a novel or a play instead of a treatise is that the author is unwilling to reduce to a formula an insight which he can present without violation only through a concrete situation whose implications he can sense but only sense. Once the meaning of a work of art can be adequately stated in abstract terms it ceases to have any *raison d'être*. It has ceased to be truer than philosophy and has become at best only the sugar-coated pill.

If those are right who maintain that the field of what we positively know and can state with precision is constantly growing, that even the uncertainties and ambiguities which still surround every insight into moral and psychological situations are destined to disappear in the light of clear and positive knowledge until there is nothing important about man which we do not know with scientific precision, then the field and the utility of art are shrinking, and the time will come when it will cease to have any function at all. But art will continue to exist and to be truer than philosophy just so long as—but no longer than—there are truths which elude formulation into laws.

On not being a best-seller

[1949]

Years ago I sat next to the editor of an exceptionally high-brow monthly who boasted that she—for it was a she—had "succeeded in whittling our circulation away until now we reach only those who are genuinely interested in aesthetics." Not long afterward the magazine ceased publication entirely, and that, I suppose, was the crowning testimony to her achievement.

It is not often that certain problems and paradoxes connected with literary popularity are presented in quite so dramatic a form, but those of us who are either "worst sellers" or at least not "best" are troubled by them a good deal. I have always envied writers who profess to consider their failure to find many readers a source of satisfaction, but I have not been able to follow them. A writer ought to be—and really of course he always is—pleased to win the largest number of readers he can get. Obviously I do not mean that he should be willing to "write down" or even that he should be willing to write "for" popularity. But when one has done one's best and done it sincerely, when one has come as close as one can to saying exactly what one wants to say, it is nonsense not to hope that many will find it worth while.

Thoreau, meditating on an unsuccessful speaking tour, tried to take the opposite attitude. "What business is it of these lecture audiences what I think?" But that is a *reductio ad absurdum,* and Thoreau himself would not have talked such amusing nonsense if the lectures had been successful. One does not speak in public and one does not "publish" unless one desires an audience. Private meditations should be private. Milton spoke of "fit audience though few," but his surprise would have been pleasant had he discovered that the few were more numerous than he expected. And in the long run, of course, they have turned out to be very numerous indeed. Even to write for posterity is to hope for a large future public, and the only escape from an ultimate trust in it is the willingness to write, as Lamb said he did, "for antiquity."

Mere fashion may be, as Oscar Wilde said, "a form of ugliness so intolerable that we have to change it every six months." It is thus that we deal with certain favorite writers, a great many of whom are obviously more popular than they ought to be or will be for long. But for the most part even time winnows out more often than it reverses. Despite such exceptions as a Robert Herrick who seems to have been almost unknown in the seventeenth century, or a Thoreau whose contemporary reputation was not impressive, enduring writers have much more often than not at least got a good deal of attention from readers of their own time. Those of us who find most of our contemporaries indifferent but who hope for future recognition are playing a long shot, since at least a considerable measure of appreciation during a writer's lifetime always makes future fame more likely.

The very best sellers at any given moment are most assuredly not always, or even usually, the very best books. Yet if the works of Harold Bell Wright and the work of Kathleen Winsor were sensationally successful, so apparently were the works of Homer and of Shakespeare. And so too, very probably, were most of those books of the twentieth century that are likely to last.

How can the public be so right and so wrong? How can it be always right in the long run and at least very unreliable in the short? How can folly grow wise while continuing to repeat its old follies? I can only say that it seems to do so and that the fact resolves not only the paradox of literary reputation but also the grander paradox upon which faith in democracy depends—the paradox, I mean, of the mob which is so fickle and so foolish but which, nevertheless, becomes in time the people who—so we hope at any rate—are always right.

At least I have never been able to understand why an age which boasts its faith in "democratic principles," why, indeed, many of those writers who proclaim, especially in verse, their faith in "the people," should so often be exalters of the esoteric in literature and thus attribute to "the people" a strange combination of political wisdom and aesthetic imbecility. Is truth somehow easier to see than beauty? Curiously enough, it was, on the other hand, the writers of the eighteenth century, the very writers who often spoke so contemptuously of "the mob," who most clearly defined "the classic" as that which makes a wide and enduring appeal. Alexander Pope, instead of exalting the slim volume of neglected verse, hailed the "bards triumphant" who are "heirs of universal praise." And it was Samuel Johnson, the Tory, who proclaimed that "where the public has thought long on a subject, it has generally thought right."

Of course the "thought long" is essential. It is the long thinking which weeds out the merely fashionable, and no doubt the chief trouble with best-seller lists is that they cover too short a period. Over any decade even dozens of classics will outsell most so-called best-sellers. What, indeed, is a classic except a permanent best-seller? The fact remains, however, that a discouragingly large number of those classics were at least pretty good sellers in their own day.

Byron waked up one morning to find himself famous. On that same morning nothing much was happening to William Wordsworth, who is now, I imagine, a better seller than Byron. But even Wordsworth, one of those writers about whom the public needed to think long, did live to find himself famous at last, and those darling examples of neglect,

Shelley and Keats, would have found themselves famous, too, had they not been cut off very young. Usually, I am afraid, one does not become immortal unless one has also had some life in time.

What is a good review?

[1937]

Of all literary forms the book review is the one most widely cultivated and least often esteemed. To many the very phrase "literary form" may smack of pretense when applied to a kind of writing which is usually so casual; and formlessness may, indeed, be the only form of many commentaries on books. Book reviewing can, nevertheless, become an art in itself and would be such more often if the ambitious reviewer would only devote himself to the cultivation of its particular excellences instead of attempting, as he so often does, to demonstrate his capacities by producing something "more than a mere review." The best review is not the one which is trying to be something else. It is not an independent essay on the subject of the book in hand and not an aesthetic discourse upon one of the literary genres. The best book review is the best review of the book in question, and the better it is the closer it sticks to its ostensible subject.

To say this is not to say that a good review is easy to write; in certain technical respects it is, indeed, the most difficult of all forms of literary criticism for the simple reason that in no other is the writer called upon to do so many things in so short a space. The critical essay, no matter how extended it may be, is not compelled to aim at any particular degree of completeness. It may—in fact it usually does—assume that the reader is sufficiently familiar with the work under discussion to make description unnecessary and it may also confine itself to whatever aspects of the subject the critic may choose.

But the book review as a literary form implies completeness; it has not really performed its function unless, to begin with, it puts the reader in possession of the facts upon which the criticism is based, and unless—no matter upon how small a scale—its consideration is complete. However penetrating a piece of writing may be, it is not a good review if it leaves the reader wondering what the book itself is like as a whole or if it is concerned with only some aspects of the book's quality.

I shall not pretend to say how large a proportion of the so-called reviews published in *The Nation* or anywhere else actually achieve the distinguishing characteristics of the book review form, but a certain number of them do, and the sense of satisfactoriness which they give can always be traced to the fact that, whatever other qualities they may have, they accomplish the three minimum tasks of the book reviewer. They describe the book, they communicate something of its quality, and they pass judgment upon it.

Each of these things is quite different from the others, but only the last is usually considered as carefully as it ought to be by either reader or writer. Adequate description implies a simple account of the scope and contents of the book; its presence guarantees that the reader will not be left wondering what, in the simplest terms, the book is about. "Communication of quality" implies, on the other hand, a miniature specimen of what is commonly called "impressionistic criticism"; it means that the reviewer must somehow manage to re-create in the mind of the reader some approximation of the reaction produced in his own mind by the book itself. And in however low esteem this form of criticism may be held as a be-all and end-all (Mr. Eliot calls it the result of a weak creative instinct rather than of a critical impulse), it is indispensable in a book review if that review is to perform the function it is supposed to perform, and if it is to become what it is supposed to be—namely, not merely an account of a book on the one hand or an independent piece of criticism on the other, but a brief critical essay which includes within itself all that is necessary to make the criticism comprehensible and significant.

Your "reviewer" often envies the more lofty "critic" because the critic is supposed to be read for his own sake while the reviewer must assume that the reader is attracted more by his interest in the book discussed than by the reviewer himself. For that very reason he is likely either to treat reviewing as a casual affair or to seek for an opportunity to write something else under the guise of a review. He might be happier himself and make his readers happier also if he would, instead, take the trouble to ask what a review ought to be and if he would examine his own work in the light of his conclusions. It is not easy to do within the space of a thousand words or less the three things enumerated. It is less easy still to combine the description, the impression, and the judgment into a whole which seems to be, not three things at least, but one.

How many reviewers of novels, for instance, seem to know how much of a particular story has to be told in order to provide a solid basis for the impression they intend to convey? And if it is decided that some part of the story must be told, how many know, as a storyteller must, whether the incidents are striking enough to come first or must be introduced with some comment which creates the interest? Yet a first-rate review, despite its miniature scale, raises precisely the same problems as long narratives or expositions raise, and each must be solved as artfully if the review is to have such beauty of form as it is capable of. Doubtless the finest reviewer can hardly hope to have his art fully appreciated by the public. But there is every reason why he should respect it himself.

The "indispensable" century

[1950]

About twenty-five years ago our generation decided that "the indispensable century" was, for it, not the eighteenth but the seventeenth. No doubt T. S. Eliot was as much responsible as any one man for the new enthusiasm, but it did not absolutely begin with him and it by no means stopped there. A good deal could be made of the fact that one of the most popular and "toughest" of modern novelists should have taken *For Whom the Bell Tolls* as a title and thereby made the name, at least, of John Donne familiar to more people than it had ever been familiar to in the history of the world before. A good half of all that distinguishes the serious literature of the past quarter-century from that of the twenty-five preceding years could be traced to the influence of the prose and verse written between 1600 and 1660. Neither the Victorian nor even the Shakespearean ages provided so much that one particular generation found usable.

No doubt much of this was all to the good. No reader with any imagination or any sense of what a way of using words can mean could possibly regret a good deal of the influence. For one thing, it redeemed poetry from the bland and tepid commonplace of the Georgians. More importantly perhaps, it revived in us a new sense of human existence as something grandiose and pretentious. The inward life of the men of the seventeenth century was one of the most intense that the English race has ever known. Their age—make no mistake about it—was an age of saints and heroes when a very great deal was expected of men's minds and spirits. They knew, for example, how to be genuinely serious, not merely, like the Victorians, how to be solemn. That was a great accomplishment and one we needed to acquire.

That we actually did acquire it fully may be doubted. But it may also be doubted whether any more of it can be acquired via mere literary influence and whether in the interests of literary health the time has not come to be again more aware of other models, of other ways in which an inward life can be lived and expressed. The seventeenth-century mode —at least when its externals are too mechanically imitated —has its limitations and its penalties. Those, goodness knows, are evident enough in at least the more pretentious second-rate writing of our day where obscurity and perversity are cultivated as ends in themselves.

Pretentious second-class writers would no doubt be what they are no matter which fashion they followed, and they are hardly worth bothering about, except perhaps to the extent of saying that their pretentious second-rateness would be more immediately evident if they wrote heroic couplets or "classical" prose. But the argument in favor of a greater awareness of models other than those of the seventeenth century has a positive aspect in the value such models would have for the good, above all perhaps for the best, of writers. We have been in the habit of assuming that good or at least "important" writing inevitably must be complex, ingenious, distorted, difficult, and, of course, "ambiguous," in the now favorable sense of the last term. We have forgot what virtues plain speaking can have, how much can be said—how much has been said—in straightforward terms whose deceptive directness conceals the fact that the writing is good for the very reason that it is hard to write rather than hard to read.

Aldous Huxley spoke recently of "the kindly shallowness of the eighteenth century." Taken as he meant it—taken that is to say unironically and in no really unfavorable sense—this is an admirable phrase. No doubt we do actually see deeper into certain things than any of our predecessors. But much that we sometimes call shallow in the eighteenth century is merely simple and clear just because the men of that century believed, as we do not, that many of the most important things in the world are simple and can be stated clearly. To assume that *everything* is simple is dangerous. But it is not perhaps so present a danger to us as its opposite: the conviction that *nothing* is simple, that the plain is the false, or at least the inadequate.

It might be well if our writers were to read a little less Donne and a little more, for instance, of Swift. Many of his opinions are certainly not mine. Kindliness, shallow or otherwise, is not his most obvious characteristic. I should not even call him "typically eighteenth century." But no man ever cultivated more successfully the art of plain speaking. His style consisted in seeming not to have any. Certainly, it is almost impossible to discuss or to describe it. If we try to talk about Swift's way of saying things we find ourselves talking instead about what he says. It is like looking through a window and then trying to describe the glass. One can say nothing except that it is transparent—which is to say that it transmits perfectly. And Swift's style is like that. It communicates without calling any attention to itself. Not only is there no obscurity; there is also not a single purple patch. Considered simply as a way of writing it is the exact opposite of both Donne and Sir Thomas Browne, and the opposite also of nineteenth- and twentieth-century stylists from De Quincey through Pater to Joyce or Stein.

Is that because Swift, or even so relatively graceless a plain-speaker as Defoe, really had nothing to say? Nowadays we especially admire what are called "devastating" books. The reviewer's preferred words of praise are "bitter," "savage," "remorseless," and "grim." But is anything the modern school has produced, even at its most indirect and its muddiest, more effectively bitter than *Gulliver's Travels,* written as Swift said "not to please mankind but to vex it"?

If the eighteenth century did not lack passion, did it then, as is so often said, lack "imagination"? In examining that question would it not be fair to say that one test of one kind of imaginative writer is his ability to create, not merely characters, but legends or myths, and that among the supreme products of imagination are those fictional personages who have detached themselves from books or authors, who lead now independent lives, and are familiar to millions who do not know even the names of the books in which they appear? Don Quixote is certainly one such character. But all the indisputable examples of such personages could be counted on the fingers of two hands, if not on those of one. Yet two of them—Gulliver and Robinson Crusoe—were created within a decade by an age which is commonly said to have had no imagination. Is either likely to be forgotten before Mr. Bloom and Alfred Prufrock?

Not everybody in the eighteenth century wrote plain like Swift and Defoe. There were also prose styles as elaborately formal as Johnson's and Gibbon's, or as elaborately informal as Stern's. But they all had at least one thing in common: *they were intended to be understood*—which is a statement not as foolishly obvious as it may seem. For if most present-day writers would profess that they want ultimately to be understood, the "ultimately" is important. They certainly do not want to be understood right off. They want to be guessed at and puzzled out. They want to be explained to the general reader by experts in their private language. They want to be disputed over by rival interpreters. And if, in the end, their meaning is still seen only as in a glass darkly, why so much the better. They have been proved "difficult," and to be difficult is hardly less important than to be "devastating."

No doubt some things are difficult to say. Possibly some are so difficult that with the best skill and the best will in the world they can never be made quite easy. And to leave them unsaid for that reason would be calamitous. I do not think that the eighteenth century did that as often as is sometimes supposed; but even if it had done so, it would hardly affect the present argument, which is only that at this moment the eighteenth century has more to teach writers than they have still to learn from the seventeenth. It is a question of aim and of ideal, of something as simple as learning how to be as clear as possible rather than how to cultivate any further whatever charms ambiguity and obscurity may have.

An important part of the difference is not something intangible or vague but something about which one may be quite specific; for it is largely a matter of that often discussed subject, the denotive and the connotive aspects of language —which obviously count for so much in poetry and which are very important in prose also. Probably no good writing which serves other than a purely utilitarian purpose fails to take advantage of the fact that words have an aura as well as a core. Certainly, all good eighteenth-century poetry, including that of Pope, is written in such a way as to take advantage of the fact that two words which mean the same thing in a dictionary do not have the same effect in a given context. Dryden, though his poetry has been very properly called "the poetry of statement," does not merely make statements. In fact, it is doubtful if an English poet was ever more successful in making what looks like mere statement actually something more.

Yet there is, nevertheless, a very important difference in poets and prose writers alike with regard to the extent to which they rely upon statement or upon implication for the major part of their communication. A Shakespeare is supremely great partly because he strikes a perfect balance, because he uses to the full both of language's two methods of communicating. A Marvel leans somewhat in one direction; a Yeats, like most present-day poets, very far in that same direction. Many another poet of today goes further still along that road until at an extreme one gets those talkers-to-themselves who employ a private language and who seek to imply or suggest everything but actually to *say* nothing.

In the eighteenth century the prose writers as well as the poets used the purely connotative possibilities of language rather sparingly and almost unconsciously. They were so intent upon being clear and precise and definite that suggestion seems merely to slip in. And for that reason they wrote what is the finest prose and verse of its kind in English. For that reason, also, what they wrote could be studied with the greatest profit today. Nothing else is so likely to teach us what at this moment we most need to learn: namely, that more things can be actually *said* than we seem to believe and that so far as prose at least is concerned the best is that whose texture is firmly denotive and which can, as statement, stand firm on its own legs.

Sometimes we hear that the root of all our trouble is that we lack any firm core of conviction. But if art imitates life, life returns the compliment, and it is surely legitimate to ask, not only how truly *Ulysses,* for example, "reflects the confusion of our times" but also to what extent it has contributed to that confusion. Where every sentence says or is at least intended to say two or three different things related only in the eccentric context of the author's mind we may possibly be curiously entertained but we seldom see any one thing clearly enough to decide whether or not we are prepared to accept it. If we really do desire to get convictions, to know what we believe and what we do not; if we are not secretly anxious to increase our doubts and our confusions; then we ought to want statements clearly defined which we can accept or reject. Poetic ambiguity has its uses, but we have had more of it than we can use. If a few more plain statements were made we might discover that we believe more than we thought we did.

Even in Pope's own day there were those who saw the danger, for that day, in his too famous definition:

> True wit is nature to advantage
>   dressed,
> What oft was thought but ne'er so
>   well expressed.

As Dr. Johnson said so precisely, such a definition of wit "depresses it below its natural dignity and reduces it from strength of thought to happiness of language." We cannot live by platitude alone. But neither can we live by paradox alone, and that is precisely what the intellectual tried to do for half a century until, more recently, he gave it up for something even less substantially nourishing. Weary of Victorian platitude, he took up paradox and then, weary of paradox, he turned to ambiguity which, sometimes at least, means only two or three simultaneous clichés parading as wit. We are solemnly assured that when Joyce asked himself "Was life worth leaving?" he meant both "Was life worth living?" and "Was it really worth my while to go into exile from the home county identified by a certain Irish river?" Neither of these questions seems in itself profoundly original. Do they become so by being asked simultaneously? Would anyone who asked them separately be a very interesting writer?

The real point of the present discourse is not, however, to

attack or to depreciate any contemporary writer for what he has found it desirable to do. It is merely to suggest that something might be now learned from models too long neglected. The eighteenth century has become indispensable again.

Great cliché debate

[1958]

For some years now I have been letting Bergen Evans correct my errors and set me right on all sorts of matters involving fact and opinion. But worms will turn and I reached my turning point when I read his warning against clichés in the July 27 issue of this magazine. Mr. Evans went out on a limb (if I may coin a phrase) and then let someone cut it off near the trunk.

Challenged to find something better than the phrase "Jack-of-all-trades," which he reprehended, he was unable to come up with anything better than "One who can turn his hand to any (or to many) kinds of work." And I don't believe even he thinks that preferable. "Jack-of-all-trades" may, as he says, have long ceased to be vivid or original; but his substitute never was. And it is fourteen words instead of four. That is going a long way about to avoid a phrase which is clear, exact, and universally understood. The same may be said of "brass tacks," "have your cake and eat it, too," and his other examples of phrases to be avoided.

In the two paragraphs I have just written there are at least five other clichés, but I submit that every one of them is economical and perspicuous. To those who still prefer one of Mr. Evans' clumsy paraphrases I can only reply that "one man's meat is another man's poison." Or, as Mr. Evans would perhaps put it, "That which, to one individual, has a pleasant flavor and is at the same time nourishing may be both distasteful and positively noxious to another."

Actually, neither "Jack-of-all-trades" nor "brass tacks" is a cliché in the most precise meaning of the term. Both started out as fresh metaphors. Then, possibly, there was a time when both had become real clichés—that is to say, phrases still used with a certain air of being novel when they were already very familiar. But by now they have passed beyond that stage. When you hear "brass tacks" you no longer think of a tack at all. It is not now a stale metaphor but simply an accepted term and no more objectionable than any familiar word used over and over again because it is both *pre*cise and *con*cise—the last two words being, by the way, a couple of clichés since the one means literally "cut off" and the other "cut short."

A very important part of the standard vocabulary is composed of words that were originally metaphors, though many of them are now unrecognized as such except by philologists. Is "dependent" a cliché to be avoided because it means "hanging from"? Should we refuse to say "palliate" because it means "cover with a cloak," "astonish" because it means "struck by thunder," or "lunatic" because it means "struck by the moon"? Their origins may be hidden by the fact that they are borrowed from a foreign language, but "brass tacks" is almost as much a word and almost as little a mere, tired metaphor as any of the examples from the Latin. And it is no more reprehensible. How about, to give a few more random examples, "easel," "sincere," "martinet," "assassin," "etiquette," "glamour," "sabotage," or "ostracize"? If we refuse all such words, we should be hard put to it to express any abstract or general idea. Anyone who is determined to avoid everything that is, by Mr. Evans' definition, a cliché had better known no Latin and stay away from dictionaries or he will find it difficult to say anything at all.

When a cliché really is objectionable, it is rarely only because it is a familiar expression. Usually, it is inept; it does not accurately convey what the user means to say. Or else it is open to some other objection—as when, for instance, the speaker brings it out with a flourish or a chuckle (e.g., "*Cherchez la femme,* as the French say") as though unaware that it is no longer surprising or witty and has become merely useful instead. "Allergic to" may someday be inoffensive—but not now, if the speaker thinks he is being up-to-date and "smart." Almost equally objectionable are phrases used as meaningless substitutes for either shorter phrases or single words, as when we say "besetting sin" and "common or garden" when we do not mean anything more than "sin" and "common."

Metaphors that recently were striking but are now in the twilight zone between genuine metaphor and mere familiar term are especially likely to be used inappropriately or to trick the users into a mixed metaphor just because the metaphorical sense is almost, but not quite, lost. "Bottlenecks must be ironed out" and "The economy of the Ruhr is bound to move within a vicious circle of bottlenecks" (both quoted in Sir Ernest Gower's *Plain Words*) are howlingly absurd, not because "bottleneck" should nearly always be avoided or because even "vicious circle" is sometimes not an accurate term; they are grotesque because bottlenecks are not ironed out and they don't move in circles, vicious or not. It is hardly necessary to add that a familiar phrase should not be used unless one can get it straight and knows what it really means. To have said "like Caesar's wife, all things to all men" was a unique achievement in ineptitude; but "psychological moment," for instance, and "to the manner born" seem to be more often used wrongly than rightly.

Anyone who undertakes to write about how one should write is sticking his neck out—if Mr. Evans will pardon the expression. And, like pretty nearly everyone who has attempted it, Mr. Evans gives us some unintentional examples of what to avoid almost as striking as his precepts. As Jacques Barzun pointed out in a recent review of Bergen and Cornelia Evans' *Dictionary of Contemporary American Usage,* an enemy of the trite phrase should not refer to someone as being "cheerfully unaware" or characterize a locution as "the darling of the pompously ignorant."

To lump together, as is done in the same dictionary, "wear and tear," "tilting at windmills," and "more in sorrow than in anger" as equally objectionable is to overlook important differences. In many contexts, "wear and tear" would be hardly more objectionable than "brass tacks." Whether "tilting at windmills" is or is not acceptable will often depend upon just how specifically it is appropriate. "More in sorrow than in anger" is usually a mere parroting of literacy at fifth hand.

Mr. Evans' besetting sin is (tut, tut, please strike out "besetting") his frequent failure to make distinctions—either those already mentioned or various others. When, for instance, he writes, "The mark of the cliché is [its] intrinsic meaninglessness . . . It simply doesn't register," he is forgetting that while "brass tacks" or, say, "pig in a poke" may not register as the metaphors they once were, they are far from being meaningless. They do, in fact, convey meaning and are preferable to the kind of roundabout substitutes he offers us.

And when he cites from an imaginary political speech the declamation that "although we cannot rest on our laurels we must not rush in where angels fear to tread," he does not sufficiently stress that while the clichés may be objectionable for other reasons, what is most offensive is the fact that the speaker is not saying anything at all. Clichés may be made to conceal the absence of thought as well as to express thought; but that is equally true of all words. We would not think the speech of Mr. Evans' politician any better if, having determined to avoid clichés, he substituted for "rush in where angels fear to tread" something like "hastily embark upon a course of action men wiser than ourselves would hesitate to enter upon without mature consideration."

Determine to avoid clichés at all costs and you are almost certain to be led into gobbledygook. To say that the race is not always to the swift nor the battle to the strong may be to adopt a cliché. But it is still preferable to George Orwell's translation into gobbledygook: "Success or failure in competitive activities exhibits no tendency to be commensurate with innate capacity." Fowler gives five rules for good writing, of which the first three are to prefer the familiar word to the farfetched, the concrete word to the abstract, and the single word to the circumlocution. Orwell's burlesque translation violates all three.

The greatest of all faults in writing is obscurity. The greatest single cause of all the other faults is self-consciousness. That is why even good rules often do as much harm as they do good unless following them has become a habit rather than the result of conscious effort. No one would ever say "her and I" if he weren't trying too hard to be correct, or "the lady's soiled garments" when he meant "the woman's dirty clothes" unless he had some absurd notion about elegance. Winston Churchill's secretary must have put a great deal of thought into how to avoid ending a certain sentence with a preposition before he achieved the result that led his employer to pencil in the margin, "This is the kind of English up with which I will not put." And I shudder to think (another good cliché) of the prolixities into which some may be led in their effort to avoid everything Mr. Evans stigmatizes as a cliché. Clichés, of course, are often painful. But I am not here going to be shamed out of saying that "the remedy is often worse than the disease."

A cliché is, in the realm of speech, what a platitude is in the realm of belief, and each has become what it is for a similar reason: the one because it is so true and the other because it is so useful. A wise man will not scorn the one nor a good writer the other. That honesty is the best policy is a platitude to which it is sometimes necessary to call attention, and when it is there is no better way of stating the platitude than by means of the cliché.

G. K. Chesterton once wrote that there are two ways of being a slave to public opinion. One way is to be afraid to disagree with it and the other is to be afraid to agree. Superior people, as he did not find it necessary to add, are particularly prone to the second fear. And that is equally true of the cliché and the platitude. Paradox and wit are delightful, but they do not always wear well. Oscar Wilde's "Nothing succeeds like excess" was brilliant as phraseology and as a half-truth. It was far better than "Nothing succeeds like success" the first time it was said. But not the fiftieth. And to use it once more with the idea that one is being clever is to use a cliché far more objectionable than the one it parodied.

Neither Mr. Evans' rules nor mine are going to eliminate all dispute. It is always said that the cultivated writer and the cultivated reader are the final judges, but there will still be cases when men with equally good claims to one designation or the other will disagree. One of them may have heard a certain phrase more often, or may differ with the other as to whether it has ceased to be a tired metaphor and become, like "palliate" or "astonish," merely the best way of conveying a meaning.

Bernard Shaw, certainly not a careless writer, used "throw out the baby with the bath," though this happens to be one

of Fowler's examples of really overworked phrases. I do not
know how we could decide who, in this case, should be followed. But I do think it is very much worth while to attempt
discrimination rather than to denounce every familiar
phrase under a "blanket indictment"—which is one more
good cliché to end with.

If you don't mind my saying so . . . [VII]

[1960]

Tradition has it that John Cleland got his royal pension in
exchange for a promise not to write a sequel to *The Memoirs
of Fanny Hill*. None of my own works is equally celebrated
(or even of the same genre) but a few years ago our own
government made *me* a similar offer. Now that my wife has
passed another birthday the offer has been—as men of
affairs are wont to put it—"upped." Not to beat further
about the bush, I am promised one hundred and eighty dollars a month to stop writing.

Those who follow my calling are accustomed to the fact
that society puts no large price upon their product, but it is
startling to find it evaluated as frankly undesirable. So far I
have not accepted the insulting offer but I shall probably
come to it in time. Or perhaps some sufficiently irritated reader will make me an even better one.

As I understand it, Washington does not care how much
"unearned income" I may have. The one condition is that
I shall stop working. And the reason for this insistence

(which would have seemed very strange at any previous period of the world's history) is now obvious: the fear of overproduction and consequent unemployment. *The Scholar,* for instance, could give a job to some younger and unemployed writer if I were not hanging about after my time has passed.

The logic is a little more persuasive when applied to situations involving the production of goods potentially constituting a more tangible surplus. But I wonder if there might not be a better way of meeting the general problem. Granted that technology has put us in a position where we are constantly threatened with more food and more "durable consumer goods" than we can use (or waste) conveniently, is there then no remedy other than the only one I have ever heard proposed—namely fewer man-hours of labor and greater consumption—the latter to be encouraged by making durable goods less durable and by fostering the concept of "psychological obsolescence" in the case of a great variety of gadgets from electric toasters to automobiles —all of which persist in refusing to wear out fast enough? I have a different plan of my own, and I will try to conquer my natural modesty if other sociological thinkers feel that in the future it should be briefly referred to as the Krutch Plan, or Principle. It does not involve either a two-day work week or a campaign to convince people that they are underprivileged if they do not have a color television set in every room, including the toilet. Briefly, it proposes the systematic encouragement of such nonproductive labor as mine; or rather, if that description seems unkind, the production of nonmaterial things that do not have to be destroyed or stored when a surplus exists. The most obvious of such sometimes durable but never physically burdensome things are the products of intellectual and artistic endeavor.

Certainly, to take as an illustration my own particular case, there would be no need to offer me a bribe to stop writing if more people read. Quite as obviously, it would not be as difficult to find jobs for people in industry if more workers were writing books, painting pictures, or composing symphonies, while fewer made electric toasters and automobiles. Of course those economists who cannot think of "consumer goods" except in terms of material things will reply that if fewer toasters and automobiles were made we should soon have an excess of purchasing power because of an insufficiency of consumer goods to absorb it. But there would be no excess of purchasing power if the public were as eager to buy books as it is to buy motorboats and television sets. Not all such purchasers would have to want for their own sakes the things they might buy. A large library or a collection of pictures conceivably might become a recognized status symbol such as they now are for a small class, and such as automobiles and the like now are for the majority of our citizens.

If it be objected that this just isn't in human nature and that human nature cannot be changed, I have two answers. The first is that societies that had a good deal more interest in things intellectual and artistic with proportionately less interest in the material certainly have existed. As Henry Adams pointed out long ago, cathedral building seemed to the European Middle Ages just what railroad building did to nineteenth-century America—namely, the one thing most worth doing. I see no theoretical reason why we might not someday turn from the worship of the automobile to the worship of books and spend as much money on libraries as we now do on clover leaves.

The second answer is that the you-can't-change-human-nature argument is obviously false. Human nature has been changed within the last generation or two—changed by manipulation and propaganda to such an extent that economy, fear of waste, not going into debt, and keeping things useful as long as possible have all come to seem shameful rather than, as they certainly were formerly, tendencies to be inculcated and admired.

What changed human nature to that extent? Some will say it was the logic of evolving technology; some that the arguments of economists were convincing; some that the clever corrupters centered around Madison Avenue are responsible. But in any case human nature did change in one direction and therefore might change in another. Would anyone like to second me in the proposal that we see what could be done, either by propaganda or by a planned shift in emphasis directed by those in government who formulate those loan, tax, and subsidy programs by which they now direct industry?

Once before I cited Robert Heilbroner's recent and able book *The Future as History* in which he attempts to predict the future by a process of extrapolation. He assumes—resignedly rather than with enthusiasm—that "with the rise of abundance" advertising will become even more important because "the nature of consumer demand has radically changed. . . . It is no longer concentrated on the basic necessities of life. . . . Indeed business is forced to create and capture the public will if it is to have any reasonable assurance of stability in the 'wants' to which it caters." But books, pictures, lectures on philosophy, and copies of *The American Scholar* are as little "basic necessities" as television sets and air conditioners, and if the circulation of the *Scholar* were quadrupled both I and the now unemployed young writer could have jobs. No doubt it is easier to "create and capture the public will" demanding television sets than it would be to create a corresponding demand for the *Scholar*. But we—and I mean the all-important "planners" —might at least try.

The Kremlin claims Mark Twain

[1960]

Mark Twain is one of the most popular writers in the Soviet Union, where a twelve-volume edition of his works was begun in 1958 with a first printing of 300,000 copies. Great writers can be a bridge of understanding between peoples, and a bridge Mark Twain has undoubtedly been. But at the moment the Soviet Union is trying to make him a bone of contention instead.

Unwittingly, Charles Neider tossed the bone when he published, last year, the *Autobiography of Mark Twain* in which he brought together excerpts from Twain's writings, some of which the author had instructed his executors not to make public until after the passage of a certain number of years.

The Moscow *Literaturnaya Gazette* has printed a vehement attack on this book, in which the compiler was accused of developing an "official American line" by excluding Twain's "brilliant, angry" pronouncements critical of American expansionism and capitalism. "Official America," the Soviet critic said, is "trying to forget" Mark Twain because he was a "critical realist." The attack was a reflection of the official view, set forth in the Great Soviet Encyclopedia, that Twain is to be admired as the "founder of critical realism in American literature," and as a "genuine people's writer."

There is no doubt that "social criticism," among many other elements, is real and important in Twain's work. But the assumption that there is an American "official line" which the editor of the *Autobiography* has followed is merely an illustration of how a Soviet critic almost inevitably misunderstands the way in which public opinion is formed and expressed in the United States. Of course, there just is no "official line" on Twain.

Its impossibility is demonstrated by the fact that there is not and never has been even a consensus here among competent and informed critics. A generation ago Van Wyck Brooks accused Twain of a certain timidity which prevented him from becoming an effective social and moral critic—something like what the Russians now say he was. The late Bernard DeVoto replied angrily that Brooks had completely missed the point of an achievement which made Twain the epic poet of American expansion. And so it has gone ever since.

To some he is, first of all, a great humorist; to others, a passionate critic of human weakness; to still others, sometimes a tragic pessimist, sometimes a creator of the most significant American "myth." Within the past few months he has been accused in a well-known literary weekly of mean-spirited "conformity" to the vulgar opportunism of his day and in the same publication defended as an individualist who bravely refused to conform. The gulf between Mr. Neider and Soviet critics is hardly greater than that which has yawned between respected American interpreters.

A second element of the Soviet view of Twain is the tacit assumption that had he lived to see the glorious new day in Russia, he might have turned his bitterness into faith in the Utopia of a People's Democracy. This, of course, is absurd. His bitterness was directed not at the American system as such but at human nature, at the world, and even at what he saw as an essentially meaningless universe.

From his earliest maturity on, the one moral aspect of Twain's work is a hatred of cruelty, first of all, and, next to cruelty, of any sort of hypocrisy. He was a man (not too common a kind, perhaps) whom any injustice he became vividly aware of put into a rage which vented itself in such blistering pieces as the posthumously published "Letter From the Recording Angel" inspired by the cruel miserliness of his wife's uncle, or another violent squib in which he compares unfavorably Theodore Roosevelt, the killer of wild animals, with a certain Western murderer who thought it only common prudence to murder all the witnesses also.

Yet he grew up in what he called "The Gilded (not the Golden) Age" of American business and by his very success was somewhat drawn into it. One result was that new mixture of political with purely moral indignation of which the Soviet critics make so much.

Many of his most explicit and violent excoriations of American business, politics, and policies occur in letters and autobiographical fragments written rather late in life. But as early as 1873, when he was just entering upon his most productive period, he published in collaboration with Charles Dudley Warner the vehement satire *The Gilded Age,* which has as its theme the unholy cooperation of predatory enterprise, national government, and the church. In it, the mastermind draws up a budget: "A majority of the House committee, say $10,000 apiece . . . for the Senate . . . the same each" and "a little extra to one or two chairmen." Another entrepreneur, anxious to put through a corrupt appropriations bill, advises on publicity:

"Your religious paper is by far the best vehicle for a thing of this kind. . . . If it's got a few Scripture quotations in it, and some temperance platitudes, and a bit of gush here and there about Sunday-schools . . . it works the nation like a charm. . . ."

Sixteen years later *A Connecticut Yankee in King Arthur's Court* contained such remarks as "Better the Almighty Dollar than a tub of rancid guts labeled King," which is evidence enough that Twain was far from being a romantic conservative. During a financial panic he wrote to his brother: "What a man wants with religion in these breadless times surpasses my comprehension." He also referred to "Those two unspeakable shams, buttermouthed hypocrites, John Wanamaker & his Sunday School Times," and again: "Satan twaddling sentimental silliness to a Sunday-school could be no burlesque upon John D. Rockefeller in his Cleveland Sunday-School."

In 1869, when a Bishop delivered an invocation at the unveiling of a statue to Commodore Vanderbilt and praised him for laying up treasures in heaven at the same time he was laying them up on earth, Twain wrote an open letter addressed to Vanderbilt which contains such phrases as "how exquisitely mean a man has to be in order to achieve what you have achieved," and "I don't remember ever reading anything about [you] which you oughtn't be ashamed of."

His attitude toward "imperialism" was plain: "We have no more business in China than in any other country that is not ours."

Of the proposal to take Hawaii, he wrote: "We must annex these people. We can afflict them with our wise and beneficent government. We can introduce the novelty of thieves, all the way up from street-car pick-pockets to municipal robbers and Government defaulters and show them how amusing it is to arrest them and try them and then turn them loose—some for cash and some for 'political influence.' . . . We can give them railway corporations who will buy their Legislatures like old clothes, and run over their best citizens. . . . We can give them lecturers! I will go myself."

The view that Twain would have been sympathetic toward Communism may even seem to be supported by his comment when refusing an invitation to congratulate those who negotiated the peace between Russia and Japan in 1905: "Russia was on the high road to emancipation from an insane and intolerable slavery; I was hoping there would be no peace until Russian liberty was safe"—and, "I am said to be a revolutionist in my sympathies, by birth, by breeding and by principle. I am always on the side of revolutionists, because there never was a revolution unless there were some oppressive and intolerable conditions against which to revolute."

These sentiments would legitimately be gratifying to Soviet critics were it not for one fact: they are their own best evidence that Twain would have considered the current Communist variety of oppression as indefensible as the capitalistic variety of his time, or any other variety of any other time. For example, if the Soviet critics are right in maintaining that Twain disapproved of United States "imperialism" in taking the Philippines, that scarcely proves that he would have applauded the Communist take-over in Czechoslovakia.

"The American dogma, rightly translated, makes this assertion: that every man is of right born free, that is, without master or owner; and also that every man is of right born his neighbor's political equal—that is, possessed of every legal right and privilege which his neighbor may attain," said Mark Twain. A man so eloquent in upholding freedom could scarcely condone a system that put the ends of the state above individual liberty.

Even a Soviet critic has admitted that, for all Twain's fault-finding, he remained in favor of democracy:

"During the almost half century of his literary activity, Twain traveled a great road of ideological development, the logical completion of which was the writer's active participation in the struggle against imperialism. . . . Creating his books in the notable decade when the United States finished its transition from 'free' capitalism to monopolistic capitalism, Twain saw and condemned the moral degradation of the bosses of bourgeois society, the rottenness of the political morals in the country, the hypocrisy and deceit of the wealthy."

Then the critic honestly added: "Twain shared the bourgeois ideals and illusions of the average American. However, his later creations reflected the destruction of these ideals and illusions. Both his world outlook and his creation in the case of this democratic writer were full of deep contradictions. Even in those years when Twain reflected the strongest disillusion with bourgeois democracy he at times again turned to it with hope."

This complaint about "deep contradictions" springs from a third element in the Soviet view of Twain. It is an effort to make him "nothing but" a critic of society, and to reduce his social criticism to the dead level of Soviet-style propaganda.

Like the young Van Wyck Brooks, the Soviet critic is unwilling to see that Mark Twain was a humorist, however "serious" his humor was, and that humor, as distinguished from mere one-dimensional satire, is always an expression of seeing-both-sides and of a certain emotional ambiguity which is bound to appear a "contradiction" or "confusion" to the doctrinaire sure that he knows what "the facts" —and even "the truth"—are.

All of Mark Twain's most memorable side remarks as well as all his richest and most mature books are the product of this humorist's ambiguity. Many of his most quoted sayings take the form of a statement that begins in the tone of idealism and then provokes the shock of laughter by turning into what looks like cynicism:

"Truth is the most valuable thing we have. Let us econo-
mize it." "Always do right. This will please some and astonish the rest." "When angry, count four; when very angry,
swear." "Man is the only animal that blushes. Or needs to."

If Beaumarchais laughed in order that he should not be
compelled to weep, Mark Twain laughed lest he should ex-
plode in contempt and anger. Such sayings as those just
quoted do not demonstrate that he was a cynic any more than
they demonstrate that he was an idealist. They demonstrate that he was a true humorist—which means that he
had that awareness of the essential confusion of human nature
which is one kind of wisdom.

One of the cruelties and injustices that hurt him most
deeply was the cruelty and injustice to which the Negro race
had been subjected. But he could be "funny" about that, too
—as for instance in this fragment of dialogue in *Huckleberry
Finn* concerning a river accident:

"We blowed out a cylinder-head."
"Good gracious! Anybody hurt?"
"No'm. Killed a nigger."
"Well, it's lucky; because sometimes people do get hurt."

Those incapable of understanding humor will no doubt
find this shocking. But artistically, at least, *Huckleberry Finn*
is worth a thousand of the *Uncle Tom's Cabin*s which a Soviet critic would admire because they were not at all "confused." And it is not certain that *Huckleberry Finn* is not
also better propaganda.

Or consider something like the following—is it any the
less telling because it makes us laugh? "It is by the goodness
of God that in our country we have those three unspeakably
precious things: freedom of speech, freedom of conscience,
and the prudence never to practice either of them."

In his political and social attitudes there was a similar
ambiguity. *The Innocents Abroad* is poised between a plain

American's scorn of Europe and a nagging suspicion that there were things about European culture he did not understand. "Wagner's music is not as bad as it sounds."

A great humorist inevitably has something in common with all other great humorists. But a great writer of any kind is also unique. And the most obvious of Mark Twain's uniqueness is a vocabulary, a rhythm, and a syntax that are unmistakably American, yet rise to a level of excellence far above that ordinarily achieved. These characteristics are recognizable even in a single phrase like Huck Finn's description of a funeral sermon—"all full of tears and flapdoodle."

But it is perhaps Bernard DeVoto who best indicated this aspect of Mark Twain's uniqueness when he pointed out that like certain other American writers—notably Franklin and Thoreau—he was capable of expressions no European could conceivably have formulated.

If only an American would have chosen to say what Franklin had to say in "We must all hang together, or assuredly we shall all hang separately"; or what Thoreau had to say in "It is not necessary that a man should earn his living by the sweat of his brow unless he sweats easier than I do"; so, too, only an American (and one particular American) was capable of Mark Twain's phrase, "The calm confidence of a Christian with four aces." All three are funny and all three have a certain air of flipness. But Twain's is the funniest and the flippest of all.

Competent American observers of contemporary Soviet life report that vast numbers of Russian school children read *Tom Sawyer* and *Huckleberry Finn* simply as the delightful tales they have always seemed to English-speaking children, and also that many adults probably continue to appreciate Mark Twain on the same level. If so, it is, as in the United States, not merely because he was a humorist, a social critic, and an original stylist. It is most of all because he was capa-

ble of an imaginative poetic sweep, not primarily either satiric or humorous, which makes him—particularly in *Huckleberry Finn* and *Life on the Mississippi*—what has been called
"a great fabulist."

Huckleberry Finn, for example, creates a fable instead of
following the easier method of autobiography, and the
great river journey of Huck and Jim makes a kind of poem
as unforgettable as the wanderings of Ulysses or the March
of the Ten Thousand.

Even *Huckleberry Finn*, though it is the most nearly
achieved of Mark Twain's books, is by no means formally
perfect as a novel. The plot line sometimes wavers; there are
improbabilities in the action; some of the incidents seem
to have been improvised as the author went along.

Decidedly Twain does not belong with the Flauberts and
the Henry Jameses who fussed and labored to remove every
slight flaw. He belongs instead with Balzac and Dickens,
the great restless creators who never strove for one kind of
perfection because perhaps they had something better to do.
They had energy and originality and gusto. Our first impulse
is to say of them what Dryden said of Shakespeare: "Here
is God's plenty."

By comparison with that copiousness and energy and originality, "faults" cease to count. To say that some of the plot-
ting of *Huckleberry Finn* is imperfect or that some of the
episodes are unconvincing is as irrelevant as it would be to
complain, as one critic did, that Coleridge's *Ancient Mariner* was "improbable."

Of his own books Mark Twain once said that they could
not be classics "because everybody likes them." Nothing he
ever said is more characteristic. It reveals the typical funny
man's contempt for the stuffy aspects of conventional culture.

There were many supposed classics that Mark Twain himself did not like and some of them—for instance, the novels of Jane Austen—really are classics. But the point here is that the best of his own works, *Huckleberry Finn* especially, are classics of the very greatest kind just because everybody does read them and does like them; because to appreciate their greatness you do not have to have any special sort of preparation; you do not have to be able to see them in relation to anything else.

Their greatness is apparent to anyone capable of reading. They justify for once the use of that tired old phrase "universally human." Any man, just by virtue of the fact that he is a man, will know what they are about.

Huckleberry Finn begins with the hero's reference to the earlier *Tom Sawyer* in which Huck had first appeared. "That book was made by Mister Mark Twain and he told the truth, mainly," says Huck. "There was things which he stretched, but mainly he told the truth."

That last is Mark Twain's best epitaph. "There was things which he stretched, but mainly he told the truth." At least it would be more accurate than the "deep contradictions" of which the Soviet critic speaks.

This was Mencken: An appreciation

[1956]

Everywhere it will be said that the death of H. L. Mencken marks the end of an epoch. But perhaps it is no less true that it marks also the beginning of something—his reputation as a writer. Mencken was a spokesman, a symbol, an embodiment, and all the other things he has been called. But he was first of all a master of the written word and, unless the world changes a great deal more than seems likely, that is the only thing which will count in the long run. Men are mentioned in textbooks because they were so right or so wrong and, sometimes, because they were so typical. But it is only because they were great writers that they are read.

Like many another such—like Shaw, for instance—he did everything he could to distract attention from the true character of his gift. On the one hand, he took up all sorts of causes, the less respectable the better, and engaged in all sorts of crusades against whatever was of good report. On the other hand, he identified himself with journalists, spoke contemptuously of what he called "beautiful letters," and violated all the canons of respectable literary taste by sprinkling his pages with outlandish words drawn sometimes from the gutter and frequently from the German—the latter being his favorite foreign tongue less, I suspect, because of his own German ancestry than because, unlike French, it was obviously not genteel. Music was the only art of which he spoke frequently with respect because only a negligible minority of his fellow countrymen respected it; beer was his hippocrene because it was neither elegant like wine nor solidly respectable like whiskey; and he loved to mix beer and music—as he did in the wonderful sketch in which he describes how he and his cronies got so befuddled in the course of their attempt to play all nine of Beethoven's symphonies between dark and dawn that they could never remember whether they finished or not—because under such circumstances not even Beethoven's music could be regarded as respectable. Finally, he built a very solid reputation as a scholar, even among the *Gelehrten* whom he loved to ridicule, by a work designed to destroy the authority of all those rules of grammar, syntax, and propriety which he himself never violated except with the deliberate artistry of which only a philologue would be capable.

Like Shaw again, Mencken developed a public role which he played so constantly that he may well have ceased himself to know in exactly what relation it stood to his original self. But he at least understood very well what was at any moment appropriate to that role and he had the toughness which enabled him to play it relentlessly even under circumstances which fatally tempt the weakly amiable to concessions. Once when an inoffensive young man asked for some corrections in a story Mencken had written I heard him dismissed with a gay but final, "Journalism is essentially inaccurate" and when, not too long after the First World War, he was about to make a tour of the South, he gave reporters a pronouncement beautifully calculated to constitute a double outrage: "No man over forty loves either his country or his wife." How inevitably a second-rate man would have thought this the proper occasion to say: "I am a Southerner myself."

It may even be that the paradoxes of his temperament and opinions are best resolved by the simple assumption that he took whatever side gave him the best opportunity to exercise his gift. When he maintained that he would rather live in the United States than in any other country in the world because nowhere else was a civilization so absurd, some took this to mean that he was a wicked man who loved to despise his fellows but it may have meant only (and understandably) that, as a certain kind of humorist, he naturally judged a culture by the material with which it provided him.

Those who saw Mencken at the Dayton antievolution trial understood this better, perhaps, than anyone else ever could. He was at the height of his popularity and this was a spectacle perfectly designed for his exploitation. Here was a monstrous absurdity which, unlike the monstrous absurdities of our own day, was merely absurd—uncontaminated, that is to say, by anything essentially evil. Mencken was like a schoolboy at a circus. Beaming with sheer delight, unable to believe that anything so like one of his own extravaganzas could really be taking place, he was everywhere at once, hobnobbing with street-corner preachers, charming the rustics with his affability and falling off his chair in the courtroom when overcome by joy. He was at the moment the happiest man in the United States, for he was not only a boy at a circus, he was also a great writer who sensed that he had his opportunity and he took it to produce what has often been called his masterpiece—his "In Memoriam: W.J.B." —though it did not become fully possible until Bryan died a few days after his declaration on the witness stand that man is not a mammal.

Many of Mencken's admirers were distressed by the attitude which he took in the thirties and forties toward Franklin D. Roosevelt and all other idealists in public life. Perhaps it would not be unfair to say that he continued to see only the absurdity of a world which had become grim and that he refused to acknowledge the existence of problems he was temperamentally incapable of facing.

Certainly it is true that his importance as a spokesman and his popularity with large masses declined as the atmosphere of the world changed. Every literate college boy read him in the twenties, relatively few read him in the forties. His disciples had once been measured by the millions, their numbers shrank into insignificance. And yet, at least when he turned from the questions of the day, he wrote as well if not better than he had ever written before. Not even the Bryan piece is more masterly or more flavorsome than some of the rich happy absurdities in the volumes of reminiscence where such sketches as that about the Italian bands which used to play in Baltimore are in the great picaresque tradition of Rabelais and Smollett.

To mar the portrait which he drew of himself by saying that he was a scholarly and, in certain respects at least, a kindly man is almost a betrayal. But there is no doubt about either the laboriousness of his scholarly work or about the genuineness of his enthusiasm for "beautiful letters." It may very well be that the *Smart Set* under his and Nathan's editorship became the most important "little magazine" in America, though neither of the editors would ever have consented to have it thought of as in the "little magazine" group. In those days at least, no one was more keenly on the lookout for new writers and there must have been scores who had reason to be grateful. I, for one, remembered too well the note with which he accompanied the first check I ever received from any publication to be hurt by the words with which he later dismissed one of my books in which he thought he detected the corrupting influence of a kind of nostalgia for God: "After all no one can be expected to come all the way from Tennessee to civilization in one generation." A good many were shocked when, a few years ago, he boasted that he had never admired Theodore Dreiser as a novelist but had used him only as a club against those whom he admired even less. But is that really any worse than Shaw's confession that in his drama criticism he was concerned not at all with the extent to which authors achieved what they wanted to achieve and asked only whether or not they were trying to do what he thought they ought?

If Mencken would not have cared to be praised for moral virtues, he would certainly have liked to have recognized those artistic achievements which were more indubitably his. No doubt it will be some time yet before he will, in all quarters, have lived down his popularity and a lack of gentility more absolute than that which even Mark Twain, his closest analogue, dared exhibit. He founded no worthy school, most of his imitators were contemptible because his style was inimitable and only he could use as a genuine instrument of expression a vocabulary and a rhythm which in other hands stubbornly refused to yield anything except vulgarity. But I risk the prediction that the time will come when it will be generally recognized, as by a few it already is, that Mencken's was the best prose written in America during the twentieth century. Those who deny that fact had better confine themselves to direct attack. They will be hard put to find a rival claimant.

Did Gide represent our time?: A review of *Portrait of André Gide* by Justin O'Brien

[1953]

The popularity of André Gide is certainly not of the widest possible sort, but among people of consciously literary interests it has grown to imposing proportions. As a matter of fact, it would not be too much to say that at the time of his death there was no other living man whom so many such people were ready to accept as *the* representative writer of our time, almost as one who might be called the Hero as Man of Letters. Mr. O'Brien's substantial study, partly biographical but with the main stress on an analysis of Gide's thought and temperament as revealed in his principal works, is likely to remain a major presentation of the subject. Mr. O'Brien is a specialist in French culture; he enjoyed the confidence of Gide, whom he saw from time to time over a period of many years; and he has threaded his way with great dexterity through the ambiguities and inconsistencies of his subject's mind. He conceals nothing, but his sympathies are never overridden by the irritations so evident in the brief excerpts recently published from the journal of Martin du Gard.

Now if Gide really was the representative man of letters of his time, what was it that made him so, or—if that question is too strong—what are some of the outstanding characteristics which were at least compatible with his position and hence of some significance in suggesting the temper, the preoccupations, and the ideals of the group which accepted him as representative?

First of all one will notice, of course, that he was preeminently a pure writer—despite the fact that he was also a moralist in the Manichean sense that Baudelaire and Huysmans were moralists, which means most aware of good in connection with evil. From childhood he was already "literary" in a sense that Englishmen or Americans rarely are and already tacitly assuming that man writing is man engaged in the occupation which best becomes him. As one reads Mr. O'Brien's account of his friendships at the Lycée Henri Quatre or of how, while still in his teens, he frequented the salon of Mallarmé, one realizes how rarely any English or American writer grows up in a similar atmosphere and how unlikely it is therefore that he will ever take literature as quite so self-evidently the final end of man. But if the literary world of England and America nevertheless accepts Gide as the representative writer, that perhaps means that it is ready to accept as an ideal a degree of absorption in literature itself, a remoteness from the everyday business of life, which is uncommon even among those native writers who are accused by the socially and politically minded of having no concern with "social significance."

That Gide flirted briefly with Communism and then revolted against it certainly helps to make him typical, but typical is not the same as "representative," and it is possibly more significant that he should further mark his separateness from the nonliterary public, that he should distrust popularity, and that in an age which, outside literature, has been fanatically devoted to the ideals of health, normality, and "adjustment" he should say: "Health does not seem to me such an enviable possession. It is merely an equilibrium, a state of mediocrity in everything. . . . A humpback is a man plus a hump, and I prefer that you should look upon health as a deficiency of disease."

Some might even maintain that his homosexuality—he preferred to be more precise and put himself in the subclass of pederasts—was another characteristic which contributed to his representativeness. He at least regarded it as a fact of primary importance, partly perhaps because it so perfectly demonstrated his anarchical "sincerity" and determination to "be himself." The tendency to "dissociate" is also certainly one of the strong tendencies of our time, and Gide early made up his mind to dissociate love from pleasure. "I have ceased," he said, "to believe in sin"; and he was convinced that both love and pleasure would be purer as well as more intense if the heart and the body went their separate ways. Following no doubt Gide's own attitude, Mr. O'Brien speaks of Gide's first experience with the pleasures of pederasty as a "liberating encounter" and of Gide's first contact with other men who shared his taste as "an important step in Gide's moral liberation."

One of the portraits which Mr. O'Brien publishes—taken in 1926—reveals a kindly and humorous face not in the least embittered or ravaged. That is not at all what one would say of a portrait of most mature "immoralists" such as, for example, Baudelaire. It certainly does not contribute to making Gide seem typical. But perhaps it makes him representative by suggesting that those modern seekers who find little except relativism and anarchy deserve for their integrity and their talents a better fate. In any event, and for whatever reason, the fact remains that the "representative" contemporary search for certain seemingly admirable things has a way of finding an awful chasm at the end of the road.

Gide is undeniably representative in that his grand goals have been sincerity, freedom, and the discovery of the real self. But does it make him even more indubitably representative if we say that in each case the nearer he came to reaching one of these goals the more clearly it seemed to reveal itself to be, not the stable absolute which it has been the best dream of mankind to find, but some relativity, or delusion, or vacuum?

What does "sincerity" reveal except what was once thought to be the shameful? What does the "real self" turn out to be except a welter of conflicting impulses in the face of which it is possible to say only that I am what I am, must do what I do, and that therefore good and evil are one? What does freedom in the end come down to but that *reductio ad absurdum* the *"acte gratuite,"* typified by the motiveless murder committed by the hero of "Les Caves du Vatican." Against the stultifying doctrine of either economic or psychological determinism Gide seems here heroically to assert the freedom of the will—but it is only in doing gratuitous evil that it can clearly manifest itself.

It is true as Mr. O'Brien points out that when the dadaists seized on the term *acte gratuite* as a slogan and made the accomplishment of such an act the most significant human achievement, Gide not only repudiated their attitude but also asserted that he did not mean to imply the reality of free will, only to distinguish between acts which have an obvious motive and those which "elude the ordinary psychological explanations." Presumably he would not approve the judgment of Guillaume Apollinaire, who when undertaking to name the "freest spirit that ever lived" chose—the Marquis de Sade. But the step or misstep from Gide to Apollinaire is easily taken. Is it, perhaps, all but inevitable unless in some way or to some extent one asks, "Sincerity *about* what?" and "Freedom *for* what?"

Many modern writers have promised to plunge into the abyss in order that, having known evil, we may come at last to understand good. While still a very young man Gide himself wrote to a friend: "Literature must be hurled into an abyss of sensualism from which it will later emerge altogether regenerated." This has a very familiar ring. Perhaps I am not the only one beginning to ask, "Just how much later is that likely to be?" Have those who proposed the program merely demonstrated again that though the descent into Avernus is easy the coming up again presents difficulties?

Whatever one may think of such questions, at least one fact seems clear. If Gide is the most representative modern writer, then literature seems to be widening the gulf between itself and the spirit of the age as that spirit manifests itself in other activities. That spirit is—and in the view of some disastrously so—pragmatic, utilitarian, instrumentalist, materialistic, and committed to the worship of norms, of averages, and of commonnesses. But it is certainly not obvious that literature will correct the extravagances of an alien age if it insists upon the fanatical cultivation of opposite extravagances instead of attempting, somehow, to mediate between the two.

If you don't mind my saying so . . . [VIII]

[1957]

The spread of American culture ("cocacolaization" the French call it) proceeds apace in the land where they used to order these things better. A returned traveler tells me that a hole in the wall adjoining the Café de la Paix advertises "Le Hot Dog Supreme," and that in revue-theaters the stripteaser is all the rage. One who has been elaborately photographed for an American magazine impersonates a *jeune fille* exuberantly divesting herself while goggle-eyed over the pages of a large volume labeled *Marquis de Sade*.

On the other hand, a French court has recently imposed a stiff fine upon the publisher of this same "divine Marquis," unmoved by the patriotic, anti-cocacolaization pleas of the defense that an American detective story is more corrupting. Whether this means that American "puritanism" also is conquering Gaul or is simply another illustration of the fact that the prosecution of famous books has been more frequent in French history than those who hold her up as an example of wise tolerance like to admit, I don't know. An American edition of translated selections from Sade was published here four years ago without, I think, troubling the police, and it was prefaced by an ardent defense of the author from the pen of that unassailable intellectual Simone de Beauvoir, who quoted Baudelaire as well as Guillaume Appollinaire's rousing opinion that Sade was "the freest man who ever lived." That he passed a major portion of his adult life in penal institutions and insane asylums is hardly relevant to the kind of freedom Appollinaire was referring to. Stone walls do not a prison make.

What really interests me in all this has to do with the proper place of that "realization of the reality of evil" which seems at the present moment to be occupying both theologians and critics of the arts. While several middle-brow magazines have been urging upon our novelists the business-man-as-hero and, in general, complaining that neither the virtue nor the happy situation of the modern American is being given adequate recognition, the high-brow organs keep urging a deeper and deeper exploration of misery and wickedness.

The general line usually taken is not quite that of the old-fashioned satirist who stressed his duty to "lash the vices of the age" nor that of the old-fashioned reformer who called for more light in dirty corners because, in the Ibsen phrase, "Evils grow in the dark." No, the current argument, like that of Mademoiselle de Beauvoir, is subtler and more existentialist—in the Kierkegaardian as well as the Sartreian version. What we need, it insists, is an adequate Sense of Sin: something to correct that false optimism which began with Rousseauistic notions about natural goodness and perfectibility and which, watered down, now persists in the doctrine that men are never criminal nor wicked but only "maladjusted" or "wrongly conditioned."

Now I am a reality-of-evil man myself. I believe that men (and that includes me) are frequently wicked, not merely "maladjusted." I agree that a good deal of contemporary political and social as well as moral thinking is wrong because it refuses to face this fact. But there are two reasons why I do not join too enthusiastically in the call for more darkness, violence, despair, and sadism in contemporary art.

One reason is simply that there is an awful lot of it already and no reader of contemporary fiction, poetry, or drama is likely to get the impression that men and women always behave nicely. No doubt one way of calling attention to the reality of beauty and the reality of goodness is to give a true picture of the ugly and the evil. And you can get this argument from a source as austere as Paul Tillich, who set it forth in an article on modern religious art on which he collaborated with Theodore Green. Defending those religious pictures which are full of "violence and anguish, anxiety and despair," the article goes on to say that "their very violence is an implicit affirmation of all the values which are being threatened and violated in these tragic times."

Once again I agree. But when we have so little except this affirmation by contrast, I wonder if it is sensible to call for more and more. Can we know the good and the beautiful only through their opposites? Don't both modern writers and their readers by now have a sufficiently adequate conviction of the reality of evil? Since we know very well that men can be beasts, would it be a surrender to shallow optimism to suggest, occasionally, that they can also be something else? Moreover, I can't banish wholly the suspicion that some who profess to be demonstrating their devotion to kindliness and chastity by copying Baudelaire and Sade are pulling our legs—and perhaps even their own. Rasputin's doctrine of Salvation through Sinning is very seductive.

The other reason that I have my reservations concerning the current doctrine is related to the first: How far, I wonder, should the artist accept the notion that he is the product rather than, in part at least, the maker of his times? Does he, as the Marxists are fond of saying, merely "reflect" an age? Or does he play a part in making it what it is? Alfred Kazin, for instance, writes: "There is sickness in contemporary literature, a very great sickness; but it is hardly self-willed, and it is bound up with the situation of contemporary humanity." Isn't the despair of our literature also and in itself a part of "the situation of contemporary humanity"? Could literature itself do something to ameliorate it? Lewis Mumford has written: "If our civilization is not to produce greater holocausts, our writers will have to become something more

than merely mirrors of its violence and disintegration." And
with that I am inclined to agree. But when Mumford goes on
to say: "They, through their own efforts, will have to regain
the initiative for the human person and the forces of life,
chaining up the demons we have allowed to run loose, and
releasing the angels and ministers of grace we have shame-
facedly—and shamefully—incarcerated," I am afraid I lose
courage and sneak away, murmuring as I go, "A large order!"

Whatever the proper answer to either of the two questions we have been asking, both of them pop up with increasing frequency in contemporary discussions. In a recent
issue of the *Illustrated London News,* Sir John Squire (a
good conservative) takes the authors of a new biography of
Toulouse-Lautrec to task for their reluctance to admit that
his "life of squalid debauch" and the subjects which it provided him are not an essential part of his genius. On the
other hand, A. L. Chanin, writing in the *Nation,* takes the
more usual contemporary position: "These brothel interiors
and the portraits of inmates, are part and parcel of the nineteenth-century goal, of novelist and playwright as well as
painter, to oppose artificiality and hypocrisy with a searching realism." The pretense in the 1890's that subject matter
is irrelevant strikes me as less unconvincing. Was Toulouse-
Lautrec being a moralist, either with or without knowing it,
or does the attractiveness of his work prove that, on the contrary, he found vice a creature of far from hideous mien?

Partly to illustrate how frequently contemporary critics
find themselves concerned with the problem, let's quote once
more, this time from Kenneth Rexroth (surely no middle-
brow apologist for things as they are) who has this to say
apropos Cocteau's *Journals*—again in the *Nation:* "A certain
clever Neo-Catholic dodge was fashionable on the café ter-
races. . . . It went like this: He sinned. Therefore he believed in sin. Therefore he believed in the Devil. Therefore
he believed in God. Therefore he believed in Catholicism.

Claudel made quite a thing of this with Rimbaud. Using a similar routine, T. S. Eliot was able to convince the less bright undergraduates back in his native corn belt that Baudelaire wrote like Racine and 'believed' like Bossuet. This has led in our day to imbecilities like 'Sade (or Genêt) belongs to us!' . . . Oh, come off it."

If you don't mind my saying so . . . [IX]

[1961]

What used to be called the War between Science and Religion was a hot war. That now in progress between Science and the Humanities is a cold one. It is being fought somewhat more chivalrously and with many protestations of respect on both sides. The scientist doesn't want to exterminate literature, and the humanist certainly doesn't want to abolish science. "Coexistence" is the catchword. But as in the case of the other cold war, the real question is, "On whose terms?" From both sides one gets something rather like the attitude of the Catholic priest who is said to have remarked to his Protestant opposite number: "After all, we are both trying to do God's work; you in your way and I—in His." There seems to be a good deal of question-begging and so many polite concessions that the terms are not usually clearly defined and the issues not squarely met.

 C. P. Snow—a champion *sans peur* and *sans reproche*—seems to rest his case not so much on the superiority of science over the humanities as upon the alleged fact that scientists are better guys. There is, he argues, more good will among them, a larger common ground on which to operate, and more willingness to make common cause. Probably this is true as long as they stay on this common ground. But scientists not infrequently are also patriots, adherents to this or that social philosophy and even, sometimes, loyal sons of some church. Those who are scientists and nothing else may be a bit *too* neutral—as, for instance, a famous rocket expert who appears to have been so little interested in anything except rockets that he was perfectly willing to make them for either side even in the middle of what less "objective" people regarded as Armageddon.

As William James said, "We may philosophize well or ill, but philosophize we must." Those who say they do not philosophize at all have usually answered philosophical questions arbitrarily and without thought. And for all the claims made that science itself can become an adequate philosophy, it seems to an unregenerate humanist like myself that such philosophy provides no answer to questions that have to be answered either thoughtfully or, as the scientist often tends to answer them, arbitrarily. We may, says a distinguished American professor of experimental psychology, take it for granted that all ultimate questions can be reduced to one— namely, what is most likely to lead to survival? But who are the "we" who take this for granted? The better-red-than-dead boys apparently do. On the other hand, there is what some regard as good authority for "He who loseth his life shall gain it." Probably there is no way of arbitrating between the two attitudes. But there is certainly no purely scientific solution, and the humanist is at least more acutely aware of the problem.

I must repeat the familiar charge that science can tell us how to do a bewildering (indeed, an alarming) number of things, but not which of them ought to be done; and I repeat it because I have never heard a satisfactory reply, and because it is perfectly evident that scientists themselves do not always agree in such decisions when called upon to make them. Of the medical practitioner it is sometimes said that medicine itself supplies him with an ethic. But take, for example, the case of the German doctors who used human beings as laboratory animals. They had learned the same medical science as those of their European and American fellows who found their experiments morally and even criminally shocking. At a medical congress both groups would have met on that common ground that Sir Charles regards as so important—as long as the discussion was confined to science. At a clinic they would have agreed on both diagnosis and treatment. Whatever the origin of their moral differences, it certainly did not lie in the field of the scientific knowledge both had mastered. Their science gave them no guidance in the making of an ethical decision.

To this objection, which seems to me incontrovertible, either of two answers is usually given. One is that science, properly understood, *would* give an answer if properly attended to. The other is that "ought" implies a concept which corresponds to nothing outside the human mind and exists there only subjectively, induced by the conditioning effect of social custom; and that, therefore, we should be content to say merely that what we ought to do must be left to whatever society evolves as a result of the wise determination to devote ourselves exclusively to scientific knowledge.

Pushed into a corner, those who maintain that only science is anything more than nonsense are likely to throw the question back into the face of the humanist. "Just how much progress have philosophy, metaphysics, religion, and poetry ever made toward establishing 'oughts' conclusively demonstrated or widely agreed upon for long? You blame us for our failures. What are your successes?" This *tu quoque* is, to put it mildly, embarrassing—so embarrassing, in fact, that I would rather drop the subject for the moment and come back to it (if I must) a little later in this discussion.

What seems to me necessary (and lacking) to clarify any general discussion of the "case for the humanities" is some clear definition of science on the one hand and, on the other, of the subject matter which the humanist believes he alone can deal with and of the methods he uses.

Originally, of course, science meant simply knowledge of any kind, and the humanities meant merely secular learning—knowledge about human affairs as contrasted with the divine, or, more simply still, the kind of thing one found in the writings of the Greeks and Romans before the Christian revelation made knowledge of the divine possible. But the meaning of the first term narrowed, and the meaning of the second grew more vague. Science came to mean a special kind of knowledge that can be acquired by certain techniques while the humanities came to mean, well, whatever is left over. What actually is left over came to seem to many less and less important if, indeed, it was important at all.

Suppose we say that science (and the definition would certainly have been accepted at a time when scientists were more modest) deals with whatever is measurable and subject to experimental verification. I cannot think of any scientific inquiry that has gone beyond that without ceasing to be completely scientific. Accept that definition, add that the subject matter of the humanities is whatever cannot be measured or verified experimentally, and it is obvious that what is left over is extensive and important.

Take, for example, the question of contentment, happiness, and joy. Pope called the second "our being's end and aim." At least some scientists would agree that it is as fundamental as survival since, if science can tell us how to survive but not how to be happy, it is wasting its time. Yet happiness cannot be measured and the assumption that this man is happier than that cannot be experimentally verified. The difficulty may not be quite as thorny as that which involves the "ought," but it is thorny enough and important enough.

Hedonists may say that what we ought to do is what will make us as individuals in our society most happy, but that still leaves happiness as one of the things that can neither be measured nor experimented with. And it is one of the things with which the literature of humanism is concerned in its own way.

The humanist does at least recognize the importance of happiness, and he does not brush it aside like the scientist whose logic is likely to run more or less thus: happiness cannot be measured, therefore it cannot be the subject of science; but since the methods of science are the only useful ones, we will just have to assume that happiness is directly proportional to something that can be measured—say income, standard of living, or even horsepower available per unit of population. That this is a monstrous assumption is made abundantly clear by the introspection and direct observation dealt with in humanistic literature. And if we are not even further than we are now down the road to radical discontent and alienation in the midst of abundance, it is largely because humane letters still affect us.

So much for the kind of subject with which the humanities can and science cannot deal. What methods does the humanist, who can neither measure nor experiment, rely upon? He cannot, of course, prove anything. All that he can do is to carry conviction. He can, for example, draw a picture of a happy man and tell a story that seems to account for that man's happiness. There is no objective test for the truth or falsity of his assumptions. For his success or failure he depends upon one thing only—the extent to which he can carry conviction, and he convinces just to the extent that our own experience confirms his. Hence my own definition of the humanities would be simply this: they are that branch of inquiry concerned with the unmeasurable and the undemonstrable and dealing with it in such a way that although nothing is proved, something is, nevertheless, believed. The truths of the humanities are, in other words, those that cannot be demonstrated but can be recognized.

Thomas De Quincey's famous definition of humane literature as the literature of power, as distinguished from the literature of knowledge, is sound although sometimes misunderstood. The literature of knowledge is that which *confers* power; humane literature, that which *is* powerful. The half-sciences of psychology, sociology, and history necessarily fall between two stools, and they would be both more useful and less dangerous if they always recognized the fact. So long as they deal only with what can be measured and experimentally verified, they rarely throw very much light upon the most important subjects. When, as all too often happens, they pretend to have proved something that their facts do not really prove, they can be disastrously misleading. They are most effective when they, like the novelist, carry conviction by statements whose truths we seem to recognize.

Sir Charles himself when he expresses the opinion that scientists are better guys than humanists is indulging in exactly the kind of loose, unsupported generalization often cited as reproachable in the man of letters. He may give random examples, but he presents no hard statistics. We may agree or not, and whether we do agree will depend upon our own experience. He is speaking as a humanist, not as a scientist.

Freud offers a more striking case in point. He was so far from establishing a science that there are by now almost as many incompatible schools of psychoanalysis as there are Christian sects. Competent physicists could not possibly disagree among themselves on fundamentals as psychoanalysts disagree. But Freud probably had as much effect upon our mental climate as any man who lived during his time, because when we read what he had to say, we experienced "the shock of recognition." What he had not actually demonstrated was recognized. We believed because our past experience had prepared us to do so.

The Lonely Crowd is, I suppose, the most widely read sociological work written in the United States during the past twenty years. Yet, as sociologists with a narrower conception of their quasi-science were quick to point out, it didnt actually prove anything. There were no measurements and no experiments weighty enough to be taken seriously. The examples of "inner-directed" and "other-directed" personalities were not selected by any controlled process of sampling but were treated merely as illustrations, much as a literary essayist might have treated them. Yet, most readers did experience the shock of recognition. *The Lonely Crowd* is a contribution to "the humanities."

Scientists fear (not without reason) the power that literature has to keep alive and to propagate all sorts of notions, including the pernicious. It can decline into mere rhetorical oratory and sometimes make the worse appear the better reason. Poets, said the American novelist and paragrapher Ed Howe, are the only prophets who are always wrong. Exasperated by Alexander Pope, Bernard Shaw exclaimed that "you can't make a lie true by putting it into an heroic couplet." But the unfortunate fact is that you can go a long way toward making it seem so. Said Mark Twain, "The history of the human race is strewn thick with evidence that a truth is not hard to kill; but that a lie, well told, is immortal." "Well told" is the operative phrase, and since to tell well is the special province of humane letters, they are no doubt responsible for more seemingly immortal lies than erroneous science ever has been. On the other hand, it is the great body of these same humane letters that have kept alive many supremely important concepts like those of "honor," "love," "duty," "the good life," et cetera, which science dismisses or at least ignores just because it has no means of dealing with them. A scientist may be and often is also a humanist, but he can be such only insofar as he recognizes the legitimacy of problems with which he cannot, as a scientist, deal. Accept science as the only legitimate concern of the human mind, and you must cease to concern yourself with anything that cannot be measured or experimented with. And a world that disregards everything thus excluded would be a world in which the human being as we know him would cease to exist.

The humanist cannot claim any success in his enterprise comparable to that which the scientist boasts of in his. He is compelled, generation after generation, to begin all over again. It is not certain that he has made any progress since the time of Plato and Aristotle or the times of Homer and Shakespeare. He may even find himself carrying less and less conviction to others, perhaps even being less and less sure himself. He never has, and he probably never will have, a method that produces results as the method of science does. But that is not because he is less intelligent and less competent. It is because the human being is more complicated than the physical world—more complicated even than the atom. But it is also at least as important to all of us; and as long as we continue to ask questions, even unanswered questions, we at least continue to recognize the reality of what the scientist tends to regard as nonexistent or unimportant just because he does not know how to deal with it. Perhaps the best defense of the humanities was made by Justice Holmes when he said that science teaches us a great deal about things that are not really very important, philosophy a very little about those that are supremely so.

"Boost—don't knock"

[1961]

It must have been about 1906 or 1907 that I first heard the slogan "Boost—Don't Knock." That was in Knoxville, Tennessee, where new waves were slow to arrive, and it came to me from the lips of a rising young real estate man who lived next door. He gave pep talks to the Chamber of Commerce, subscribed to Elbert Hubbard's *Philistine*, bought Mission furniture, and in every other respect conformed to a newly established pattern. Bruce Barton with his Jesus as salesman was just around the corner.

I would not like to draw too sweeping or too hasty a conclusion but the sad fact is that this booster came to a bad end. He took his own life shortly after 1929 when it was revealed that the real estate and loan firm of which he was a leading member owed a good deal of its prosperity to some dubious practices. All the loans were, he hoped, sound. Besides, in a community as progressive as Knoxville was just becoming, property values were sure to rise so rapidly that all the mortgages would soon be safely covered. My neighbor was a small victim of a philosophy which brought destruction to more powerful men and almost to our whole civilization.

The real moral is, I suppose, not that knocking is better than boosting but that one should choose carefully what he is going to boost. Life, joy, and accomplishment come more often to the yea-sayer than to the nay-sayer—provided he says "yea" to the right things. And the rule holds as true today as it did in 1907 because it is the sickness of our age that so many of its best minds play it safe by saying "nay" to everything.

Anyone who practices the two trades which have been mine—journalism and teaching—must find himself either boosting or knocking a good deal of the time, and I have done both. I suppose, however, that if my Knoxville optimist were here to judge me he would say that when the record was balanced I would find myself dismissed to the left-hand side, along with the other goats who had done more knocking than boosting.

Of this fact I am not proud. On the whole, the writers I admire most are those who have managed to find words for their love, and wonder, and hope. I would rather have written (if so absurd a possibility can be entertained) "The loveliest pair that ever yet in love's embraces met" than Swift's "Nymph Going to Bed," than *Tropic of Cancer,* or, for that matter, than the collected works of Sigmund Freud. I would rather, if I could, believe that "The world's great age begins anew" than to find myself asking, "What rough beast, its hour come round at last, slouches towards Bethlehem to be born?" Should anyone ask me—as no one ever has—to choose some page of my own by which I would most like to be remembered, it would certainly be one where I paid tribute to a great man, a great book, or to some wonder and beauty of the natural world. Like Thoreau I would wish my journal to be "the record of my loves." But like Thoreau (whose rejection of his time was a bit unusual) and like most of my contemporaries (among whom "alienation" is epidemic) I have complained and scolded more often than I have celebrated.

Is that, I sometimes wonder, exclusively the fault of the age in which we live or is it some lack of courage in ourselves?

Few believe any longer in the reality of the good old days. The optimist whom one still occasionally meets has little good to say of the past and little more to say of the present —only of that future which he thinks may be better than either. Yet there is no denying the fact that from the art and literature of the past one gets an impression that serenity, joy, and peace were far more prevalent than they are today. Its creative spirits managed to see catastrophe as tragedy, not as the increasing nihilism of the most admired playwrights of the present day. And having purged their souls with pity and terror they could also laugh a hearty laugh or repose themselves in serenity. What did they have to laugh at or what to be serene about?

Anyone who turns from the contemplation of most European literature or of any of the other arts to study the record of its social or political history will find it hard to believe that the art was created in such a world. What we know of life in the Middle Ages—even for the relatively privileged—seems to us to have been composed of perpetual discomfort and quick, recurring horrors. Yet even the fortresses built during the darkest of the Dark Ages are grimly beautiful.

Do you reply that, after all, they had no hydrogen bomb to fear? Surely the individual life was at least as precarious as it now is and most of those who contemplated their short span professed, at least, to believe in the eternal torment of Hell—the most terrifying conception ever invented by man, not excepting that generated by the hydrogen bomb itself, which, at worst, would put an end to all human suffering along with all human life.

Look at Chartres or any of the other cathedrals built as the Middle Ages came to an end. Over the central portal you will probably find a vision of the Last Judgment with emperors and bishops being tossed along with humbler folk into the hell-mouth. Look elsewhere and the scholars and saints gaze out from their pedestals with eyes which seem to reflect the peace which passeth understanding. What then becomes of the theory that art reflects the times in which it is created? Is there any possible conclusion to be reached except that in the Middle Ages at least art reflected a human spirit which somehow transcended the world in which it had its being?

Move down to London into the filth and barbarism of the eighteenth century. Dr. Johnson, nearly blind, tortured by scrofula, proclaims roundly that life is a state in which more is to be endured than to be enjoyed and that the natural progress of the human mind is not from pleasure to pleasure but from hope to hope. Yet he never denied that there was something to be enjoyed as well as to be endured and it is a far cry from the pessimism of *Rasselas* to the nihilism of, say, *Waiting for Godot*. Henry Fielding saw and pitied more of the misery of his time than most. One of the most quietly terrible passages in literature is his calm description of the jeers from depraved brutes which greeted him, an obviously dying man, as he was hoisted onto the ship taking him to death itself. Yet *Tom Jones* is a cheerful book.

If you think that it was only the writers who managed somehow to rise above their times, then listen to the music from Byrd, through Purcell, to Handel. What relation, if any, does it have to the variously troubled times of any of them? How it seems to speak of sweetness, serenity, and confidence! Where on earth did they find them? Mozart, who knew at first hand all the spurns which patient merit from the unworthy takes, who was struggling so unsuccessfully with poverty that he was soon to be buried in an unmarked pauper's grave, gives us as one of his very last gifts *The Magic Flute*—an opera so serene and also so merry that Shakespeare's *Tempest* is the only work of art which invites comparison.

Your present-day composer—though he travels a harder road than any other creative man is today condemned to follow—not infrequently gets a scholarship, a grant, or a commission from some endowed orchestra, only to find himself expressing in the acrid sounds of his music the same disgruntled comment on human life, the universe, and even music itself which one hears from the novelist and the poet. There are exceptions of course. Swift was "modern" in his loathing for the human race and in his love of dirt for its own sake. Robert Frost, on the other hand, is quite old-fashioned in apparently finding the world still worth living in. But there is no doubt about the general tone of either the old art or the new.

In the past there is little *except* its art, and the spirit which created it, to which I would wish to return. But if the good old days weren't even comparatively good, then why, if we knew only their art, would we conclude that they must have been? Was it merely because the artists had courage or because (to borrow another phrase I heard fresh from the lips of the Knoxville optimist) they looked at the doughnut and not at the hole?

I can think of four or five other possible answers to that question but none is convincing. You could say, for example, that the old poets, painters, and composers were mere escapists turning their backs on reality and compounding an opiate which enabled them to take refuge in dreams instead of trying to make this a better world—which last is, as we have discovered, a discouraging business. Or perhaps that they were honest victims of various delusions which we have got rid of and that therefore we are compelled to face at last the horrid truth that man is a failure and the universe he inhabits meaninglessly cruel. Is it possible, on the other hand, that they were somehow right and we somehow wrong?

Another curious aspect of the situation is this: If it is art that gives us the most attractive picture of the past, contemporary art gives us the most dismal view of the present. Many an unthinking man in the street seems relatively cheerful, and the artist of today addresses himself almost exclusively to a very special audience—in part just because his dark thoughts seem to so many common men very much over-drawn. Among even the most respected political and social thinkers hope, at least for the future, is not unknown. Such thinkers do include, to be sure, pessimists who range all the way from the dead black of a Sir Charles Galton Darwin to the somber gray of a Harrison Brown who continues to cherish a faint hope that there may just possibly be a solution to our difficulties even though he can't quite see what it would be. But there are also those who stoutly maintain that the world's great age could—perhaps even will—soon begin anew if we reform the world as it could be reformed. It is only among the respected artists that that "alienation" tends to be complete and unreconcilable.

I am not unaware of the defense often made for them, sometimes in unexpected quarters. Pointing out how bad things are is, so some say, the first step toward making them better—even if the possibility is not explicitly acknowledged. That vice is a creature of hideous mien is, the defense goes on, best demonstrated by an accurate portrait. Like Baudelaire, your modern celebrates virtue and beauty by describing vice and ugliness. Still, that is not the only way in which it can be done. Your beatnik represents the most recent phase of the Manichean theory that vice is the most important thing in the world because it is the shadow which makes goodness stand out in relief. An admiring reviewer of a recent novel describes its hero as one who "takes an alcoholic revenge upon society," though just how such a revenge can either damage or reform society is not very clear to me at least.

I am, as I have just said, familiar with such defenses. In fact I was already familiar with them in 1929 when I wrote a book called *The Modern Temper*. Despite the logic of Gnosticism—Judas was as necessary as Jesus to our salvation —"It is," I wrote, "rather difficult to carry on trade with a man who may be planning to revivify your Idea of justice by cheating you unmercifully, and rather difficult successfully to bring up a family when the father illustrates benevolence indirectly by beating the children or the mother sets out to secure a clear Idea of purity by prostituting all her daughters." This still seems to me something which might be remembered by those existentialists who set out to practice unmotivated acts, by beatniks who take "an alcoholic revenge on society," and (not to mention names) by certain contemporary American novelists who boast how they thumb their nose at a corrupt society by being as disorderly as possible.

Perhaps this present age of world crises, anxiety, and despair really is only the darkness before the dawn of a life more worth living than any human life ever was before. Perhaps, as some optimists think, it will be brought about by better organization, national and international, by socialism, by Communism, or by a world federation. Elsewhere and more than once I have expressed my own opinion that none of these things, good as one or more of them may be, is enough. I have said that since, in my opinion, man makes society, not society man, he can be saved only by being born again; by recovering that respect for his own nature and his own powers which so much modern thought, scientific and sociological, has tended to deprive him of; by forming some concept of the good life which is not merely prosperity, comfort, convenience, and power. But it is with the present, not with a possible future, that I am concerned here; not with how to live in Utopia when and if we achieve it, and not with how to promote that possible Utopia. What I am concerned with is rather how to live better than we now do while waiting for the glorious day which may or may not come.

After all, even if such days do arrive, that will probably be after most of us are dead. What shall we do in the meantime? Shall we retreat into the art of the past or live in a dream of the future? Or shall we try, as so many of our ancestors seem to have tried, to take some satisfaction in the world we are compelled to live in, no matter how bad it may be? It is just possible that no hydrogen bomb will ever fall upon us. If it does not, then how foolish we shall seem even to ourselves if we have permitted fear of it to overshadow all we might have enjoyed and done. Bomb or no bomb, we are all, as that difficult optimist Robert Louis Stevenson once remarked, merely enjoying a reprieve from the condemnation to death which nature has passed upon us. If we accept one reprieve, why not the other? As Samuel Johnson once wrote, "He that sees before him to his third dinner, has a long prospect."

One group of contemporary socialists has recently complained that our thinking is not sufficiently Utopian. Sometimes I am inclined to believe that we would be happier if it were less so. Those who find life not worth living because it is not perfect are not likely to find it so in the foreseeable future and they might do better to resolve, as Thoreau said he did, that his first business was to live in this world be it good or bad.

There is, it seems to me, an attitude which is neither "eat drink and be merry" nor a sullen refusal to take advantage of what goods an individual life affords—either because some others are deprived of them or because we have a duty to think of nothing except how to improve the world. Indifference to the suffering of others and to the fate of humanity is one thing. Refusal to accept gratefully what benefits we enjoy is another. And this last is what Catholic theology calls the Sin of Melancholy. It is, strangely enough, one of the sins to which the contemporary intellectual seems most prone. Between callousness and melancholy there is surely some golden mean. Perhaps it was because they had achieved this golden mean that so many artists of the past were able to find the bad old days not intolerably bad and that they were not, like us, "alienated."

What is the moral of all this so far as the contemporary

artist is concerned? It is surely not, as some of the more popular magazines seem to have suggested in their editorials, that he should fix a grin on his face and adopt as uncritically as my boyhood neighbor the twin slogans "Boost—Don't Knock" and "Look at the doughnut but forget the hole." The duty of the artist is to state the truth as he sees it and that duty comes before any supposed duty to cheer up his readers. What I am asking him to consider is simple: (1) Does he tell the whole truth as he sees it or only that part of it which it has become the fashion to dwell upon exclusively? Is, in other words, his own condition and that of his acquaintances as bad as his works suggest? (2) If the answer to both these questions is in the affirmative then could he, perhaps, make it otherwise by reconsidering his premises, demanding less of the world, and being also less unwilling to make the most of what partial and temporary goods it still affords— even to those of us who find ourselves assigned to the age of anxiety?

Something like this is what I find myself trying to do. Sometimes I fail but sometimes, also, I succeed. I try to remember that (and it was again Thoreau who said it) God did not send me into this world without some spending money.

Challenge to an unknown writer

[1962]

"When half-gods go the gods arrive." So at least said Emerson in words which summed up well the attitude of the Victorians. They were reeling under the impact of their century's multiple skepticisms but they were still able to believe that it must all be "somehow good."

We who were young in the twenties did not quote Emerson very often but we were very busy getting rid of half-gods and we believed in our job because we assumed—without always bothering to say so—that the gods were waiting to take their place. First of all, we said, let us get rid of Puritanism and Provincialism, the two great enemies of the freedom to be ourselves. And we were sure that we had selves which deserved to be free.

Almost every work of literature in any form was iconoclastic. Edgar Lee Masters and Sherwood Anderson we admired because they destroyed the idyllic image of the village; Sinclair Lewis because he did the same for the image of the small town. We admired Lytton Strachey because he revealed the clay feet of heroes and we imitated him clumsily in biographies which degenerated into that vulgarest form of idol-breaking which we all too appropriately named "debunking." If we were at least hectically cheerful that was because we cheerfully assumed that our gods (pagan gods, we hoped) would come. The new world was to be a merry one.

Freud we greeted with enthusiasm; and by selecting only the negative portions of his doctrine we assumed that he, too, was important chiefly because he exposed errors and seemed to encourage us to scrap the long-accepted patterns of behavior. Those critics and philosophers who dealt with concepts more abstruse than Puritanism and Provincialism were also largely concerned with clearing the ground. Remy de Gourmont—once much read but now apparently almost forgotten—popularized the general term "the dissociation of ideas," by which he meant the most radical possible dissolution of the habitual patterns associating one idea with another. Consciously or unconsciously, Proust was following him when he undertook to "dissociate the ideas of love and permanence"; Pirandello, when he attempted to dissolve the concept of a continuous personality or ego. When Eliot wrote "April is the cruelest month" he was dissociating one of the oldest associations, spring and renewed hope. Aldous Huxley was doing the same thing rather more obviously when, for instance, he described his lovers "quietly sweating palm to palm."

Incongruity rather than congruity became the accepted form of the metaphor and "the moon shook like a piece of angry candy." In much fashionable poetry, syntax was thrown to the winds. James Joyce all but destroyed language by making it a succession of incongruous puns. In Paris they proclaimed "the revolution of the word" and dadaism went the whole way by insisting upon radical meaninglessness. But just as the gods were expected to step in when the half-gods went, so, too, new associations were supposed to form once the old had been broken.

Like Emerson, Matthew Arnold also had tried to believe that though one world was dead there was another waiting to be born, and we, who thought ourselves so new, were unconsciously echoing him also. But the new world has not been born and the true gods are slow in arriving. Sinclair Lewis could expose Provincialism but he failed to create "a cultured heroine" who convinced anyone. We were no longer Puritans and we hoped that we were no longer provincials. We were free. But we did not know what we were free for. When the ground was cleared only Eliot's wasteland was left. We are now waiting, not for God, but for Godot. And even he is not expected to arrive.

The most obvious aspect of the new freedom was, of course, the sexual; and it was to some extent a sort of symbol of all the others. He who rejected in that department the mores of a preceding generation would be prepared, we thought, to reject all the others. Dissociation was again the method. If we could dissociate the ideas of love and permanence we could also dissociate "sex" from "domesticity," from "fidelity," and, of course, from "sin." Freed from all the arbitrary associations which had resulted in the frustrations, repressions, and guilty misery of the Victorians, it would form other and happier ones. Ultimately, so we believed, the idea of sex would associate itself cheerfully with such ideas as playfulness, joy, fulfillment, and even just plain fun. In certain previous ages it had at least come somewhere near doing just that. And we assumed (a bit unhistorically perhaps) that pagan Greece represented an even more desirable synthesis and set of associations.

If we were ever actually successful pagans during some years of the twenties, we did not remain such for long. If one may take today's novels as evidence, we get precious little joy, fulfillment, or even fun out of sex. The heroes of Tennessee Williams are more bedeviled by it than the Pilgrim Fathers ever were. If there is anyting which the heroes of contemporary fiction in any form most assuredly are not, it is happy pagans.

Just how those who neither write nor read fare in this respect is harder to know. "Popular culture" is certainly not timidly puritanical in its exploitation of "sex appeal." Almost all popular songs treat of love. The most improbable products—toilet paper, for example—cannot be advertised without the cooperation of some voluptuous female. The moving pictures try desperately to outdo one another in being "frank, explicit, free," or, as they say, "adult"—this last being, curiously enough, the exact opposite of what the marriage counselors call "mature." Moralists are prone to assume that all of this means that we are abandoned devotees of the Venus Pandemos and that the man in the street, unlike the intellectual, is reveling in pagan orgies. But I am not quite sure that this is what all this desperate emphasis upon the delights of sex really means.

Anthropologists tell us that in primitive societies fertility cults involve erotic dances, and the exhibition of realistic or symbolic representations of the sex organs. But some of them, at least, add that this means, not that primitive people are obsessively attracted by sexual activity, but that they are not. The purpose of the rites is to work up an interest in something they tend to forget all about.

I am now about to ask a question rather than to make a statement. But I cannot help wondering if the dutiful wolf whistle and mammary fetishism do not suggest a similar state of affairs. If we were really so randy as we pretend to be, would we need all this stimulation? Certainly the names of and the publicity for the more expensive perfumes suggest that women are compelled to use desperate means to provoke even the most libertine of proposals. After all, the night clubs, the musical shows, and the "continental" movies are only Barmecide feasts. Do most of the spectators proceed from them to their private games or (depending upon age) do they either resume their longing for a sports car or their perusal of the *Wall Street Journal?*

So far as intellectuals are concerned, their plight seems to be, in part at least, due to the fact that instead of finding any idea which can be pleasantly associated with any other, they go from dissociation to dissociation. Once we were content to say that we did not understand the universe. Now we declare that it is radically incomprehensible. Mr. Mencken set out to prove only that the "American Way of Life" was absurd; now, as existentialists, we have given "absurd" a technical meaning and accept it as the primary characteristic of the universe.

"Only he who has chaos within," said Nietzsche, "can give birth to a dancing star." But though we have chaos aplenty the dancing stars are few. "Nonconformity" is, I suppose, a middle-brow rather than a high-brow ideal but it, too, is characteristically negative. Like "freedom" it is meaningless unless you know for what purpose you refuse to conform. "Mother," runs a current quip, "why aren't you a nonconformist like everybody else?" If "existential," "absurd," and "alienated" are the three most fashionable adjectives, the phrase which will best establish you as "projecting a contemporary image" is "the search for identity." And that is the latest way of saying that you feel lost. Being lost is the inevitable result of being free and nonconformist without knowing what you are free or nonconformist for. To have an identity it is necessary to know what you belong to as well as to what you do not.

Ideally, the business of the "intellectual"—in the special, narrow sense of that word—is to define ultimate values. The business of the statesman, the sociologist, the economist, and the lawmaker is to devise the means by which they can be made to prevail. But rarely have the two groups paid so little attention to one another. The first are still predominately iconoclasts verging toward, if not actually accepting, a nihilistic despair. Many, at least, of the second are full of hopeful plans to abolish racial and economic inequality, to raise still further the standard of living in our own country, to develop the undeveloped countries, and thus to fulfill the hopes of the world.

In a recent issue of a scholarly magazine the director of a large foundation addressed himself to the question of "Our National Purpose." What aim, he asked, lies beyond the immediate, almost solved problem of securing the benefits of our affluent society to all citizens of our republic? And the answer which he finally came up with was this: "Why, to confer upon the inhabitants of the whole earth the benefits of our own prosperity and our own way of life." But are we so sure that we Americans lead not only a good life, but the very best life, and that an adequate national purpose is simply to spread it far and wide? To some of us it seems that we could do with some of the kind of fundamental questioning which intellectuals are supposed to provide but which we do not get much of in any usable form. It is hardly fair to blame the doers for not consulting the thinkers if the latter will tell them only that a Good Life is impossible in an "existential" and "absurd" universe.

The two groups are literally poles apart. At one pole is the social engineer who relies upon economic reform and "proper conditioning," which latter is to be achieved by the application of those methods of manipulation that "the behavioral sciences" have developed and which (when applied by our enemies) we call "brainwashing." At the other pole are the intellectuals who recommend only that we strive toward that existential resignation which makes the absurd acceptable. If the former actually are on the right track; if society makes men and if most men would be happy in a world where they would find "things" sufficient if only we have enough of them, then we seem to be headed for a civilization in which everybody will be content except the thinkers—who have grown desperate.

Perhaps that is, indeed, the civilization we now have. The consciously "alienated" are certainly a very small minority. The majority may be, as the minority insists, vaguely and subconsciously anxious and discontent. But so far as I can observe, those who have fast cars to drive, TV sets to look at, and cake as well as bread to eat do not consider their world "absurd" and if they long for anything it is not usually something the intellectuals promise them. Nor is this to be wondered at. If the only choice is between a sort of comfortable barbarism and despair, then I suppose that the first is a wiser choice.

Would it be reasonable to hope that literature might do something to rescue us from nihilism on the one hand and from thoughtless adjustment to a kind of life which is abundant without being good? Would it be reasonable to ask, even, that it should make some effort to do so?

Many will reply that to ask such a question is to bring out

into the open at last the Philistinism they had suspected from my first paragraph. The business of the writer of fiction is, they say, to describe life as it is lived. All art "expresses" or "reflects" the world in which the artist lives. If contemporary literature is confused, dispirited, and ugly, why, so is the modern world. It embodies the spirit of the age. To do anything else would be to betray its function.

Before we accept that answer as final we might dare to question two of its assumptions. Does contemporary literature adequately describe life as it is led in the twentieth century? If it does, then is this all that the literary art should be expected to do?

Actually, of course, no literary work in any form describes all the kinds of life being lived at any time. The writer could not, even if he would, do that, and he rarely attempts to do so. He selects aspects, puts his emphasis on one thing rather than another, describes what he himself finds most interesting or even, in some quite respectable instances, what is most readily marketable. The heroes of our O'Haras, to say nothing of our Mailers and Joneses, may be, as their creators would maintain, the most characteristic and the most significant of our age. But they are certainly not the only kind of people who exist. William Dean Howells has been often ridiculed for saying that it was the business of the American novelist to describe only "the more smiling aspects" of American life. But absurd as that was, it is no more absurd than the assumption that he should describe only those which grin and grimace and gnash their teeth though they never smile. A generation ago G. K. Chesterton defended Dickens against a charge that his geniality and optimism were exaggerated by saying that they undoubtedly were; but no more exaggerated than the gloom of Dostoevsky. It merely happens, he added, that today exaggeration in one direction, but not in the other, is regarded as reprehensible.

More crucial is the question whether to "express" or "reflect" the spirit of the age is indeed the only proper function of literature. Does it not also, and should it not also, at least influence if it does not create that spirit? We still use the phrase "creative writer" but if he only "reflects" and "expresses" then what does he create?

Perhaps the almost unquestioning acceptance of the theory that art is "a reflection" is another example of the extent to which Marxist theories have tended to dominate the thinking even of these who would not call themselves Marxists. If all philosophies and all convictions are mere "ideologies" and therefore mere reflections of the dialectic of an evolving society, then a reasonable corollary is that literature is, in turn, a mere "expression" or "reflection" of both the society and the ideologies that society has generated. But if one believes that art leads some kind of independent existence, that men make the societies they are in turn made by, then the creative writer, like the thinker of every kind, is not merely acted upon. He also acts. "As a man thinketh so he is" embodies at least as much truth as any Marxian assumption that what he thinks depends merely upon what he (and his society) are. To a considerable extent, at least, we see life as it has been presented to us in the books we read. The spirit of the age has been created by its artists at least as much as it has created them.

"If it were not for poetry few men would ever fall in love." So declared La Rochefoucauld in one of the most often quoted of his proverbs. If you understand "love" to mean an emotion which grows out of the association of a whole complex of ideas with nascent sexual attraction, then the epigram is as true as an epigram need be. The poets whom La Rochefoucauld had in mind made the associations. His saying is also rather truer than what is implied by those who maintain that literature can only "reflect." No man can write love poetry, they seem to say, because nobody falls in love any more. But perhaps more modern intellectuals would fall in love if more of their favorite poets taught them how.

If this really is a meaningless universe—and I am not existentialist enough to be sure that it is—then one thing is certain: great literature describes life in terms which confer meaning upon it. Twenty-eight years ago, when I myself had recently ceased to believe that getting rid of half-gods was sufficient to assure the arrival of the true ones, I wrote in a book (*Experience and Art*) a paragraph by which I will still stand:

> If Love and Honor and Duty can be salvaged, then someone must write about them in a fashion which carries conviction. If we are to get along without them, then someone must describe a world from which they are absent in a fashion which makes that world seem worth having. And it is just the failure to do either of these things quite adequately which reveals the weakness of contemporary literature.

At the end of a recent and much admired play by Ionesco the hero proclaims that he himself, all alone if necessary, will refuse to turn into a rhinoceros. That is a good beginning. But what is it that he intends to remain? Just not being a rhinoceros isn't enough.

What I learned about existentialism

[1962]

When I first came upon the magic word "existential" I didn't know what it meant. To be perfectly frank, I am not at all sure that I know now and I suspect that some (mind you, I don't say by any means all) of those who stick it in here and there to give weight to their utterance do either. In the twenties when we wanted to attach a vague but inclusively laudatory adjective we fell back upon "civilized" or even "sophisticated." Sometimes at least, "existential" seems to perform the same useful function. When, for instance, I read (as I did not long ago) an art critic's comparison of two avant-garde painters and come to his summation, "By comparison with Mr. A, Mr. B is more parodistic and existential," I am willing to give him the benefit of the doubt but he doesn't, as it would be fashionable to say, "communicate" very effectively.

Seeking some quick enlightenment, I consulted the *Encyclopaedia Britannica,* where I find the following sentence: "Since existentialism is a tendency or attitude rather than a philosophical school there are few doctrines common to all exponents of it." This is putting it mildly. A designation which fits, let us say, both Paul Tillich and Samuel Beckett is not very illuminating when applied as a merely undefined label.

Why, if I am as befogged as I confess myself to be, do I have the impudence to write an article about "existential" and its ism? Faced with such a difficult question, I often fall back upon Samuel Johnson, and it therefore comes to mind that he once said, when ridiculing Alexander Pope's *Essay on Man,* that Pope had read Bolingbroke, and not understanding him was naturally anxious to explain him to others. No doubt I am at the moment moved by the same natural impulse.

I do know, of course, that Kierkegaard (whom it doesn't hurt to refer to from time to time) invented or popularized the term. Also that it did not spread very far outside theological circles until Sartre made it atheistic instead of Christian and thus much more "contemporary"—very much as

Marx turned Hegel upside down by attaching "of matter" to "dialectic."

Moreover, if I understand both of them aright, the two transformations were almost equally transmogrifying. Kierkegaard rejected rationalist descriptions of the universe in order to make the human being free to exercise a Christian option; the Sartreian version also rejects rationalism—not in order to permit us to be Christians but to demonstrate that the universe is "absurd."

Though they agree that the human being is free rather than the helpless victim of forces outside his control, Sartre, unlike Kierkegaard, uses this thesis to move "beyond good and evil" and (to quote the *Britannica* again) seems to suggest "that human freedom is sometimes best displayed on occasion by acts of singular atrocity." Kierkegaard appears to urge men to use their freedom to become rational in an irrational universe; some of the disciples of Sartre appear to urge man to abolish the distinction between the two. Thus, at least some of them plunge into nihilism.

One of the best American expositions of atheistic existentialism chooses as the epigraph of its penultimate chapter this quotation from Samuel Beckett: "Nothing is more real than nothing," and then it proceeds to amplify this statement with the mock prayer from a Hemingway story: "Our nada, who art in nada, nada be thy name; thy will be nada as it is in nada." (Nada is, of course, Spanish for "nothing.")

To me, however, the deepest meaning (or meaninglessness) of the whole doctrine lies in the metaphysical contention that "existence precedes essence."

In Sunday School, I was introduced to the mysterious statement which begins the Gospel according to John: "In the beginning was the Word and the Word was God"—which, I suspect, was not so very much clearer to my mentors than it was to me. Here, however, is the translation of the statement and what follows it in the somewhat more perspicuous language of the recently published *New English Bible*: "When all things began, the Word already was. The Word dwelt with God and what God was, the Word was. The Word, then, was with God at the beginning and, through Him, all things came to be." Most of us did have it explained to us in Sunday School that the Greek term translated as "word" is "logos" and that logos means not only "word," but also "idea," so that one might have translated the opening sentences as, "In the beginning was the Idea and the Idea was with God and the Idea was God." This is another way of saying "essence precedes existence."

Now, I am no Greek scholar but I dare point out that the English descendant of the word logos, or rather a word already related to it in Greek, is "logic." And therefore, with all realization of my incompetence in such matters, I ask if the best translation would not be: "In the beginning was the logical and the logical was with God and the logic was God."

If this be a permissible translation it gives me my key to the meaning of existentialism. The Neoplatonism of the Gospel according to John represents one extreme position. What Sartre called atheistic existentialism represents the opposite. To him the thing, not the idea, comes first and neither God nor logic is anywhere except, perhaps, in man. Instead of saying that the universe is all meaning he says that meaning does not exist anywhere in it—except perhaps in so far as a man, all alone in an absurd universe, is able to lift himself by his own bootstraps and create what does not elsewhere exist. Hence, the truest picture of human life is, one must conclude, given by such surrealistic dramas as Beckett's *Waiting for Godot* and literature must give up the struggle to find the meaning of life and resign itself to simply presenting and accepting its meaninglessness.

Whatever else you may say about this new philosophy it

is certainly radical. One of the most persistent assumptions of the human mind has been exactly the opposite; namely, that there is some sort of logic and meaning to events. Man has always been aware that he could not always discover them but he has tended to assume that this was due to the defect of his mind, not to any meaninglessness in the universe itself. Now we are told not only that all the meanings we have ever read into this universe or into human life were figments of the imagination, but also that the whole search for them is that famous seeking of a black hat at midnight in a dark cellar, the hat not being there. Wisdom consists merely in knowing that it is not—though presumably we are free to supply its lack by creating out of our own imaginations a hat of whatever color we prefer.

Obviously the image of man which existentialism "projects" (this last word is, by the way, another very fashionable one) is about as contemptible as possible. It is, in fact, the latest and apparently the ultimate stage in the progressive degradation of the "image of man" which took great leaps forward under the influence of Marx and Darwin—or at least under the influence of the simplifications and misunderstandings of their doctrine.

When Darwinism pictures man as the climax of the development of living organisms which took place as an inevitable process with which aspiration, purpose, and so forth have nothing to do, he plainly foreshadows the existentialist doctrine that the universe is without meaning or purpose. And if, on the other hand, existentialism seems to restore that freedom to choose which Marxism deprived us of, it then reaches by its own different route an equally gloomy conclusion; namely, that though man can choose, his choices are purely arbitrary and can be justified as good or bad by no external criteria.

The dead end of the tendency represented by Darwin and Marx is reached in some such pronouncement as the following by Professor Skinner, professor of experimental psychology at Harvard. Denying categorically and absolutely that man has any control over his destiny, that he has any power to choose or determine, Professor Skinner writes in his *Science and Human Behavior:* "The free inner man who is held responsible for the behavior of the external biological organism is only a prescientific substitute for the kinds of causes which are discovered in the course of scientific analysis. All these causes lie outside the individual. . . . It has always been the unfortunate task of science to dispossess cherished beliefs regarding the place of man in the universe."

From this dead end, existentialism seemed at first to offer an exit by restoring free will to the human being. But it seems to close promptly another door behind him. Though man may, by the exercise of a purely arbitrary option, create purpose and establish morality and meaning in a universe where neither exist, it is impossible to decide except by an arbitrary choice *which* purpose or *which* morality should be chosen. There seems to be no reason why an individual should not, like Milton's Lucifer, exclaim: "Evil be thou my good." And thus we are back again in a world of moral nihilism.

This explains those "unmotivated acts" which play a conspicuous part in some of the imaginative literature created by the existentialists and which are typically what the *Britannica* refers to as "acts of singular atrocity." The reasoning seems to run thus: Man's most important characteristic and that which bestows upon him his dignity is his freedom to choose. But this freedom is as adequately exercised in an act of arbitrary atrocity as it would be in one of arbitrary benevolence. Therefore man may demonstrate his essential freedom and dignity by being a monster.

Very ingenious, no doubt. It is as ingenious, indeed, as the argument advanced by the expounders of that early Christian heresy who maintained that Judas should be revered as much as Jesus because, without his betrayal, Jesus would not have been crucified and would not have been able to bring salvation to mankind. But does the argument of either the existentialist or the Manichean really deserve to be taken seriously?

Of all the theories which attempt to account for man's aspirations, sense of purpose and of right and wrong in a world which does not clearly correspond at all times to all of them, the existential theory seems to me the most improbable and indeed to be a logical monstrosity. On the one hand transcendental religions assert that man is not merely part of a natural world and is capable of exhibiting characteristics found nowhere in it because a God of one sort or another has bestowed them upon him. On the other hand, various species of naturalism reject everything transcendental but maintain that the seemingly unique characteristics of the human being are in fact not absolutely unique since in one form or another they are actually somewhere existent in nature itself. Either of these theories is at least logically tenable. But to say that the transcendental does not exist, that man is nothing but a part of a meaningless universe, but that, nevertheless, he can create meaning and purpose, seems to me to involve a self-contradiction. Where did he acquire that remarkable capacity?

Those who scorn the poet and all creators of imaginative fiction regard them as spinners of more or less pleasing fancies. Literature itself then becomes largely what Oxford used to be called—"The Home of Lost Causes"—and no more than a retreat for those who do not have the courage to face reality. To some of us, on the contrary, it seems that modern literature has been rather too ready to surrender its claim to be a method for pursuing truths which escape the scientist and even the formal philosopher.

The naturalistic novel from Zola to Dreiser accepted the

determinism of the psychologist and the sociologist. It was thus the child of Darwin and Marx and it anticipated Professor Skinner. The hero of Dreiser's last major work, *An American Tragedy,* presents us with a hero who murders the girl he has seduced, not because he is weak or evil, but simply because the forces of society to which he was subjected made it inevitable that he should do just this and that he could not possibly have done anything else. Now the most "advanced" contemporary literature has moved away from determinism to Sartreian "freedom" which leaves man, if possible, worse off than determinism had left him.

Perhaps the last major literary voice to be confidently raised in either England or the United States against the drift toward the degraded image of man and the acceptance of a meaningless universe was that anti-Darwinian evolutionist and somewhat un-Marxist Marxian, Bernard Shaw. In *Back to Methuselah* he presented his own version of evolution and in the first section, which takes place in the Garden of Eden, Raphael, paying a visit, explains it all to Adam. The two capacities inherent in the living creature which account for the development of man and which reach their highest point to date in him and assure him a glorious future are these: first, Imagination, which enables him to dream of what might be; second, Will, which enables him to see to it that what might be shall become what is.

How neatly and how completely this disposes of the determinism of Marx. How it gives us again a glorious image of man by putting his fate once more in his own hands, and how it restores to the universe a "word" or a "logos."

Is Shaw's theory actually more difficult to accept than the inherent paradoxes of existentialism? Like the latter it assumes for man the power to choose. But by the very fact that it assumes also a direction inherent in the evolutionary process it implies that the choices man is now free to

make are not arbitrary or neutral. He may choose to become
either more or less human and one of these choices is more
desirable than the other. The universe is no longer "absurd."
We need only (though it is a big "only") dream the right
dreams and accept the fact that the reality of Will can free us
from the predestination of all determinisms—including that
of "evolving technology."

Confessions of a square

[1964]

A generation ago John Jay Chapman remarked that the man
from Mars would get a truer idea of human life from Italian
opera than from the essays of Emerson. For one thing, he
would learn that there are two sexes, and that, said Chapman, is a good place to begin.

Emerson and Italian opera are both a little behind the
times, but if the man from Mars is anything like us, our sex
life is one of the first things he will inquire about. If we want
him to be as confused as we are, I suggest that we expose
him to a few of the things we are exposed to: first a few
"adult movies," a few issues of our most popular "magazines
for men," and a few popular Broadway comedies. Then, by
way of contrast, let's give him some specimens of the work
of our most esteemed "serious writers"—Tennessee Williams, for example.

Long before he had finished with the adult movies and
the magazines for men, he would be convinced that "that

old debbel sex" has turned out to be only an amusingly mischievous imp. On the other hand, he would not get far into Tennessee Williams without being driven to the conclusion that, to put it mildly, our sex life could still do with a good deal of "adjusting."

Shortly before the Profumo case broke, the *Manchester Guardian* reviewed a book called *Sex in Society,* by one Alexander Comfort, M.A., M.B., Sc.D., in which the author characterizes sexual intercourse as simply "the healthiest and most important human sport." No magazine for men could make it much simpler than that, and to those of us who are numbered among the rapidly disappearing survivors from the twenties, Dr. Comfort seems to go just a little bit further than we then went—but not very much further and certainly in the same direction.

Puritanism was our great enemy. Its fear of sex was one of its most malignant manifestations. Lovemaking, we said, had been at various times regarded as (1) a sin, (2) a mystical experience, (3) a somewhat humiliating biological necessity, (4) the delightful game that the eighteenth century called "gallantry." We proposed to get rid of sin entirely and to make a new synthesis of the other attitudes. Lovemaking was to be a delightful form of play, heightened by the haunting presence of certain mystical overtones.

Today, two generations after the heyday of the anti-Puritan revolt, I can still say that I suppose this ideal is better than one that raises the sense of sin too high. But what puzzles me is the conflicting evidence concerning the actual character of contemporary American "sex life." This last is a rather depressing phrase, but its habitual use is suggestive in itself.

The great popularity of "adult movies" and "magazines for men" seems to support the contention that sex, being no longer associated with sin, has become a mere "fun thing." But nearly every novel, play, or poem written by any one of

198 | WRITERS AND WRITING

the writers most admired by "serious critics" and most read
by those seriously interested in literature points in a contrary
direction.

None of them, to be sure, ignores sex or treats it as unimportant. Some, beginning with D. H. Lawrence and coming on down to critic Leslie Fiedler and social commentator
Paul Goodman, seem to find the cancer eating at the vitals of
modern American man to be a fear or hatred of the sexual
experience. But whether they celebrate our escape from Victorianism or protest that we haven't really escaped at all, their
characters, far from finding their amours a "fun thing," seem
to be more bedeviled by that old debbel than the Puritan
fathers ever were. Some of the characters created by Tennessee Williams, for example, have no conscious scruples
regarding even the most perverse and sadistic manifestations,
but St. Anthony himself never found his fantasies more agonizing than these characters find their imaginings. And, to
take another example, let's ask just how much fun the four
dramatis personae of *Who's Afraid of Virginia Woolf?* seem
to be having?

One may patiently search the pages of Williams (to say
nothing of Beckett, Ionesco, Genêt, Albee, and the rest) without finding a single example of happily "pagan" lovemaking.
Yet these writers are typical of those whom a large section
of the public seems to find most clearly "speaking to their
condition." Even at their least desperate, they follow the
guidance of D. H. Lawrence (that Puritan in reverse), for
whom sex was not so much either a game or an ecstasy
as a sort of duty that, according to him, his contemporaries
were neglecting to fulfill in any fashion acceptable to the
Dark Gods. At their worst, our most typical artists are wallowing in a very hell of frustration and violence.

Do I exaggerate, or do I perhaps miss the intentions of
the serious writers I have been referring to? If so, my failure
to comprehend is shared by both those who admire and those

who attack them. In a single issue of *Commentary* I find (1) a letter defending the "fun thing" attitude, (2) an admiring review of William Burroughs' much discussed novel *Naked Lunch*, (3) a less admiring and somewhat ironic article called "The Innocence of Tennessee Williams," and (4) a dismally effective story called "So I Am Not a Lady Chatterley, So It's Better I Should Know It Now," in which the heroine is desperately frustrated in her efforts to find a male capable of joining her in a joyous celebration of a "sex experience," which, one gathers, she was curious about because she had read so much about it in the *Reader's Digest*.

What does the reviewer of *Naked Lunch* have to say about it? For one thing, he says that the novel resembles those by the greatest writers of our day—namely, Camus, Genêt, Beckett, and Robbe-Grillet—in that all of them are completely "alienated," have given up "the quest for a moral position," and therefore find themselves in a valueless and absurd universe. But, he adds cheerfully, Burroughs is "more fun to read." He then proceeds: "Camus, the most traditional, the gentlest, and the wisest of the four writers I've named, has his Stranger find, or fabricate, good in the idea that his own beheading will amuse others. Genêt, the wildest and loveliest, still recognizes the need for a moral position, but unable to find one, he inverts the traditional one: dishonesty is better than honesty, cowardice is better than bravery, betrayal is better than loyalty, homosexuality is better than heterosexuality, and so on."

Now, whatever else these writers may be, they are not "pagans" (in the very special sense usually assigned the word during the twenties and implied in "adult movies" and "magazines for men." Their god of love usually manifests herself as a Fury much like Racine's *"Vénus toute entière à sa proie attachée."*

What puzzles me is the impossibility of reconciling the two classes of evidence. The "serious novelists" are as far as it is possible to get from what we of the twenties preached as a healthy and sane "paganism." Is it these serious novelists, is it the "adult movies" and "magazines for men," or is it neither that presents a true picture? Does a significant public absorb and appreciate both? How, if such a public does exist, does it reconcile them? Or do we have two separate cultures that have no comprehension of one another? How should I describe to my bewildered Martian what sex in the United States is really like? What is the relation, if any, between the audience of "magazines for men" and that of our "serious" writers?

Some moralists of the sterner sort would no doubt say that the connection between them is obvious enough. The first leads to the second. A Tennessee Williams character is merely what a "pagan" turns into after he has played too long. But that is a little too simple for me because, for one thing, I have known a few aged playboys who went right on playing with apparent, if diminishing, success and, on the other hand, a few young men who were riddled with guilt while they were still boys thinking of the sins they had not yet committed.

It is, of course, possible that we always tend to take literature too seriously as evidence of what people really believe, feel, and do; that literature is more fantasy than representation; that we can't really take it seriously and that we applaud its extravagances and exaggerations because they push to logical extremes the impulses and notions we would never actually accept; that, in other words, one may read the "magazines for men" without aspiring to imitate the more exuberant of their characters' adventures, just as we may read an existentialist novel without seriously considering the possibility of committing some atrocity just to prove that we are indeed "free to choose."

I suppose a suspicion that something like this may be true explains my own lack of full commitment to the prophets of any school of literature and has led me to take a hopelessly middle-brow stance when I have had occasion to review the plays of Tennessee Williams—to take him again as an example. On such occasions I have said merely that no other contemporary American playwright has his irresistible storyteller's gift, that when he begins a tale "one cannot choose but hear," although the world into which he plunges us is not one I recognize as familiar, or which, I suspect, exists anywhere except in the minds of a few eccentrics.

Perhaps this is merely a complacent superficiality on my part. But whether it is or not, the fact remains that many of our most talented explicators and presumably many of their readers reject absolutely such a dismissal. To them the writers whom they most admire are not merely storytellers, however talented and however extraordinary their themes and attitudes may be. They think it our duty to probe deep and to learn what it is they have to teach. I doubt that any nineteenth-century reader took Edgar Allan Poe seriously, considered his sadistic fancies as parables, or was led by his obsession with dead maidens to solemnly consider the question whether or not necrophilia was indeed the most exalted manifestation of the erotic impulse. Today essayists of one sort or another do dive deeper and deeper into the moral implications of their preferred writers and are at least half convinced that abnormal sex appetites (homosexuality especially) are actually the most normal and that Ionesco and Genêt are profound philosophers.

However legitimate or even sternly necessary it may be to consider such writers as thinkers rather than merely as tellers of extravagant tales, the fact remains that analysis in depth results in such different and often contradictory conclusions concerning what they mean and what we can learn from them that there is no limit to the number of articles each critic who tries to dig a little deeper than anyone had ever dug before can fabricate for the pages of the more intellectual periodicals.

Consider first an essay entitled "The Desperate Morality

of Tennessee Williams" (*American Scholar*, Spring, 1962). According to the author, Williams is, first of all, not a story-teller, but an unconventional moralist who takes off from D. H. Lawrence but differs from him in his prejudice in favor of homosexual rather than heterosexual love. The essay is a long and very searching analysis. But I think I do not oversimplify by saying that it finds Williams' fundamental thesis to be that for anyone to reject any sexual advance, no matter how distasteful it or the person who offers it may be, is to be guilty of a sin that will surely bring punishment.

On the other hand, Marion Magid, author of "The Innocence of Tennessee Williams," undertakes to dig even deeper in his comments. He comes up with a diagnosis that may not be entirely incompatible with the preceding one but is certainly quite different. According to him, the real source of Williams' agony is his hatred and fear of all sex —a fact that explains not only the ugly appearance sex has in his plays but also his obsession with what most people regard as perverse manifestations. He hates and fears normal eroticism so intensely that homosexuality, sadism, and the rest seem relatively acceptable! For this reason Williams is really not an atypical but a sort of crypto-typical American.

Mr. Magid continues: "Williams has, one must recall, the reputation for being our sexiest American playwright. What could, in fact, be more innocent!"

A story by O. Henry concerns a Western miner courting a widow by mail. He has come across a copy of the Rubáiyát, and he copies out for her benefit the quatrain, "A book of verses underneath a bough, a loaf of bread, a jug of wine and thou . . ." The result is unexpected. The very respectable widow breaks off the correspondence with this parting shot: "You can go on your scandalous picnics alone!"

Conveniently for my purpose, Robert Graves has explicated the same verses by pointing out that in Arabic "bread" is a symbol of wisdom and "wine" is a symbol of ecstasy.

Omar was not inviting his beloved to a scandalous picnic but to a sacrament in which wisdom and ecstasy are joined to create a mystical experience. The two interpretations give us a splendid example of the contrast between a superficial interpretation and criticism in (possibly) too great depth.

I am not saying that Graves or, for that matter, Magid is wrong. Only that if superficiality is one danger, another is the danger of approaching the edge of overinterpretation and that overinterpretation can result in a paradox. Dig as deep as Magid has dug and you are in danger of reaching a conclusion that is the same as that of the most superficial reader—namely, that Williams is just a dirty writer who invites us to picnics very scandalous indeed.

Perhaps the soundest interpretation of his character and role is not that he is either an example of our deep corruption or a super-Puritan moralist to be taken seriously, but that he is merely, as was previously suggested, the teller of *outré* tales so well told that we are tempted to take them seriously in an inappropriate way.

Two of the greatest goods that literature can confer are these: showing us the world and showing us ourselves. Unfortunately, it can also persuade us to believe that the world is different from what our own experience tells us that it is and that we ourselves are what we are told by fashionable writers we are. The more talented a writer, the more likely he is to persuade us that his own possibly eccentric convictions ought to be (and finally are) our own.

At the risk of being dismissed as pathetically unperceptive, I feel bound to say that the world of Sartre and even Camus —to say nothing of that of Williams, Beckett, and Genêt— is simply not the world I know and that their most pressing problems are not mine. I am not convinced that homosexuality is more beautiful than love between the sexes, that the universe is meaningless, or that the choice between cruelty and kindness is a merely arbitrary one.

Do most of those who try to learn from these writers really believe any of these things either? I doubt that they do; and I suspect that those who have come really to accept such premises have been persuaded by writers who have created rather than revealed the fictional world in which they operate. Perhaps this means only that I am a hopeless square incapable of understanding the world I live in. Perhaps, on the other hand, it means merely that I am right in so unsensational a way that I can hardly hope to persuade the many who would rather *épaté les bourgeois* (and themselves) than be tamely sensible.

Many of our unhappy geniuses defend homosexuality. From that we are sometimes prone to assume that homosexuality is what has made them geniuses. Perhaps it is only what has made them unhappy.

The last Boswell paper

[1951]

SCENE: THE ELYSIAN FIELDS. *Dr. Samuel Johnson, standing, looks up from a book whose pages he has been ruffling impatiently. He puts it back on a shelf which exists for him alone and turns to a stranger seated on what the stranger thinks is a large stone.*

JOHNSON: Sir, not less than two hours have passed since I first observed you. You have said nothing. Are you rational? Are you capable of articulate speech?

THE STRANGER: I have not thought anything worth saying this week.

JOHNSON: Sir, I have run about the world more than most, and I have never yet met anyone whom such a consideration restrained. You are affecting a singularity which you hope will bring you into notice. Cant is cant and no better for being of a new kind. You could say that it is a fine day. You would not care whether it is a fine day or not, and I would know that you did not care. But it is out of such nothings that most conversations are made. No man need *be* a fool, but in civilized company it is often proper that he should behave like one.

THE STRANGER: The little I have seen of civilized company makes me regret that I have ever seen anything of it. That this is a fine day is a fact too inexpressibly important to be mentioned lightly.

JOHNSON: Then, sir, you *are* a fool and that is worse than seeming one. No sensible man really cares whether the weather is fine or not. No civilized man is out in it for long. You are not an Englishman.

THE STRANGER: I am a citizen of Concord.

JOHNSON: And what, sir, is this Concord?

THE STRANGER: A village in Massachusetts. I came from America.

JOHNSON: That, sir, does not surprise me. I am surprised that anyone should *stay* there.

THE STRANGER: I was born at the most favored spot in the world, and just in the nick of time, too.

JOHNSON: Pooh. Bute was a Scotchman and therefore a fool. Otherwise we should soon have taught the rebels all that rebels need to learn. But the Americans are punishing themselves. Converse with no one but red savages and you will soon *be* red savages. Who ever wrote a book in America?

THE STRANGER: I did.

JOHNSON: And what was this *American* book about?

THE STRANGER: A year by a pond side.

JOHNSON: Ho, ho. In England we learn wisdom from books; in America you learn it from ponds. No one can take anything out of his head that he has not first put into his head. Put pond water in and you will get pond water out. I wager, sir, it was a very *watery* book. But perhaps *Americans* like pond water. Did it sell? Did the printers get their money back?

THE STRANGER: I did not write it to sell.

JOHNSON: No one but a fool ever wrote for anything except money.

THE STRANGER: No one but a fool ever sold more of his time than he had to. I have sold less than most. I have proved that no man need live by the sweat of his brow unless he sweats a great deal more easily than I do. I built a house and I lived in it for a year at a total cost of sixty-one dollars and ninety-nine cents.

JOHNSON: Sir, you did not live, you existed. I pay my black servant Francis more than that.

THE STRANGER: I keep no horses to feel my oats for me and I keep no servant to do my living for me. I find it too sweet. I would do it myself.

JOHNSON: And what, sir, did you *do* while existing by a pond? By what occupation did you avoid the contemplation of vacuity? How did you palliate the evils of existence?

THE STRANGER: I watched the pond freeze in autumn and I watched it thaw in spring.

JOHNSON: Bozzy should hear you talk. He, too, would have it believed that he likes "wild prospects"—when his father or his wife keeps him from London. Once, sir, he undertook to compare a Scotch inlet with the Bay of Naples. Water, I told him, is much the same everywhere. And what, pray, is so different about this American pond?

THE STRANGER: I do not want water to be different. Because it is the same everywhere I can do all my traveling in Concord.

JOHNSON: London, sir, would make five hundred of your Concords. The full tide of human existence flows at Charing Cross. It is a microcosm. He who is tired of London is tired of life.

THE STRANGER: Everything is a microcosm. All Africa and India are within me. A man who is tired of London is not tired of life. He is tired of too many men too much alike. When he leaves it he may begin to live. And of that he will not tire so easily.

JOHNSON: Monboddo, sir, is interested in such "natural" fellows. Perhaps you Americans are that tribe with tails he is always expecting to find. He would be pleased to examine you. But what man who ever dreamed of murmuring brooks and bleating flocks did not return to London Bridge as soon as ever he could? The emptiness which the Pharaohs could not fill with pyramids cannot be filled with mere rustic pursuits. The remedy for the ills of life is palliative rather than radical. The soul must be distracted. And London is the great metropolis of palliatives.

THE STRANGER: Even by Walden Pond I was distracted too often. Would that I never was for one instant. Life is too short as it is. Even *I* may die without knowing that I have lived.

JOHNSON: Life, sir, is a condition in which there is more to be endured than to be enjoyed. Americans are not exempt from the human condition.

THE STRANGER: I find mine inexpressibly sweet.

JOHNSON (*With sudden vehemence*): Have you ever considered, sir, that you may go to Hell?

THE STRANGER: No.

JOHNSON (*Earnestly*): I should not like to be in your condition.

THE STRANGER: And I should not like to be in yours.

JOHNSON: Are you so sure that you have made your peace with God?

THE STRANGER: I am not aware that we ever quarreled.

JOHNSON (*Mutters frantically to himself and touches what looks like a post to him, like a stump to the stranger*): Sir, I would not discuss generosity with Chartris nor chastity with Lady Diana, and I will not discuss religion with you. A whore is a whore and an atheist is an atheist. . . . But even Americans must eat. Food is a universal topic. Are there taverns in Massachusetts? Has the art of cookery penetrated there? What is your favorite *American* dish?

THE STRANGER: Whichever one is nearest me at table. In the woods I once felt a strong desire to devour a woodchuck raw. At Walden I ate molasses and Indian meal. I drink no alcoholic liquors lest they should spoil my taste for water.

JOHNSON: He who has no care for his belly is not likely to care for anything else. (*Thoughtfully*) De Mullin has charge of my kitchen. But I have no spit.

THE STRANGER: No more have I. Perhaps we will agree at last.

JOHNSON: I doubt it, sir, and I should not be well content if I did not doubt it. You are an enthusiast. You think all mankind before you wrong. Or perhaps you have taken a fancy to pretend so. No man can talk nonsense well who does not know that it is nonsense. Whatever has never been thought before is not likely to be true. Nothing that is odd will do for long. Common sense will reassert itself. You, sir, like the poet Gray, have found out a new way of being dull and you expect, therefore, that people will think you are great. In a word, sir, you are extravagant.

THE STRANGER: My only fear is that I shall not be extravagant enough. The wild goose who breaks his fast in Canada and plumes himself for the night in a Southern bayou is not extravagant. It depends on how you are yarded. The sun is extravagant, and God is extravagant. Would I could equal them!

JOHNSON: Sir! Will you not talk about Tom Thumb or the Punic Wars? I will abstract my attention. The cant about ancient Rome is not worse than the cant about Nature. I would as soon read a pastoral poem. Have you read "Lycidas"? *You* would like it.

THE STRANGER: I am a graduate of Harvard College.

JOHNSON: I am a doctor of Oxford University, where all the branches of learning are cultivated.

THE STRANGER: As at Harvard, no doubt—all the branches and none of the roots.

JOHNSON: In a land where no learning is to be found you are no doubt wise to despite it.

THE STRANGER: On the contrary, I learn something every day. There is more going on in Hubbard's meadow than even I suspected.

JOHNSON: Do you not reverse the wisdom of the ages?

THE STRANGER: The wisdom; but not the folly.

JOHNSON: And is all that, sir, to be found in ponds? Is not some of it in books?

THE STRANGER: Decayed literature makes the richest soil.

JOHNSON: Have a care, sir, or you will deviate into sense. You have very nearly forgot to be extravagant. Fools do not attract attention in their moments of sanity. No one would visit Bedlam if its inmates were not dependably mad. Did they, sir, ever lock you up in Concord?

THE STRANGER: Once. But it was for refusing to pay a tax.

JOHNSON: That, sir, I find is an American mania. Was this tax on tea?

THE STRANGER: It was on black men.

JOHNSON: Ha! How is it that we heard the loudest yelps for liberty among the drivers of Negroes? I should think the souls of the Africans would sit heavy on the swords of Americans.

THE STRANGER: So, sir, should I.

JOHNSON: And yet, sir, no man is much distressed by public affairs. We say that our heart bleeds for our country, but we eat our dinners none the less.

THE STRANGER: It interfered with the pleasure of my walks.

JOHNSON: But not, sir, with your dinner. I gave poor Noll Goldsmith the moral for his poem.

> How small of all that human hearts
>   endure,
> That part which kings or laws can
>   cause or cure.
> Still to ourselves in every place
>   consign'd,
> Our own felicity we make or find.

THE STRANGER: I did not so much regret the condition of my country as I regretted that I had ever heard about it. I did not come into this world to make it better but to live in it, be it good or bad. I have tried doing good, and I found that it did not agree with my constitution.

JOHNSON: No man, sir, knows for what he came into this

world. It is not for him, sir, to say. I have neglected my duty and I have no doubt that you have neglected yours. May God forgive me. Several poor wretches live in my house. They do not contribute to its peace. But if they did not live there I do not know where they would live. Have you fed the poor?

THE STRANGER: I have offered to make several poor families as rich as myself, but they preferred to stay as they were. No man can be saved who will not save himself. It is hard to have a Southern overseer; it is worse to have a Northern one; but worst of all is when you are the slave driver yourself. How many a poor immortal soul have I met well nigh crushed and smothered under its load, creeping down the road of life, pushing before it a barn seventy-five feet by thirty, its Augean stables never cleansed. The luxuriously rich are not simply kept warm but unnaturally hot; they are cooked à la mode.

JOHNSON: Sir, you have read that scoundrel Rousseau.

THE STRANGER: At Walden I read in an older book and I needed no Rousseau to turn the pages for me.

JOHNSON: If you *will* talk the common cant of "luxury" I shall bid you good morning. Go converse with your red savages. They, sir, have not been corrupted by luxury. They may take your scalp, sir, but hair, sir, is a luxury.

THE STRANGER: I could learn as much from red savages as from white ones.

JOHNSON: *You* could. But I, sir, am not an American. We, sir, have outlived many heresies. You must not expect us to be astonished by strange doctrines. Milton was a heretic, but Milton himself could not triumph for long over sense.

THE STRANGER: The mass of men lead lives of quiet desperation.

JOHNSON: All rational creatures lead lives of desperation.

Between the distresses of this life and the terrors of the life to come how, sir, should a man not be desperate?

THE STRANGER: One world at a time!

JOHNSON: I perceive, sir, that you are an atheist only as a dog is an atheist. You have never thought about the matter.

THE STRANGER: Tom Tyde, the tinker, standing on the gallows was asked if he had anything to say. "Tell the tailors," said he, "to remember to make a knot in their thread before they take their stitch." His companion's prayer is forgotten.

JOHNSON: I trust, sir, that God will not forget mine. Not an hour passes that I do not think on my maker.

THE STRANGER: He that thinks much of tomorrow is not well employed today. Do not concern yourself about your health, even in this world. For all you know you may be dead already. God did not send me into this world without some spending money.

JOHNSON: If I had not thought of futurity, I should spend my life driving rapidly in a post chaise with a pretty woman. And no man, to be sure, is compelled to do as much as he can. He has a right to some time to himself. He who can see his third dinner ahead may be said to enjoy, as this world goes, a lengthy prospect. But a man *is* required to do *something*, and I trust God will consider that I have done enough.

THE STRANGER: Even the Bible is a somewhat provincial book. A new man will not need ancient wisdom.

JOHNSON: There will be no new man. Human nature, sir, is known, and so are the ways of the world. What five thousand years has not changed will not be changed by five thousand more. You must not suppose that the laws of nature will be suspended for you. God did not intend that human life should be passed in a state of felicity. Existence at its best is mediocre. Man could not endure either the trials of his daily life or the terrible prospect of death were he not diverted.

Some diversions God has forbidden or, like the pleasures of sense, permitted only under certain circumstances. To others he has set wider limits. But it is not possible for man to be content. Like the beasts, he is hungry and thirsty, but, though, like them, he is pained with want, he is not, like them, satisfied with fullness. He has some latent need for which this place affords no gratification, some desires distinct from sense which are not fulfilled. The remedy for the ills of life—I repeat it, sir—is palliative rather than radical.

THE STRANGER: I have heard no such bad news. The heavens rejoice and so do I. My life, like the rain, is unspeakable. I have had such joys as a Homer or a Shakespeare could not tell of. My only regret is that I have not been radical enough. What demon possessed me that I behaved so well? The universe is wider than our views of it. We have not truly explored either the world or ourselves. Half of Africa is white on the map. Who knows how much of our own souls is the same? Only that day dawns to which we are awake. There is more day to dawn. The sun is only a morning star.

JOHNSON: Kit Smart, sir, had some such notions. But we sent him to Bedlam.

THE STRANGER: When the asylums are too small to hold all the sane and the prisons too small to hold all the righteous, then sunrise will be near.

JOHNSON: The state of nature is the state of war. Any government is better than no government. Madness is to be pitied, but society has a right to protect itself. Had you a stick in your hand I should knock you down first and pity you afterward. But words hurt no man. You may talk for effect, sir, and I will talk with you.

(*At this moment James Boswell steps from behind the bookcase. The notebook which he thrusts into his pocket suggests that contrary to his usual custom he has been taking notes in the field, as it were.*)

BOSWELL: Gentlemen, your very humble servant. I had hoped that I might have the distinction of presenting two such remarkable men to one another, but I see that chance has been before me. (*To the Stranger*) Your pardon, sir, but I bear a message to Dr. Johnson. (*To Johnson*) Mr. Dilly, sir, has asked me to inquire if he can have the pleasure of your company for dinner tonight.

JOHNSON: I shall be honored.

BOSWELL: You mean, I assume, that you will come if the company invited is agreeable to you.

JOHNSON: What do you mean, sir? Do you think I am so ignorant of the world as to imagine that I am to prescribe to a gentleman what company he is to have at his table?

BOSWELL: I beg your pardon, sir, for wishing to prevent you from meeting people whom you might not like.

JOHNSON: Let us have no more of this. It is treating me strangely to talk as though I could not meet any company whatever, occasionally.

BOSWELL: Even, let us say, Voltaire?

JOHNSON: Voltaire, sir, or the Devil, sir. If there is any difference between them.

BOSWELL (*Smiles the smile of one who has accomplished his purpose. He turns to the stranger*): You will pardon us, sir. Mr. Dilly did not know that I should find you with Dr. Johnson.

THE STRANGER: You need not excuse yourself. I myself am engaged for this evening—to an elm tree.

Thoreau on Madison Avenue

[1955]

Not long ago the shade of Henry David Thoreau visited me at midnight, as it occasionally does. As usual I broke the silence, but our conversation seems to me worth reporting.

ME: Well, Henry, this is an important day for you.

HENRY: I never knew a day that wasn't.

ME: The same old Henry, I see. I really should have anticipated that one. But I had something less transcendental in mind. I mean that it was just one hundred years ago that *Walden* was published.

HENRY: It was also just a hundred years ago today that I met in a bean field the plumpest woodchuck I ever saw. I didn't eat him, but I thought to myself that if I did eat meat I would want it to be some such savage meat as that.

ME (*Dryly*): I have read your *Journal*. But you were a writer after all. You did hope for some readers—for rather more than it seemed likely you would ever get. How do you like being the author of an accepted classic?

HENRY: A classic is a work which everyone acknowledges the obligation to read and nobody thinks it necessary to take seriously. The New Testament is generally regarded as the most indispensable of classics. It is read every Sunday in churches and, occasionally, even in private. But if it were once actually heard by any congregation not a stone would be left standing of that church—or of any other.

ME: Oh! Come, come. It is generally admitted that your influence has been tremendous. Your writings are said to have been accepted as Bibles by many modern reformers, including the founders of the British Labor Party.

HENRY: And I have just reminded you how much influence Bibles really have.

ME: At least it must be a satisfaction to remember that your defense of John Brown carried some weight. And the slave was freed.

HENRY: From one of his masters, but not from himself. It is hard to have a Southern overseer; it is worse to have a Northern one; but worst of all when you are the slave driver yourself. Abolition may possibly have saved the souls of the masters in the other world; but I cannot see that it contributed much to saving the souls of the slaves in your world or the other. Nowadays they hope they will someday be regarded as "just as good as anybody else." I never heard of a less exalted ambition.

ME: Well, there's still the Labor Party, anyway. You were a kind of socialist. And all Labor Parties applaud when you say, "I cannot believe that our factory system is the best mode by which man can get clothing . . . since, as far as I have heard or observed, the principal object is, not that mankind may be well or honestly clad, but, unquestionably, that corporations may be enriched."

HENRY: Yes, indeed. And when I lived in Concord many of the neighbors who existed there with me picked and chose among the Gospel sayings. But they never took enough to change essentially their way of life. I never heard it maintained by any sensible man that anywhere in the United States life was lived as Jesus intended it should be. And I doubt that life in any socialist country would please me better. Where today are men any less exclusively concerned with getting and spending? What else does what they call "a higher standard of living" amount to? What necessities of the soul that money can't buy are they trying to attain? Where have they learned that what mankind needs to know is not how to be rich, but how to live well in poverty?

ME: Perhaps all that will come in time. One must begin somewhere.

HENRY: What I *do* know is that one must not begin at the wrong end. One should put first things first.

ME: What *is* the right end? Where *should* they begin?

HENRY: Simplify. Simplify. Wise individuals have done that from time to time. But what society has ever voluntarily taken one step in that direction? More things for more people is the noblest ideal any modern reformer has ever been able to think of. He supposes the curse will no longer be a curse if only everybody is cursed with it. But that is not what is implied in *Walden*—or in a much older book. Who can truly say that he was ever "influenced" by either my life or my writings if he still believes that the need of mankind is for still more *things?* In my day the mass of men led lives of quiet desperation. The lives of such men are less quiet in 1954, but they are no less desperate. And this is what you call Progress. The mud-turtles in Massachusetts have not changed. But they are no worse than they were when I admired them for their persistence in the ways that mud-turtles had found best for their kind. Would I could say the same for those men who are now said to live in New England.

ME: But, Henry, our society could not possibly simplify— even if it wanted to, which it certainly doesn't. That agricultural economy which was one of the few things in Concord village you approved of could not serve the needs of one-third the population of the United States—to say nothing of those in distant parts who now depend upon us for so many things.

Not all the machines yet invented are more than barely sufficient to keep abreast of the needs of a constantly growing population.

HENRY: And neither will all those you may manage to invent in the future do more. It is for want of a Man that there are so many men.

ME: You can hardly be serious. You are extravagant.

HENRY: It is because I am serious that I always try, in vain, to be extravagant. No extravagance can be adequate to the plight of man. His potentialities are so great that no one can imagine them; his actuality something that makes angels weep and sent even me to mud-turtles and woodchucks for fellowship. How can such facts be moderately stated?

ME: It is not your judgment upon us that I question so much as the practicality of your proposals for improving our condition. Do you think that letting most men die of want would produce a Man? Do you hold even ordinary lives that cheap?

HENRY: Not so cheap as your world holds them. Does not that world show plainly enough that it regards them as freely expendable? Has is not improved the methods of mass destruction even more spectacularly than it has improved the methods of agriculture? Does it not act as though it had come finally to the conclusion that it is simpler to slaughter populations than it is to feed them?

ME: Perhaps, perhaps. At least it is a platitude to say so.

HENRY: That honesty is the best policy is a platitude also. And none the worse for that.

ME: I suppose so. But I still don't see how we could possibly simplify. It has become too difficult. We have gone too far.

HENRY: It will not get any easier. Is having gone too far a good reason for going further? Or is that an act of desperation? It is not the part of wisdom to do desperate things.

ME: Not all men today feel desperate or even pessimistic. The future looks very bright to some. Only the other day some representative of a highly optimistic group sent me through the mail a whole sheaf of optimistic pronouncements by a very successful citizen.

HENRY: And in what calling or profession was this optimist so highly successful?

ME: Advertising.

HENRY: Indeed. And what Gospel, what Good News, does he bring us? I can hardly imagine that he is a prophet of simplicity. Or is it some necessities of the soul that he is advertising just now?

ME: No—not exactly. Or perhaps I had better say not at all. In fact, I don't think he would agree with any of your premises or your proposals. He sees the future as bright chiefly because men in his profession have learned how to persuade people to want more and more things—even things they would never have dreamed of wanting before.

HENRY: And he thinks that will make them happier?

ME: I am afraid, Henry, that you do not understand the modern world. You see . . .

HENRY: Are you so sure that it understands itself? But go on.

ME: Thank you. The truth of the matter is that in your day nobody understood the role played in a modern economy by Consumption as the underlying cause of Prosperity. As a matter of fact, in your world it did not play this role. At that time it was not yet possible to produce enough to meet the needs of your fellow citizens. Therefore, it was a virtue in the individual to use no more of anything than he needed and not to think that he needed anything he did not. But technology has changed all that. If everybody did not demand that Higher Standard of Living which advertising has taught us all to insist upon, we should soon plunge into the deepest Depression our world has ever known. To supply it with only what you would call necessities would not keep one-tenth of the workers busy half the time. To use up what they are making in increasing quantities is a necessity which even the advertising man finds it difficult to persuade us to meet. The first duty of a Good Citizen in our republic is to be a Good Consumer. Sometimes we call a man who doesn't vote a bad citizen. But society can get along passably well even if a third of the people don't vote; but if a third of them stopped buying what you call superfluities catastrophe would be upon us. Simplify indeed! To a modern economist it is perfectly evident that unless we keep on complicating more and more exuberantly the whole of our world will come tumbling down.

HENRY: What I call Economy I understand well enough. It means the way in which men get a living, how they are fed and clothed and sheltered. But when you change Economy to Economics—another one of those modern words with a paralysis in its tail—it seems to be a very different matter. Somehow the right of men to food and clothing has got itself transformed into their duty to use up as much food and clothing as possible.

ME: That to begin with. But it is only a beginning. It is also their duty to buy hundreds of things never heard of in your day and then to buy new ones before the old have worn out. Only a society which operates on this principle can be healthy today.

HENRY: And does your very successful optimist say this in so many words? I should like very much to know what words he finds to say such things with.

ME (*Extracting from my pocket a report on some of the pronouncements made in Salt Lake City last June 27 at the Fifty-first Annual Convention of the Advertising Association of the West*): Well, the most general statement was made by the director of advertising for a California public service corporation: "We of the advertising world are custodians of the indispensable key to the mass selling that must accompany production."

HENRY: The words are English but it doesn't sound like English to me. But please go on. There is nothing I ever valued more than getting new thoughts.

ME: I think a few sentences by the chairman of the board of a large New York advertising agency will make it all clearer. "Perhaps the most dynamic and unique contribution of American economy to the world is . . . that in a society which emphasizes psychological obsolescence rather than the physical wearing out of products, we have helped to achieve the most productive economy in human history."

HENRY: Give me a moment to translate that. I understand that we are going to be told what America's greatest contribution to the world really is. But I am not sure that I understand what that emphasis on "psychological obsolescence" rather than "physical wearing" really means. Can it really mean what I think it does? Does it really mean that our most valuable contribution to the world is our method of persuading men to throw things away while they are still just as good as they ever were? And is this "most productive economy in human history" something to boast about principally because it provides us with things to throw away and could not produce so much unless we did throw them away?

ME: Well, if you want to put it that way. It means, for instance, that the ordinary housewife must buy another vacuum cleaner just to keep the production of vacuum cleaners at a high level. It also means that the better class of citizen must buy a new automobile every year because the changed chromium ornaments make it obvious that last year's model is "psychologically obsolescent."

HENRY: And you say that all this wasting is necessary to our prosperity? I should think it would keep everybody's nose to the grindstone a good deal more constantly than is necessary.

ME: But when you work hard to buy things you don't need and thereby keep other people working hard to make them we don't call that "keeping noses to the grindstone." We call it "maintaining employment at a high level." Let me go on. As the gentleman I have just been quoting goes on to say, advertising has been "a constructive and facilitative force. . . . By creating a psychological desire to own—as opposed to that of necessity—advertising has increased the number of jobs available; raised the standard of living by reducing selling costs; increased company profits as well as company security." By way of a gloss the editor of this report adds: "Of some 500 classified psychological wants only ninety-six are necessary. . . . New markets—newlyweds, the bumper crop of babies, etc.—are constantly developing. To tap these markets desires must be created. And advertising is the means." As you see, an annual bumper crop of babies is necessary because every newborn child is potentially a consumer—of what goods and what future, God only knows.

HENRY: And this gentleman is convinced that desires ought to be created and that "the psychological desire to own" should be fostered. Mankind is not yet sufficiently devoted to material things! Upon such treasures it should be encouraged to set more irrevocably its heart. But tell me something else. When I was young and inexperienced I was tempted for a foolish moment to take some stock in the prophecies of a German immigrant named Etzler, who dreamed of a machine-made Utopia in which all necessary work would be done by steam engines and men would have unlimited leisure to cultivate their souls. Now, if I understand your modern optimist aright, he wants to increase "the psychological desire to own" so that everyone will be so busy satisfying these artificially created wants that he will not need to bother at all with his soul. Has Etzler no disciples today?

ME: A few. You remember that Mr. Shaw you once told me you met just after he erupted into heaven? You two did not hit it off too well together, but he imparted to you his vision of tomorrow's world: "The only hope for any kind of artist is a society so thoroughly organized and regimented that he can always earn a living by three hours of brainless, robot labor like machine-tending and then have twice that long left over to write his books and paint his pictures."

HENRY: I see. And even now three hours of labor would be enough to "earn a living," though it is not enough to satisfy all the "psychological desire to own" that has been created, not enough if everybody insists upon throwing things away not when they have been used up but as soon as they become "psychologically obsolescent." Does not anyone rebel against the trick that has been played upon them?

ME: A few individuals rebel. But I am not sure I admire them. They may be artists or thinkers or whatnot. But they are not good citizens. They are not Efficient Consumers. And in this age the efficient consumer is what we need most. We already make more of everything than we can really use up. Getting rid of the stuff is our problem.

HENRY: I see. I do indeed.

ME: And what, may I ask, do you intend to do about it?

HENRY: I don't need to do anything about it. Where I now dwell there is no obsolescence, either physical or psychological. And the psychological desire to own seems to have been left somewhere behind by all those I have had occasion to talk with. But I know what I would do if I were alive in your world.

ME: Which is?

HENRY: I refused to live in the bustling nineteenth century. I said that I would stand, or sit, quietly while it passed by. I would refuse even more firmly to live in the still more bustling twentieth.

ME: You would not mind being called a bad citizen? You would refuse to contribute to Progress?

HENRY: I refused in my own day, and I was called a bad citizen for doing so. "Skulker" was, I think, the word Mr. Stevenson, the romancer and essayist, chose. But according to you I am a classic now.

ME: Would not a rebel be better advised if he worked instead for that better world in which leisure rather than a superfluity of goods had become the consequence of mechanization?

HENRY: I once knew a would-be poet who proposed to get rich so that he could devote his time to poetry. He should have gone up to the garret immediately.

ME: Really, Henry, you dodge the question. Why, if everybody . . .

HENRY: They won't.

G.B.S. enters heaven (?)

[1952]

SCENE: THE AFTERWORLD. *Thoreau is seated quietly on a pumpkin. To Mozartian strains the ectoplasmic form of Ber-*

nard Shaw is taking shape. Before it has become recognizable
he begins to speak.

SHAW (*Triumphantly*): I talk, therefore I am. But let no one
seize this occasion to tell me that I was wrong about Eternity.
With my usual perceptiveness I realized it before anyone else
had the gumption to do so; with my usual frankness I admit
it at once. The truth of the matter is that simple honesty has
always been my chief distinction though no doubt the angelic
hosts will take up the babble about my paradoxes and my
brilliance, instead.

Nevertheless, I am disappointed. I had hoped that the Life
Force had used me up. What I want is to be thrown into the
dustbin. If necessary I will consent to spend a few eons in the
contemplation and ecstasy appropriate to an ancient. But
on all the Dominions, Principalities, and Powers I hereby
serve notice. I will *not* explain anything further to them or
to anyone else. Besides, it ought to be evident to the meanest
intelligence not befuddled by romantic nonsense about Music, Beauty, and the other excuses for parasitic idleness that
what the angels really need is an honest day's work—something which will give them the sense of being used for a noble
purpose. (*He is struck by a sudden doubt.*) The atmosphere
here is distressingly suggestive of the third act of *Man and*
Superman—(*To Thoreau*) this isn't by any chance Hell, is it?

THOREAU: I have never taken the trouble to ask. Whatever
it is, it suits me very well. One world at a time, you know.

SHAW: A surprisingly sensible remark. It is what the churches
forgot when they made the simple common sense of Jesus an
excuse for shirking their responsibilities. You must be that
American backwoodsman who caught a glimpse of the truth
and then lost sight of it among the trees. Marx would have
made a man of you.

THOREAU: I never doubted that I was one—except perhaps
when I saw too many men about me. This Marx, I suppose,

was one of those reformers who would have too benevolently insisted upon doing for me what I had much rather do for myself.

SHAW: Marx was the greatest mind between John Bunyan and me. Of course, he was wrong about many simple things, the real nature of rent, for example. What is even more important, he never made it clear that there is no contradiction whatever between economic determinism and Lamarckian free will. Thus, the only trouble with the poor is poverty, while at the same time the only trouble with the poor and the rich alike is their failure to realize that man can make of himself whatever he has the will to become. But I explained all that in plays which Shakespeare would have written if he had not, unfortunately, been born brainless. Nevertheless, I owe much to Marx, and because I have no foolish pride in the fact that the Life Force happened to make me its chosen instrument, I acknowledge the debt.

THOREAU: I find that I got along very well without him. He could not have told me how to spend an afternoon. That, like every other really important thing, I had to learn for myself, not from my elders or my contemporaries, from whom I never heard one sensible piece of advice. Since the seventeenth century there have been no really manly writers in the line of Homer and Shakespeare. They all use words like "determinism" and "evolutionary"—words which have a paralysis in their tails. As for rent, I know well enough what *that* is. It is the tribute one man pays to another for doing for him what he would have better done for himself—build a house, for example. To what a sorry pass has this division of labor led us! The mass of men slavishly do things not worth doing in order to escape the opportunity of leading their own lives. Every man for himself, say I! Even the Devil won't want the hindmost.

SHAW: Would you tear down the Brooklyn Bridge and let

every man carry his own plank? That is the only logical alternative to Communism.

THOREAU: I did not know that there was a Brooklyn Bridge. But it does not surprise me. No doubt there will some day be an Atlantic Bridge and a Pacific Bridge too. But it will not be a good thing. How many dismal days will have been spent in slavery just to pay for what most would be better without! As for carrying your own plank, I can easily imagine a man worse employed. Besides, most men need do nothing of the sort. They would be better off staying on their own side of the river.

SHAW: You almost persuade me to go on all fours. Even Voltaire—despite his dirty little mind—saw that this is what all the babble about simplicity would logically come down to. Man can go up or he can go down. The Life Force says "Go Up." For my part I am with it. What you call simplicity is only the inefficient, romanticized. Life is a great deal simpler with bridges and sewers than without them. They help free men for nobler work.

THOREAU: I have not often seen them engaged upon any. Noble is not the term I should apply to what I saw of men's daily labors when I was so unfortunate as to visit New York or Boston. They seemed busier—and busy to less purpose— than Minot, the farmer of Concord. For all I know the Indian before the white man came may have known better than either how to live. I was a writer, and I learned more from woodchucks and snapping turtles than I did from my most civilized neighbors.

SHAW: The ghosts of dead ideas still haunt the regions of the blest! I would never have dreamed that even Hell could be so far behind the times. But writers have always been half-sage, half-fool. They do not even know which side their bread is buttered on. Most of them have some silly hankering after anarchy instead of realizing that the only hope for any kind of artist is a society so thoroughly organized and regimented that he can always earn a living by three hours of brainless, robot labor like machine-tending and then have twice that long left over to write his books and paint his pictures. Until socialism has achieved that for him he will remain the begging, borrowing, stealing, self-pitying parasite he is at present.

THOREAU: Three hours of robot labor per day would be more than I could stand, and it is far more than I had to force myself to perform. Besides, and as I would have known, I was dead long before this Utopia of yours could come about. I remember an acquaintance who devoted himself to accumulating money in the hope of getting enough to enable him to become a poet. I told him that he should have gone up to the garret at once. That is what I did. If other men were sensible they would do the same.

SHAW: Like nearly every other artist who has ever lived, you were a parasite and not ashamed to be one. You took advantage of a security and a stability which others had established. A world full of Thoreaus is unthinkable.

THOREAU: There is no danger of that; there were never even two. As for taking advantage of the society I found, I did it exactly as I took advantage of the sun and rain, the earth and water. How I should have conducted my life on some other planet I do not know, but I think I would have managed. God sent me into a peculiar world, and I took my principal business to be to live in it—be it good or bad. That was at least a better way of spending my time than dreaming of different and impossible ones. I consider myself remarkably fortunate, and I was certainly remarkably happy.

SHAW: Are you so besotted as to think *that* important? Happiness and Beauty are by-products. I was too busy to ask whether or not I was happy. That must mean that I was.

THOREAU: On the contrary, it must mean that you died without ever knowing that you had lived. I feared I might do that but I escaped it.

SHAW: I very much doubt that you did. One must live before one can know that one has. Contemplation will be for those who have grown older than Methuselah. Three score and ten is too short a span to be wasted in idleness. Come to think of it, four score and thirteen is not so very much longer. But I did make a beginning.

THOREAU: I died at forty-five. One year would have been enough. But ten thousand would not have been too many.

SHAW: You are more extraordinary than I thought. I doubt if any man before you was ever so wrong twice in two successive sentences. One year would not have been enough because, as the world grows more complicated, there are more and more things that must be learned. Ten thousand would have been too many because if the Life Force is to satisfy her passion for improvement she cannot permit the earth to become too cluttered with her discarded experiments.

THOREAU: He who has not learned all that is really important by the time he is twenty will never learn it. Even I forgot much that I had known very well in my youth.

SHAW: You were merely putting away childish things and had not the wit to know that dreams are well exchanged for realities.

THOREAU: And do you really think that you really know what the most important realities really are? From all you have said so far I doubt that you do.

SHAW: I know that growth and change are real. I know that neither human life nor human society is what it will become. As Nietzsche—another of Life's unsuccessful attempts to create me—proclaimed, "Man is something which must be surpassed."

THOREAU: If man could once understand the unspeakable truth about himself and the equally unspeakable truth about the world of nature in which he lives, then there would be no need for him to surpass either himself or it.

SHAW: All my doubts are resolved! Only in Hell could a man utter such blasphemies against the Holy Ghost—an old name for the Life Force—and not be incontinently blasted. But I solemnly warn the Prince of Darkness that I have no intention of spending Eternity in happiness and contentment. I will *not* become a romantic lover or a musical amateur. Even in the infernal regions there must be a borough council in need of a clerk. And if this Choctaw here is a typical specimen of the citizenry, then the affairs of Hell must be in a hellish state. (*He rushes vigorously off left to a flourish of trombones. Thoreau remains exactly where he was—on a pumpkin.*)

III
THEATER

The not-so good old days

[1953]

"Theatrical reminiscence," so Max Beerbohm once said, "is the most awful weapon in the armory of age." Having been exposed myself to those who "remembered Booth," I know what he meant. But age has few weapons, and it must use what it has. Now that I have completed more than fifty years of playgoing—more than half of them professional—my capacity to bore must be imposing. I have, I am afraid, reached the Age of Reminiscence.

In any group the proportion of those who remember *The Hairy Ape* at the Provincetown or even the first night of *What Price Glory?* grows smaller and smaller, though one is by no means safe in assuming that a few do not. But should I live to be ninety—as my mother and my grandmother did —then I shall have little competition to fear when I boast, truthfully enough, that I saw Maude Adams act, Pavlova dance, and John Drew "behave." Perhaps that is not enough to wait for, but it is better than nothing. Only persistence, they say, is required to become in time the oldest living something-or-other.

At five and a half I first saw a curtain go up on *Si Pluncket,* a rural melodrama so obscure that among all my acquaintances only George Nathan remembers it. In the last act the villain is disposed of when he falls (I don't think he was even pushed) into a threshing machine, and fragments of his clothes come out with the chaff. But what I remember most vividly is a sense of disappointment. The advance posters showed the machine belching smoke, and there was no smoke on the stage. Perhaps that disillusioning first experience accounts for the fact that I have never been able to surrender completely to what the more enthusiastic call the glamour of the stage. I have never ceased to be suspicious that someone —playwright, performer, or even scene painter—is out to do me.

Not long thereafter I exposed myself to the whole repertory of the traveling ten-twenty-thirty. Time and time again I saw the dirty little coward shoot Jesse James in the back while Jesse was straightening the picture of a race horse on the wall. And what a lesson that was in the if-he-only-knew technique for creating suspense! All through the scene that picture was glaringly askew. We of the godlike audience, gifted with foreknowledge, knew that it was poor Jesse's death warrant. But we could warn him no more than our guardian angels can warn us. Willy-nilly we go to our predestined fates.

At almost the same time, the heady world of musical comedy was opened, again with an unimportant specimen, the forgotten *Telephone Girl.* But it was not so very much later that *The Merry Widow* came along, and to many thousands it must have been, as it was to me, the first intimation that there was supposed to exist somewhere a wickedly gay world which presented all sorts of opportunities unavailable to the less fortunate. How happy were those who, to solve emotional difficulties—even those of blighted love—need only "go off to Maxim's where fun and frolic beams." If Knoxville, Tennessee, had even a rough equivalent of Maxim's, I didn't know about it, though I was soon to learn that the

institution was recognized in New York. The rough equiva-
lents there sounded rather innocent when the temporarily
exiled George M. Cohan sent his nostalgic regards to Broadway and poured scorn on New Rochelle.

Other musical comedies hinted broadly that these same
resorts were haunts of glittering sin. A violent rash of *opera*
with such titles as *Madam Sherry* and *The Girl from Rector's*
broke out and managed to suggest that real New Yorkers accepted as a regular feature of their mores the existence of
these glittering hells to which nice girls inevitably drifted
but from which they were rescued—before they were ir-
reparably damaged—by disillusioned young men who sought
wine, women, and an occasional song only to find, before the
last curtain, that they were headed back to respectability
with some brand snatched from the burning. The number
of champagne goblets which were suddenly dashed to the
floor just as a hero or heroine was about to take the first of a
series of maddening swigs must have been a boon to the glass
industry. They certainly succeeded in establishing in many
young minds an inevitable symbol of the moral crisis.

Reginald de Koven had sung of the nut-brown ale, which
was safely literary; beer, celebrated in many a song like
"Down Where the Wurtzberger Flows," was somewhat more
authentically jolly, but the new generation of sophisticated
heroes who had heard about Paris and Vienna never thought
of anything except champagne. For the old melodrama, stage
property men could manufacture their own whiskey out of
cold tea, but for a smart musical comedy you had to put in a
large order for ginger ale in fancy bottles. As a result many
young men and women who went off from a small town to
New York ostensibly in search of colleges, art schools, concerts,
or whatnot were really looking for Maxim's.

But even in the provinces, the theater was not all stock
company and musical comedy. That eminently serious play-

wright Charles Klein could invite serious thought about the evil deeds of great corporations with *The Lion and the Mouse.* Try reading it someday! Determined to lose our innocence, we patronized *Bought and Paid For, The Easiest Way,* and even *The Yellow Ticket.* Meanwhile, the genteel could see John Drew and Laura Hope Crews in *The Tyranny of Tears* and perhaps wonder whether *Everywoman* really was as morally instructive as it was said to be or somehow rather different in style and tone from *Everyman,* of which it was supposed to be the modern analogue.

As for Ibsen, Shaw, and the rest, one got them if one got them at all chiefly from the printed page. But Shaw was breaking through to some sort of public even outside New York rather earlier than is always remembered. Before the First World War, *Androcles and the Lion* appeared in a popular magazine—*Everybody's,* I think—and inspired me to my first attempt at dramatic criticism: a defense of Shaw's religious attitudes against an attack in the literary magazine of some Catholic college. Too bad that Shaw did not know what an ardent disciple ready to go to bat for him he had made. Or perhaps it was just as well. Nearly a quarter of a century later when I praised *The Simpleton of the Unexpected Isles* as good fun but not really meaning anything at all, he dismissed that opinion in the program to the Malvern Festival with the pronouncement that "The trouble with Mr. Krutch is, he has an insufficient respect for the Apocalypse." A somewhat cryptic remark, perhaps, but a final dismissal nonetheless.

"Ugh-hugh and so what?" Thus, and without making any effort to the inaudible, one of the younger members of my disappearing audience remarks to another. Of the ability to recall a good deal of theatrical history, perhaps we can say only what was said by one of the characters in *The Chorus Lady,* I think, about an actress who has learned "technique." "Technique is what, by the time you have got it, they don't want you any more."

Would they, I wonder hopefully, be any more interested or impressed if I moved forward from prehistory to history? Would they like to hear about the night when *Bound East for Cardiff* first introduced Eugene O'Neill to New York or how Helen Westley blacked her behind as well as her face to appear as the Ethiopian slave in Philip Moeller's *Helena's Husband* at the Bandbox, where Lawrence Langner and Theresa Helburn were getting their first taste of theatrical production? They at least are still very much alive.

Not interested? Then how about the night when Caruso and Farrar, after a well-publicized falling out, made up publicly before the curtain at the Metropolitan to the great delight of the audience? Still less so.

But I do have a generalization to make. If someone will ask me, even ask condescendingly, if I really am as besotted as those other ancients who maintain that nothing has really changed, that modern plays are just as bad as the old ones, I may surprise him by saying, "No, I do not hold that opinion —at least not quite."

No one needs to be told that here is plenty of hokum, nonsense, and naïveté parading as sophistication on the contemporary stage. It is also evident enough that not all the plays of, say, the twenties, which then seemed so remarkably good, hold up as well as we hoped they would. But there is a real difference. Sometime round about the beginning of the First World War, audiences had begun to tolerate a real seriousness and real frankness which had long been expected in the novel but was still not looked for in the play. The general level did rise. A man could now put his best, whatever it was, on Broadway. The ideals of an Arthur Hopkins or a Theatre Guild really were different, and better than those of a Belasco or even a Charles Frohman. O'Neill, to say nothing of Arthur Miller and Tennessee Williams, may or may not seem two generations hence permanent parts of dramatic literature. But they cannot possibly cease to exist, or rather cannot possibly reveal the fact that they never did exist as, say, the plays of Charles Klein, George Broadhurst, and perhaps even of Eugene Walter never existed at all. The difference, though not so great, is the difference between a contemporary play and a soap opera.

It's not merely a matter of increased slickness and dexterity. To some extent we really have grown up. We are more knowing and more mature even if not necessarily more wise. If we fall into insincerity we are not so complacent about it. Plays written between 1915 and the present really are better than those written during the same number of years before that period opened.

This, I maintain, is quite an admission for an old dodo. I like to think that it may even prove that I am not one—yet. The theater of my early youth was good fun in its way, but a later generation was in many ways more fortunate. Perhaps as I approach ninety, I shall begin to doubt that this is true. When and if I see that opinion beginning to dawn upon me, I shall say to myself, "You really have reached the last of the seven ages now."

When a colleague at Columbia once told me that he did not expect to retire until he was put out, I asked him how he was going to feel when the time came that he could not conceal even from himself the fact that his students regarded him as a tiresome old fossil. "It is," he replied, "a wise provision of nature that that time never comes." In general, he was probably right. But I like to think that nature is not quite that protective to all of us.

The first twenty-five years

[1949]

Twenty-five years ago this autumn [1924] I wrote my first drama review for *The Nation*—of *What Price Glory?* by Laurence Stallings and Maxwell Anderson. One needs no virtue higher than persistence to become in time the oldest living something-or-other, and while I am not yet quite even that, I believe that I am, in point of service and next to Mr. Nathan, the oldest practitioner in New York of a somewhat unusual profession. Acquaintances aware of the fact are about equally divided between those who say, "What a delightful life!" and those who inquire, "How on earth do you stand it?"

The latter are very likely to be persons who take literature seriously, and they not infrequently point out with ill-disguised condescension that at least nine out of ten new theatrical productions are below the artistic level which a man of intelligence and taste ought to be able to endure. They assume—what I think is actually open to dispute— that the average quality of contemporary plays is considerably below that of contemporary belles-lettres in other forms, and they conclude that I must be either heroically self-sacrificing or merely comfortably vulgar. Neither judgment can I accept. The theater does have a legitimate appeal which is not strictly proportioned to the literary merit of the words being spoken, and I should like, perhaps by way of self-justification, to try to say what one basis of that appeal is.

In my case it has very little to do with what is commonly meant by the "glamour" of the stage. It is true that I saw my first adult play before I was six years old and that I have attended the theater pretty persistently ever since. People who can say that are generally expected to add that they have never lost the special thrill of anticipation, that when the house lights dim and the footlights go on they become as little children again, etc., etc. If I ever experienced anything of the kind—which I doubt—it was too long ago to be remembered. In my youth I did take advantage now and then of the special facilities I had for going behind the scenes, but I do not believe that I was ever in the slightest degree stagestruck. Since then I have known some interesting playwrights and met some attractive actors, but I do not think in either case that the fact that they were part of the theatrical profession made them for that special reason any more "glamorous" than anyone else.

Yet for all that, it remains true that a play which one follows in the company of one's fellows is something more than the words spoken, something more, even, than the words plus whatever of special meaning or passion a good performance puts into them. One participates not only in the play but also in the reactions of the audience. One senses as one can never sense while reading a book that one is sharing an experience. It is impossible to feel wholly isolated or completely alone. One's fellows are indeed one's fellows—just in so far as they are, at any moment, being moved by what is moving oneself.

The most obvious proof that something of this sort takes place is the phenomenon of laughter. Everyone who has ever both seen and read a comedy knows that something which can at best provoke a smile when met on the printed page may be irresistibly hilarious when shared with an audience. And it is absurd to say that "it seemed better than it was," or that it wasn't "really funny." Seeming was its business, and its function was to make possible that essentially social thing called laughter, which binds men together at least as truly and as importantly as any other impulse they can share.

Those who are fond of saying that drama began as ritual and that it ought to become ritualistic again are wrong in the assumption, for acted drama has never been anything else, and those who assemble in Forty-fifth Street are publicly worshiping one of the oldest gods even when they are shaking with communal laughter at the ageless predicaments of the victim in a farce. If group emotions other than those which express themselves as audible mirth had equally obvious outward expressions, we should know no less surely that people come to a theater to feel many things which they cannot feel alone, that what they seek in tragedy is not merely the experience of pity and terror but the experience of experiencing it publicly, of paying open tribute to the humanity which can thus confess in assembly its membership in a cult.

Perhaps the theater is, indeed, the only truly catholic temple still standing and gathers the only worshipers undivided. The church is sectarian; nearly every other public meeting is partisan. People attend the political rally to express their separateness from certain of their fellows as much as to express their agreement with certain others, and the churchgoer is by no means always exempt from the limitations of the same attitude. But an audience laughing or weeping at a play is truly united. On what other occasion does it confess that all the members are meeting on a common ground? On what other occasion is it so openly acknowledged that human beings can agree? And for that reason it may be that those plays whose subject is honor, or pity, or fear, or love are actually more significant than those which deal with what are called "problems." They generate the most inclusive solidarities.

Those who scorn the theater often complain that there is in it too little opportunity for any except mass appeal. I am

certainly not one who would want all art to be limited to
that which is immediately accessible to all. But to find some
excuse for one institution where nothing even approaching
the esoteric can survive is not necessarily to defend the
cheap, the hackneyed, and the obvious. All question of absolute merit aside, would anyone have ever guessed that *A
Streetcar Named Desire* and *The Death of a Salesman* would
have mass appeal? Yet obviously each strikes some chord, and
the audiences which respond to it in unison are undergoing
an experience radically different from any possible to the
reader of any best-seller, good or bad. They are agreeing
publicly about something they did not know that they
agreed about, and even now could not define. In a society
which seems about to fly to pieces this is not unimportant.
Perhaps no group has completely lost its chance of survival
as long as its members continue to recognize that they agree
in at least one thing: they are members of the human race. It
is something which can be forgotten.

The Twenties: Theater of body and soul

[1955]

A famous cartoonist now deep in his sixties has covered the
walls of his country house with theatrical mementos. Gazing
one day with misty eyes at a photograph of the Floradora
Sextet, he exclaimed, "I'd give *anything* to see again one of
the musical comedies of my youth."

The reply was obvious. "What you really mean is that you

would give anything to see *any* musical comedy with the eyes
you had then." And as the sad light of dawning disillusion
spread over his face he sighed: "Perhaps you are right."

Everybody knows that distance lends enchantment. But
then, sometimes, certain distant things really were enchant-
ing. And there's the rub. As Shakespeare knew, the prosperity of a jest lies in the ear of him who hears it. But how
shall those of us who look back distinguish between the
richness of a joke or the eloquence of a drama and the recep-
tiveness of our ears? How, especially, when the thing remembered lived on a stage? We can re-examine the text or hum
the tune. But the presences which gave it life can live again
only in memory—which is notoriously full of tricks.

As for *Tell Me, Pretty Maiden,* that was so long ago that
I cannot be sure whether I remember it or only remember
that I once did. But what of the nearer twenties, apparently
now in the process of being rediscovered? Only a few years
ago that epoch was regarded as outmoded at best, morally
reprehensible at worst. Now the high-brow quarterlies write
about Scott Fitzgerald almost as frequently and almost as
reverently as they do about Henry James. Off-Broadway theaters have revived plays of that era, and not all have been by
O'Neill. One of the hits of the current season, *The Boy
Friend,* is a musical deliberately "in the style of" the twenties, and a revival of *Good News* has been contemplated.
There is even quite a lot of talk—and apparently serious
talk about new editions of the *Ziegfeld Follies, Vanities,*
and *Scandals.* Is this mere nostalgia, if not a sort of desperation? Or did the twenties—to use its own phrase—really have
something?

Suppose we start with the musicals. The first thing to remember is that it had a lot of them. There were approximately twice as many theaters as there are now; eight or nine
openings a week were not unusual at the height of the season, and even the second-string critics on the dailies were

kept busier than holders of the chairs are now. And a goodly proportion of the openings were musicals, not of one kind but many.

The great team of Guy Bolton and P. G. Wodehouse (an instinctive American who soon rectified the mistake he had made by being born in England) still had some book shows to write, either together or with others, and to go with the music of various composers. Irving Berlin and Vincent Youmans reached the heights of their careers. Richard Rodgers and Cole Porter were beginning to be heard of. Difficult as it may be to believe, there really was a time (1924) when *The Student Prince* was a new show, and its composer, Sigmund Romberg, went on to *The Desert Song* and *The New Moon,* which helped to popularize a rather lush romanticism opposed to the tenuous gentility of the Wodehouse-Bolton-Kern formula. But perhaps the revue was most characteristic.

Here in those *Follies, Scandals,* and *Vanities* and the rest was the true unabashed expression of a mood not likely to be recaptured soon again—an orgiastic explosion of luxury, sensuality, and ribald humor. What made them unique was the fact that they were not born, as such things often have been, out of fear and desperation; rather they came out of the conviction that wealth and abundance had come to stay. We cannot possibly understand them if we assume, as we almost inevitably do, that they were either produced or enjoyed by people who were saying to themselves, "After us the deluge." Ironical as the fact may seem, these people were repeating instead what statesmen told them—that the "new era" of permanent prosperity and luxury for everybody was just opening.

When the revues were vulgar—and some aspects like Ziegfeld's parading giantesses loaded down with tons of costume were the essence of vulgarity—there was a kind of innocence about them too; the innocence of the *nouveau riche* whose orgies are not at all the same as the orgies of the decadent. But the revues were not all vulgarity either. At moments they were genuinely Dionysian instead, and I can still remember a celebration of one edition of the *Follies* in which so serious a critic as Ludwig Lewisohn was moved to quote Horace and to think of pagan festivals. And what comedians there were to banish what, without them, might easily have become—the phrase is Aldous Huxley's—"the imbecile earnestness of lust." Ed Wynn, W. C. Fields, Bobby Clark, and the absolutely incomparable Fanny Brice are just four leading examples. Of the absolute excellence of these comedians I have no doubt. Nostalgia need contribute nothing to our memory of them. If my cartoonist friend and I should be granted by some niggardly fairy one revisit and one only to the past, he might choose *Floradora*. I should take Fanny Brice doing, say, her interpretive modern dance "Rewolt!"

When the thirties put on sackcloth and ashes (and how some of even the most frivolous did go in for them!), this new period not unnaturally preferred to denounce or forget the more reckless of its revels. What is less excusable is that it perversely forgot that there had been, at the same time, a great deal of aspiration. Not only the new generation but even those who had every reason to know better talked as though the previous decade had been remarkable for nothing except gangsters, bathtub gin, and petting parties. To hear their diatribes one would never have guessed that a real renaissance of the arts had been in full swing; that, for instance, the Provincetown Playhouse and the Washington Square Players had, just as the teens were ending, ignited the most fundamental and most rapidly developing revolution which the American theater had ever known; that a single year in the twenties, 1924, had seen the first productions of *The Show-Off, What Price Glory?, They Knew What They Wanted,* and *Desire Under the Elms;* and that of two of those plays, if not indeed of all of them, it might truly be said that they were intrinsically superior to any play ever written in America before. Even if you think only of the theater, you cannot dismiss the twenties as the Jazz Age unless you cherish the strange delusion that Sidney Howard and Eugene O'Neill, to mention only two, were jazz babies. Nor were the great performers all clowns. Nobody who saw them is likely to forget, say, Pauline Lord in *They Knew What They Wanted,* Helen Hayes in *What Every Woman Knows,* or Lynn Fontanne in the "My Three Men" scene of *Strange Interlude.*

What was it that the theatrical workers of the twenties had, and that they shared with other artists? It was, first of all, a generalized enthusiasm and a belief in the future of their art. At times, and especially at first, that enthusiasm seemed uncertain of its direction. The Provincetown and Washington Square people seemed to be surer that they wanted something than they were about what it was they wanted. They produced almost at random plays by the recent European masters and near masters at the same time that they snatched at anything which looked like a new native American. To the Provincetown, Edna Millay and Mike Gold, for example, were all one. Even so, it seemed indisputable that the Fabulous Invalid had never looked less an invalid or on the point of becoming more fabulous.

Besides this general confidence and enthusiasm there was something else. When you consider the best remembered plays, say those by Rice, Anderson, Kelly, Behrman, and O'Neill—it becomes apparent that for all their diversity, they had something in common which distinguished them sharply from their immediate predecessors. Moreover, that something puts even the tragic O'Neill and the comic Behrman in the same universe.

What was it? Was it indeed something more than the shared conviction that the theater could be more than merely show business, and playwriting more than the mere trade which it has been called by one of their successful predecessors? It was all that; but it was something more. And paradoxically, that something was partly conditioned by the same sense of security which had so much to do with the Babylonian gaudiness of the *Follies* and the *Scandals*.

The paradox is resolved in the fact that the sense of security meant different things to different people. To the tycoons, the soldiers of fortune, the bootleggers, and the playboys, it may not have meant much more than the conviction that money would always be plentiful, to be picked up by all who had the gumption to take what was lying so abundantly about. But to thoughtful men it meant something else.

To understand what that was, we must, by an effort of memory, make ourselves realize that to thoughtful as well as to reckless men, the twenties seemed to be an age when the primary problems of survival in the world had been solved. The last great war had been fought, and the economic system had been stabilized. Peace and prosperity had become permanent at last. A busy world was full of careers for the young. Those launched in the busy world would follow to the ends of their lives the lines they already had laid down. The youth starting out had merely to decide whether he would be doctor, lawyer, or merchant. There was room for everybody and prosperity for everybody. There were no major threats, military, political, or economic.

Such a conviction that the primary problems of survival have been solved may make the materialistic, the sensual, the unimaginative merely complacent or recklessly self-indulgent. But it is not in the nature of thoughtful men to be satisfied with that. Freedom from desperate problems of survival, a life that seems in those ways secure, permits them to ask the questions which lie beyond that kind of security. What, they ask themselves, of the problems of man himself? What is he when he is no longer threatened from without? What of his soul, if he has one? Can he be as much at home in the universe as he seemed to have become in this world? Now that we have security and prosperity, what are we going to do with them? Where do we go from here?

Different as they were in temperament, all the major playwrights of the twenties were alike in that each in his own way asked this kind of question. Though Elmer Rice made his first success as a serious dramatist with *The Adding Machine,* a nihilistic fantasy whose thesis and tone were borrowed from a despairing Germany, he was so much an American of the twenties that cheerfulness soon broke through. His next important play was *Street Scene* in which, despite the catastrophic conclusion, he wrote a celebration of the emotional potentialities of the common man. Maxwell Anderson explored romance in his historic plays and then in *Winterset* wrote a play which is only incidentally about the Sacco-Vanzetti case, fundamentally about the nature of justice—which is something hardly to be bothered about when mere survival is at stake. Kelly and Behrman ask the same sort of questions with comic intelligence and in connection with secure, middle- and upper-class people whose problems are those which begin when the primary problems have been answered, whose way of living can be studied because making a living is no longer their chief preoccupation. And of course the case of O'Neill is the clearest of all. His now famous declaration that he was not interested in "the relation of man to man," only in "the relation of man to God," is hardly explicable except on the assumption that man is already assured of his survival in the world of men.

What withered in the chill wind that blew out of 1929 into the thirties was, then, not merely the Jazz Age but also the conviction that we could afford to take the soul rather than the body as the chief subject of literature, art, and philosophy. The Federal Theater and its Living Newspaper seemed about to become what the Provincetown and the Washington Square Players had been for the previous generation. To the economic problem and the political problem, the military was soon added. Marxism tinctured at least every serious play, and the premise of Marxism is the exact opposite of O'Neill's premise. It says that we should be interested in nothing *except* the relation of man to man because there is nothing else real we can possibly be interested in.

Most of the "plays of social significance" written on that assumption have already been forgotten, and it would be unkind to mention the names of some writers who were then held up as those to whom the future belonged. Of the two who are still vividly remembered, Odets adopted the then obligatory role of social critic but breathed into his best plays a warmth and compassion none of the others seemed capable of; Saroyan managed somehow to generate a world of fantasy which was uniquely his own.

At this present moment we have left the twenties, left the thirties, and finally the forties. Where do we stand? Obviously we do not have that confidence in either the world of the theater or the great world outside which dominated the twenties. Hardly less obviously, there is no longer much interest in the limited kind of play which the thirties believed it should write. Arthur Miller and Tennessee Williams are the current writers who have made the greatest impression, but neither would have quite fitted into either the twenties or the thirties. The first has an obvious relation to "the drama of social consciousness," but he is not so dogmatic as he would have been twenty years ago. Williams is more ambiguous still. His characters have their most vivid lives in their private, often their secret worlds. Neither seems quite sure how his sense that our civilization is crumbling can be reconciled with the desire, strongest in Williams, to deal with what transcends any immediate situation.

If, as seems not unlikely, we are in for some sort of major

revival of interest in the twenties, then the question is this: Can they, can we, can the playwrights yet to emerge, learn anything from it? Is there any past there which is genuinely usable?

Few, I think, would like to revive the Jazz Age or now think affectionately of bathtub gin except as part of a period piece. Hence one kind of revival might be rather like previous revivals of interest in the Gay Nineties. Or for that matter, like the still earlier revival of the Victorian. But it is not of anything of that sort that I am thinking. What of the serious plays, of the possibility of taking them seriously and of making useful what we can learn from them?

That any considerable number would prove still viable in our theater I am not sure. Even when they were new, many of us were not so convinced that they were masterpieces as we were that they promised soon to become such. But there is something in their spirit which might speak to our condition and set us on a promising road again. And the reason why they might do so is this: Though our present situation is in some respects so different, yet we do feel the need of approaching their chief preoccupations, even if from a different angle.

We no longer believe that this world is, or is likely soon to become, secure. Yet we no longer find satisfactory those plays of the thirties which were concerned chiefly with such security. Perhaps what we feel is that if we are to spend the rest of our lives in insecurity, if we must continue to live our human lives on the brink of an abyss, we should nevertheless like to keep them human. We would like, in our changed atmosphere, to take up again the pursuit of the kind of truths the artists of the twenties were in pursuit of. If we do so we may again recapture their convictions. We may again come to believe that the theater has an important role to play in contemporary life, that even if it does not solve our world problems, it can help us lead human lives, not only with but beyond those problems.

Why novelists go wrong

[1959]

It is a commonplace of the American theater that neither critics nor novelists write successful plays. To that generalization there are more exceptions in Europe than there are in the United States, and even here there are some conspicuous ones. After all, the longest New York run chalked up during the nineteenth century was that of *A Trip to Chinatown,* which was the work of a reformed drama critic, and *Tobacco Road* (an adaptation) also broke a record. Still, if the exceptions are only comparatively rare, they are sufficiently so to raise the question of what the phenomenon means.

In so far as the critic is concerned, the answer seems easy: The analytical and the creative habits of mind, the tendency to be interested in generalizations rather than concrete instances, are sufficiently opposed to interfere with one another. But a novelist tells stories and he is very likely to write scenes that are loosely called "dramatic." Why does he often find it difficult to write them for the theater?

Moreover, it is a historical fact that the rise of the novel in English coincided with the decline of the drama as a literary form. Prose fiction seemed to offer new opportunities and it pushed both the playwright and the theater into a position of third-rate importance. Several major poets of the nineteenth century tried to write in the dramatic form—notably Shelley, Byron, Browning, and Tennyson—without producing anything very theaterworthy, while the novelist left the stage pretty much alone until relatively late in the 1900's.

The very word "theatrical" had come to mean (as it still sometimes does) "sensational," "tricky," "overdone," and "false." As long as that situation continued, the tendency was to regard playmaking as a kind of meretricious carpentry unworthy of a serious artist. "Plays," it was said, "are not written but rewritten." Another proclamation, attributed to an American artisan and often quoted, was this: "Playwriting is not an art but a trade." Brander Matthews, the first "Professor of Dramatic Literature" in an American university and himself a highly unsuccessful playwright, used to tell his classes that one of his efforts "enjoyed a continuous run of one successive night." He was a bit rueful but also a bit proud. The implication was that he was too gifted and too sincere to succeed.

At the time, we may grant, there was some justification for his attitude. But when Ibsen, Shaw, and their contemporaries brought the theater back into the intellectual and artistic main stream, when they banished the mechanically "well-made play" and made playwriting again an art rather than a trade, one might have expected the poet and the novelist to step in and take advantage of the new opportunity. Some of them did. Tolstoy and Chekhov in Russia, Barrie and Galsworthy and Arnold Bennett in England (to name just a few) wrote important or theatrically successful plays. But is there any comparable American example? Is it also not true that in England, as in the United States, distinguished novelists who write distinguished plays are sufficiently rare to suggest that there is some fundamental difference between the novelist and the playwright *as creator*? That it is not merely a matter of a teachable technique or, even more simply, of an interest in the form?

Since playwrights and novelists are as humanly prejudiced as anyone else, they are inclined to sneer a bit at one another; each is apt to imply that he could be successful in the other's profession if he were willing (in Dr. Johnson's

phrase) "to abandon himself to it." Henry James, after trying hard and repeatedly to write a successful play, shrugged
off his successive failures by announcing that he simply
would not consent to descend to the superficial trickery that,
so experience had convinced him, was essential for success in
the theater. On the other hand Bernard Shaw (downright as
usual) roundly proclaimed that *anybody* could write a novel.
"But a play . . . is a different matter—different, too, in the
sense of being weightier, not lighter." He did not care at the
moment to remember that he himself had written five un-
publishable novels before he turned to the theater. Obviously he, at least, wasn't the "anybody" who could write
novels.

Is there, then, some clearly definable quality or method of
presentation, properly called "the dramatic" that the playwright exhibits or has mastered, and that the novelist finds
it impossible to exhibit as a quality or to practice as a
method except sporadically?

We toss about the word "dramatic" very freely, as though
we knew just what we meant by it. A novel is "dramatic";
an incident is "dramatic"; and even (in the advertisements)
a lipstick or a floor lamp is "dramatic." But if you turn (as
I did a few minutes ago) to a desk dictionary and then, disappointed there, to the Oxford, you will discover that even
the latter dodges the problem of definition and walks around
in a circle. "Dramatic" is "of, pertaining to, or connected
with the, or a, drama; characteristic of, or appropriate to,
the drama, theatrical." "Drama" is "a composition in prose
or verse adapted to be acted on the stage." And yet we think
that Polonius is funny when he pontificates: "for, to define
true madness, what is't but to be nothing else but mad?"
The essence of the drama is to be dramatic, and the meaning of "dramatic" is "appropriate to the drama"!

To escape this dilemma, which consists in whirling about
with our tails in our mouths, and, incidentally, to throw

some light on the question of the difference between a drama and even a "dramatic" novel, we might bring in Aristotle. In fact I shall probably do so before I have finished. But a certain playful squib from Shaw is a better introduction. It is less abstract and also illustrates rather than explains what the difference is. And to that extent it is itself "dramatic."

In 1916, when Shaw was reaching the height of his powers, the editor of the London *Nation* sent him for review a book called *The Author's Craft* by Arnold Bennett, in which, according to Shaw, one of the most successful of English novelists "talks shop and debits harmless tosh about technique for the entertainment of literary amateurs" which is, I hope, not what I am doing. Shaw saw no reason why he should bother with the book until he came across the phrase, "One reason why a play is easier to write than a novel . . ." That set him off. With the quick, copious inventiveness that is likely to be characteristic of the greatest novelists and the greatest playwrights, he contrasted a scene from *Macbeth* with a parody example of a chapter of a novel "in the style of my friends Bennett and Galsworthy when they are too lazy to write plays."

The whole thing is wonderfully effective and illuminating too, but I think the point can be made by a single brief excerpt. Macduff has just found Macbeth on the battlefield, and Shakespeare, in order to convey the fact that Macbeth has no heart to fight because he is weary of all slaughter and also because Macduff is still another of the same tribe he has vainly attempted to exterminate, makes Macbeth say:

> Of all men else I have avoided thee.
> But get thee back; my soul is too much charg'd
> With blood of thine already.

Bennett, says Shaw, would have written it thus: "He decided to give Macduff a chance. He was tired of killing people named Macduff. He said so. He advised Macduff to go away." Now, of course one difference between "my soul is too much charg'd with blood of thine already" and "he was tired of killing people named Macduff" is the difference between strong poetic language and prose. But that is not the point here. Quite aside from that is a more important fact—the one is "dramatic," the other isn't.

A few years later, when Shaw was discussing the question of the printed play and the failure of Henry James on the stage, he wrote: "There is a literary language which is perfectly intelligible to the eye, yet utterly unintelligible to the ear . . . Of that English James was master in the library and slave on the stage." No doubt that was indeed one reason for James's unsuccess. But like the question of prose versus poetry, it does not go directly to the heart of the distinction between what is "dramatic" and what isn't. The parody of Bennett does.

Nearly two millennia and a half ago, Aristotle had the same distinction in mind when he used a word that is variously translated as "imitation" or "representation," and when he called it the essence of the poet's gift, he did not mean "realism" or "naturalism" or "a copy of the literal fact." What he did mean was "presentation" as opposed to description or explanation, and "presentation" is precisely what Shakespeare achieved and the pseudo Bennett did not. The one creates the mood and the mental processes of Macbeth; the other attempts to tell us about them; and that is what makes the first "dramatic" and the other its opposite.

So far as mere external form is concerned, the obvious difference is, of course, between dialogue on the one hand and narrative, description, or analysis on the other. But to adopt the external *form* of dialogue does not by any means guarantee truly dramatic creation. To take an extreme and absurd example, it does not help a playwright to be dramatic when he makes the maid say, "As you well know, it was just ten years ago that the young master shook the dust of this road from his feet." A great deal of the dialogue written for the stage is merely a somewhat less obvious attempt to disguise the fact that the author is "telling about" a character or a situation that he has been unable to "present" or "create." And it is the failure to create that is often the real, as opposed to the apparent, reason for the "undramatic" character of an unsatisfactory play.

We often complain of such a play that it "lacks action," that it is "too talky" or "too didactic." Some of Shakespeare's plays (though hardly *Macbeth*) get along with very little of what we call "stage action." Shaw is endlessly talky and relentlessly didactic. But Shakespeare can dispense with "action" and Shaw can get away with talk and sermonizing because the dialogue of both is usually dramatic in the important sense that the words, thoughts, and emotions of the talkers are dramatically realized.

For a modern example of what the method of "presentation" is, one could not do better than to choose the opening scenes of *A Streetcar Named Desire* or *Cat on a Hot Tin Roof*. In neither case is the heroine a familiar type easily identifiable by a few simple clues. Both are complex individuals in an unusual and highly complex emotional state. Yet both appear on the stage before anyone has had a chance to tell us anything about them. But from almost the first words they say, we begin the process of understanding them, and the process continues steadily as the play proceeds because Tennessee Williams has "imitated" them so successfully that no description or analysis is necessary. I doubt that that implies any conscious awareness on the author's part of just what he is doing. At least such awareness is not necessary. What is necessary is twofold: the talent and the instinct of a true dramatist.

All good novels have dramatic scenes. In between them are the passages in which the novelist narrates, describes, or "tells about" characters or events, and it may be remarked incidentally that the much-admired "stream of consciousness" is often, though not always, a mere device for pretending that something is being represented when we are merely being told about it. But why doesn't the novelist give us everything dramatically?

Shaw says it is because the novelist is "lazy," because "telling" is so much easier than "creating." The novelist himself will give more respectable reasons. He will say, perhaps, that nowadays we understand characters and events in terms of psychological and sociological concepts and that therefore we cannot make them interpret themselves as the dramatist attempts to do. Perhaps. But two facts remain. One is that "imitation" in Aristotle's sense is still the most vivid, the most arresting, and the most satisfying of all the forms of storytelling; the other, that novelists are often unsuccessful in the theater because they will not or cannot fully "dramatize" their stories.

Theater: Cultural common denominator

[1956]

People who love the theater usually don't spend much time thinking about why it is important—they just know that it is. And that is probably the reason they usually do so unconvincing a job when called upon to explain the importance to some skeptical public. Send them down to City Hall, to Washington, or even for an appearance before some less august assembly, and what do they do? They talk somewhat

apologetically about "entertainment," and with a good deal
of awe about "culture." But legislators, social workers, and
even public-spirited benefactors are often pretty vague about
what "culture" is, and I don't think they usually get much
enlightenment. They are left with the feeling that it is something ornamental, agreeable, and apparently quite pleasant
to those who have a taste for it, but a good deal less than a
necessity of life. In their hearts most of them think of it
as a luxury we can get along very well without when we have
to, and of theater as "culture" of a singularly expensive kind.

What are commonly called the more serious arguments
don't seem to me much better. Plays do sometimes—nowadays quite frequently—"discuss social problems." In the
theater you can find corrupt politicians being attacked, juvenile delinquency examined, and intolerance disapproved
of. You can even get a popular exposition of Freudian psychology. But you can also get all these things from sociological treatises, newspaper editorials, lecture courses, and radio
panels. No doubt the dramatic presentation may be especially effective on occasion, but I can't honestly say that I
think the American public would be very significantly less
well informed about any of them if the theater were dead as
a doornail. Neither the drama nor any other art form is an
instrument of first importance when it comes to helping people decide whom to vote for or what legislation to approve
of.

And yet, for all that, there is a lot of truth in the old saw
about the importance of those who make the songs of the
nation—especially if you include all those songs which
are painted and danced, written and spoken, as well as
those that are sung. It is the "songs" in this broad sense
which formulate and transmit the pattern of opinions, habits, and emotions which constitute the "culture" and thus
determine the character of a civilization. Homer had rather

more to do with what Greek civilization was like than either Lycurgus or Plato did; Shakespeare, rather more to do with what England was like for three centuries than did Bacon or Sir Edward Coke. At this very moment our own arts, good and bad, exercise a stronger influence upon our citizens than either schools or churches. And it is nearly always so. If legislators and educators really knew what "culture" is and does, they would know that no society could endure for a year without it, and that the only question is what kind of culture you have. They would know also that the theater can make a unique contribution to that culture.

If these two statements seem a bit farfetched, let's examine them, one after another.

Suppose we consider, for example, a certain social group which is immersed in the texture of a very dense culture of a very inferior sort: the group, I mean, composed of upper-middle-class teen-agers in contemporary America. Where do they get the code they live by; their idea of what conduct, what tastes, and what beliefs are proper? How do they know what attitude they should take toward parents, members of the opposite sex, constituted authorities? How do they know what is up-to-date, what is smart, what is admirable? Is it from what their parents tell them, from what they learn in day school or in Sunday school—if they go to one? A very little they may get from each of these sources, but only a very little. Most of it they get from television, the movies, popular songs, and whatever magazines they see. These establish the fundamentals of their culture. Any child who had been isolated from all of them since infancy would be completely lost in the society of his fellows. He might, if he had been immersed in a better culture instead, have higher standards, higher ideals, and better tastes. But he would be rather more remote from his companions than a Greenland Eskimo is remote from an African Bantu.

Moralists and social workers who view these teen-agers with alarm usually miss the really important part. They wish that popular art taught better lessons. They think that the important thing is the ostensible moral. But of course it isn't, and that is why "industry codes" mean so little. What really count are the implications, the often intangible assumptions about values. The movie which puts two characters to bed only after they have been properly married may in other ways convey a much worse idea about what the relation of the sexes can and should be than one less careful about what it says in so many words. A vulgar culture is vulgar not so much because it preaches vulgar lessons as because it exemplifies crude thinking, obtuse sensibility, and clumsy manners.

It is not only the teen-agers who live by the works of art they admire. So do all of us. La Rochefoucauld made the famous remark that few people would ever fall in love if it were not for poetry. That is true enough, in a sense. The emotions we feel are pretty largely those we have been prepared in advance to feel. And it is from poems, plays, and novels, far more than from teachers or preachers, that we learn what to expect. But why single out "falling in love"? What is true of that process is equally true of almost every other human experience. Few people would fall in love if it weren't for the poets, but just as few would be heroes or, for that matter, "hardheaded businessmen" or "sophisticated men about town." Indeed few would be "ladies" or "gentlemen" either, because it is works of art, good or bad, which transmit more effectively than anything else the prevailing conception of, say, gentlemanliness as opposed to boorishness, no less than of virtue as opposed to vice.

Many a man will tell you today that he has no religion and no philosophy. He may even tell you also that he has no morals. If he is an intellectual he may go on to argue that morals are nothing but mores, and that nothing is good or evil except insofar as some particular society says that it is. Does such a man follow no conventions? Doesn't he act as though he thought certain things were *comme il faut,* and certain things not? Would he steal candy from a baby? Not necessarily, or even usually. But why not? What is the something he lives by? Is it habits and prejudices lingering from the days before he became emancipated? To some small extent, perhaps. But principally it is because, though he may have no religion and no formal philosophy, he has absorbed moral and aesthetic ideas as well as traditions of mere manners from novels, plays, and all the other forms of art.

In an age when the influence of specific religious and moral teaching has declined to as low a level as it has reached today, the role of the arts in formulating what men live for—and by—is even more important than it usually has been. Take away from even the unimaginative, stolid citizen —one wholly without intellectual interests and completely devoid of what is ordinarily called culture—take away from him the things that he unconsciously has absorbed either from the popular arts or from contact with those who have absorbed them from those arts, and the civilization in which he plays so important a role would lose its shape. No man would be predictable enough to make part of a functioning society. We should have a barbarous anarchy impossible to imagine. Take away from the cultivated and intellectual classes everything which they have accepted from the art they have experienced at first or second hand, and an even worse anarchy would result. The arts are not just more or less desirable. They are indispensable. You could not get rid of them even if you wanted to.

Not unfrequently both men of action and philosophers have convinced themselves that human life is essentially meaningless; that good and evil are one; and that there are no rules except those which the strong man makes for himself. Many men of action and many philosophers have, in other words, tried to live in a world from which all value judgments had been banished. But no work of art, popular or exalted, can possibly exist except against a background of explicit or implicit assumptions concerning good and evil, beauty and ugliness. In fact art might be defined as an account of human life presented in such a way as to involve value judgments. And it is for that reason that as long as we have art, we shall still find ourselves making such value judgments even though philosophy should wither away and religion die.

Of all the instruments ever invented for communicating an artist's vision, the printed word is still the most versatile. Yet even it cannot communicate everything as well as certain other instruments can. Especially it cannot create certain effects which only the acted drama can create. I am not for the moment thinking of what the actor and the *mise en scène* contribute. I am thinking rather of what the audience itself contributes by virtue of the very fact that it has gathered as a group to enjoy certain experiences which it is conscious of sharing with other beings. For such an audience a play is more than the words the playwright wrote, and more than the life the performers give them. When we are part of such an audience we are participating not only in the play itself, but also in the reactions of the other members of the audience. It is impossible for us to feel isolated or alone. Our fellows are indeed our fellows just insofar as they are being moved at the same moment by the same emotions.

The most obvious illustration of this fact is the laughter which rings out at moments when, even if we were watching a rehearsal, we should smile at most. The laughter is an acknowledgment of the presence of others, and of a sense of unity with them. If other subtler emotions had equally obvious outward manifestation, we should be equally aware that they too are reinforced by this same sense of community. What we seek when we come to a tragedy is not merely the experience of pity and terror, but the experience of experiencing it publicly, and of thus acknowledging our common humanity.

Is there any other institution in our society which draws men together in the same way? Political rallies join us with our fellow partisans and separate us from our opponents. Even churches are usually more or less sectarian. But a laughing or weeping audience is truly united. On few other occasions does any group confess in the same way that it meets on a common ground.

Those who say that the theater began as a ritual and that it should become ritualistic again are both right and wrong—right in their first assumption, wrong in supposing that it ever has been anything but ritualistic. Perhaps, indeed, the theater is the only truly catholic temple still standing. Those who assemble in it are worshiping some of the oldest gods and confessing a faith fundamental enough to be shared by those who go to different churches, vote for different candidates, and accept different philosophies. That they can unite in laughing at the same farce or weeping at the same tragedy is a surprising fact. They are agreeing publicly on something they did not know they agreed on, and could not define if they tried. They are testifying to the fact that they belong not only to the human race but to a civilization which, beneath all of its divisions and diversities, is united by modes of feeling and standards of value more fundamental than any of the things over which it is divided. To do that is not only to enrich the life of that society. It is also to increase greatly its chances of survival.

Unfortunately not even the movies perform the same function in the same way—partly because of the dark isolation of the movie theater, partly, perhaps, because the shadow of an actor is more of a symbol and less of a warm fact than the actor himself. Even less is the so-called audience of radio and television an audience at all. It absorbs ideas, convictions, and prejudices. There is no doubt about the extent to which it is being what is called in the jargon of sociology "acculturated." But just because the whole process is private and mechanical it is dehumanized rather than humanized. The audience is a lonely crowd, not, like a theater audience, a truly social one.

It is a curious fact that the Puritan enemies of the theater understood better than its modern proponents the true nature of the theater's influence. They opposed ostensibly "moral" plays almost as bitterly as they did those which they regarded as immoral. And they did so because they realized, as apologists for the theater often do not, that the ostensible themes and theses are less important than the implicit. The Puritans wanted no church but their own, and no culture not based directly upon the Old Testament. They were aware of the fact that the most innocent-seeming play broadened culture and united men in the acknowledgment of values not always recognized in their religion. It seems a pity that those who value the modern theater should have a less adequate understanding of the role it plays.

If you don't mind my saying so . . . [X]

[1962]

When I published my first little book about the New England countryside, Charles Poore (thinking I suppose of my fellow drama critic, Brooks Atkinson) dismissed me with amiable flippancy as "just another Broadwayite doubling as Connecticut Yankee." That was in 1949. Nowadays when I pay one of my brief visits to New York, taxi drivers usually ask, "Where are you from?" Even the shills employed by the rubberneck buses sometimes address me hopefully. Evidently that much of the big-city look can be rubbed off in little more than a decade.

Just what combination of stigmata now mark me as a provincial I am not sure. Do I gawk at the tall buildings? Do I wait before crossing the street for the light to turn green instead of sensing, as the true New Yorker does, that traffic has just been halted by a yellow and that I can save a few seconds if I jump the gun and am willing to disregard the possibility that some equally hurried automobilist has also decided to take advantage of the neutral seconds? Of course, I should prefer to think that the things that distinguish me are less humiliating. Is it just that I have lost that harried look? Or even, perhaps, that my hat (although of not more than a quarter-gallon capacity) does have a slightly Western brim. I don't know. It may even be that I unconsciously assume the famous it's-a-nice-place-to-visit-but-I'd-hate-to-live-here look.

I am writing this some weeks after my latest visit during which (falling again into the pattern of the provincial) most of my playgoing was confined to the long-established hits. Who living in New York and going to the theater at all did not see *My Fair Lady* before 1962? And the nearest I came to being up-to-date was to explore some of the off-Broadway productions that had been running long enough for even me to have heard of them. This newest of Little Theater movements was just getting started when I bowed to an inner voice that whispered, "Go west, old man," and I was mildly curious to know to what extent the phenomenon resembled the off-Broadway movement of my own younger days when we reviewers put the Bandbox, the Provincetown, the Neighborhood, and the New Playwrights Theatre on our visiting list.

To those young enough to regard the experimental theaters of that age as something belonging to a dead past when even those who supposed themselves sophisticated were actually hopeless squares, I would like to insist that so far as the "New Wave" dramaturgy is concerned there are parallels fairly close. What we called "expressionism" had adopted a method (or lack of method) quite similar to the *non sequiturs* of existential surrealism. Beckett and Ionesco (especially the latter) may be a good deal more gamy than, say, Dos Passos in his *The Moon Is a Gong* or John Howard Lawson in *Roger Bloomer,* but they are hardly less realistic and I doubt that any "modern" director has thought of anything more irrational than the incident in one play (whose title and author I have forgotten) where young ladies costumed as monkeys rushed down the aisles to distribute lollipops to the audience. Since this particular production was supported in part by a certain eminent financier, it led Alexander Woollcott to observe that the greatest all-day sucker of them all was probably Mr. Otto Kahn.

Among the new productions I was most impressed—if that is the word—by Jean Genêt's long-run hit, *The Balcony.* As I suppose everybody interested in such things knows by now, this work concerns a creative bawdy house that stages (for pretty high fees, I should imagine) elaborate fantasies designed to gratify the special erotic obsessions of the customers and in which they may participate as actors. Most of these customers want to dress up and pretend that they are someone else. A judge wants to be judged, condemned, and punished by a sadistic beauty. A clergyman wants to dress up as a bishop and then couple with a young woman who pretends to be St. Theresa. But from the standpoint of the audience the most rewarding of these eccentrics is the one who must imagine himself a general on a bloody battlefield and is in love with his horse—the last delightfully acted by a handsome dancer provided with a magnificent tail and trained to prance like a mare. On the other hand, the profoundest psychological insight is provided by a chief of police on his way to dictatorship who realizes that he will never have achieved self-fulfillment until some patron of the "House of Illusions" wants to take part in a charade in which he can imagine himself to be this very chief of police.

This last strikes me as being neither more nor less profound than a gag of the twenties that declared, "You can't call yourself really famous until somebody goes crazy and imagines that he is you." As a wisecrack it may just possibly pass muster but as the foundation for a philosophical drama it is hardly adequate.

For these and other reasons my summary judgment as a retired and outmoded reviewer is simply that *The Balcony* offers several moments of sensational effectiveness in its erotic scenes but that its strained and contorted philosophizing is sheer piffle. What I shall longest remember is the dancer with the tail. And, if the best thing about the old show with the free lollipops was Woollcott's comment, so, I am inclined to think, the best thing about *The Balcony* is *Time* magazine's tribute to the equine grace of the dancer above mentioned. This tribute, exhibited in a gigantic blow-up outside the theater, reaches its climax when it calls the young lady in question "the first whorse in history."

What is one to make of the vogue of such plays as *The Balcony?* Is it to be taken, as Moscow would no doubt like to believe, as evidence of the utter decadence of Western civilization and a sure sign that we are on the point of collapse? Or shall we shrug it off by remarking that art has a tendency to go to extremes and that audiences are actually little affected by such eccentricities? My own guess would be that the correct estimate is somewhere in between and that it is not uninteresting to inquire what is new and what isn't in such writers as Genêt, Beckett, and Ionesco.

A few sentences back I quoted *Time* with approval. Although I do not take most of my critical opinions from either that publication or its sisters, I think a survey of the off-Broadway phenomenon that appeared in *Life* put its finger on a very significant fact. The new surrealistic play, it said, resembles in both theme and method some of the classic "bits" of the burlesque show and it cited a very famous one known in the business as "Flogel Street." In this sketch an inoffensive and innocent lost stranger asks a passerby how to get to the street in question. Thereupon the stranger turns upon him, reproaches him for being a panhandler, grows more and more vehement, finally pulls the victim's hat over his eyes and departs in a rage. This is much the kind of irrational thing that happens to the innocent and the lost in Beckett or Ionesco. It embodies the Kafkaesque obsession with a punishment that cannot fit the crime because no crime, except that of being innocent, has been committed.

Life's comments, which I have already somewhat expanded, seem to me important enough to be worth pursuing further. Not only the theme—man bewildered in a meaninglessly hostile world—but also the method is the same. Like the surrealist play, the typical burlesque bit asks us to abandon any pretense to the literal "imitation of life," and to accept the wildest improbability. Take for example the endlessly repeated situation where a tramp who poses as the Count de Something-or-Other is accepted at the aristocratic reception despite the glaring decrepitude of his clothes and the grotesqueness of his manners. What happens could happen only in the wildest of dreams. But, as in a dream, there is what Freud called the latent content. Here is a fantasy that embodies hopes and fears as well as what it is now fashionable to call the essential "absurdity" of existence.

Actually, of course, the whole tradition of the clown—whether he be a classic clown in whiteface or a highly individual clown like Charlie Chaplin—is the same. He is always in search of both identity and dignity. He cannot "belong" because he is not like other men. He is perpetually rejected and he has every sort of indignity thrust upon him— from the kick in the pants to the pie in the face. *He Who Gets Slapped,* he was called in a second-rate but somehow revealing Russian play. And that is precisely what the existentialist hero, like the eternal clown, usually is.

Why, then, aren't the plays of Beckett, Ionesco, *et alii,* merely burlesque bits or circus interludes? The difference is, I think, the difference between laughter and self-pity. For one thing, most clowns, including Chaplin, have their brief moments of triumph. Sometimes they rebel and, throwing caution to the winds, do exactly what they want to do, and even get away with it for the moment. Hope springs eternal. The clown's head is bloody—also drenched and full of custard or wallpaper paste—but it is unbowed. The existential hero, on the other hand, can't trip up a policeman or land a custard pie in the face of his tormentors. He is always and invariably "he who gets slapped," never he who slaps in return.

An even more important difference is this: We are not asked to identify so completely with the clown. We rejoice, as Lucretius has it, not because we enjoy the pains of others but because we say (or try to say) that they are not ours. Of the clown we may think, "There but for the grace of God go I." The existentialist hero asks us to conclude instead: "Since there is no God to grant the grace, there in fact I am."

Some time ago Benjamin De Mott published in the pages of this magazine an extremely shrewd and interesting analysis of the current style of "sick" humor—which is of course not too distantly related to surrealistic plays by its pessimism and its morbidity. Two footnotes I should like to add—one of them in mild protest, the other a mere addition.

Since I myself have just been treading the same dangerous ground it hardly becomes me to point out that the solemn analysis of jokes has its dangers. Shelley, whose sense of humor was by no means overdeveloped, is said to have declared that *The School for Scandal* taught him at last to understand what is meant by the comic spirit. When, he said, you present as likable a dissipated and dishonest young man while ridiculing his sober brother you have what is called "a comedy." And without wishing to question the general soundness of Mr. De Mott's contention that there is perversity and corruption in some "sick" comedy I think that in a few instances he overstates his case.

No doubt audiences take in diverse ways such jokes as those he cites ridiculing the health drives. ("Help Stamp Out Blackheads; Put the Squeeze on this Dread Disease!") But to me it seems that the ridicule is here directed, not against the aims of the health drives, but (and very properly) at the methods used to publicize them. We have far too much faith in the effectiveness and propriety of the clever slogan, too little in a rational appeal. The jingle may be suitable for selling a toothpaste but it degrades and makes trivial any serious enterprise. Slogans always arouse my suspicion and I think they are dangerous tools for those whose aims are completely honest. Religion, so it seems to me, is in a bad way if the most effective method of promoting it is by putting up billboards that proclaim, "The family that prays together stays together." The comedians who ridicule such procedures as those now usual in the promotion of presumably worthy causes are not so sick as the philanthropy that rests its case on a jingle.

So much for my mild objection. As for my mere addenda to Mr. De Mott's article, it is simply this: Sick humor, although it is indeed enjoying a vogue probably unprecedented, is by no means new, and parallels to the modern examples are even closer than those between the clown and the existentialist hero. Mr. De Mott cites *A Modest Proposal* as proof that

Swift cannot be misunderstood and that he is clearly on the side of the angels. But could he say the same thing of Swift's vision of judgment in which God dismisses all human beings as fools not worth damning or of any one of the various "sick" descriptions of the foulness of physical love? Swift is at the moment one of the most admired and defended of classic writers but it is difficult to make him seem consistently "healthy."

More recent but not contemporary examples of "sick" humor are also not hard to find and Ambrose Bierce will supply half a dozen. I think for instance of one piece called "An Unsuccessful Conflagration" in which a wife murderer bewails the bad luck that overcame him because he put the *corpus delicti* in a cabinet he didn't know was fireproof.

Some years ago a psychoanalyst solemnly warned parents against *Alice in Wonderland* as a dangerous invitation to neurosis because it involves a constantly recurring "threat to the integrity of the body" and thus encourages a typical neurotic anxiety. What, I wonder, would he have thought of Mark Twain's sketch, "Amelia's Unfortunate Young Man." Amelia's fiancé, one Williamson Breckinridge Carruthers, is an outstanding example of what the psychiatrists call "the accident prone." He catches smallpox which destroys his manly beauty and erysipelas which makes him blind in one eye. He loses one arm by the premature explosion of a firecracker, the other by falling into a well while watching a balloon ascension. Still later he loses both legs. Then: "Shortly before the time set for the nuptials another disaster occurred. There was but one man scalped by the Owen's River Indians last year. That man was Williamson Breckinridge Carruthers of New Jersey. He was hurrying home with happiness in his heart, when he lost his hair forever, and in that hour he almost cursed the mistaken mercy that had spared his head." Mark Twain's problem as an editor is to advise the young lady whether she should or should not marry the unfortunate young man and it involves, as the conscientious editor says, "The lifelong happiness of a woman, and that of nearly two thirds of a man." "It does not seem to me," is his conclusion, "that there is very much risk . . . because if he sticks to his singular propensity for damaging himself every time he sees a good opportunity, his next experience is bound to finish him, and then you are safe married or single. If married, the wooden legs and such other valuables as he may possess revert to the widow. . . ."

Gruesome and therefore, I suppose, "sick" humor is at the moment exceedingly popular with children and in fact it was, I think, from childish lips that I first heard it in its modern form. Only recently a ten-year-old acted out for me with great glee the tale of a little boy who returned crying from school because his companions had called him "a three-headed monster." His mother (distributing three properly placed pats) replies: "There . . . there . . . there." Yet even from the mouths of babes—who are notoriously not squeamish in such matters—I have never heard anything more continuously and cumulatively heartless than Mark Twain's tale. I don't think, nevertheless, that I have been brutalized or corrupted by it. In fact, I regard it as one of the most overwhelmingly hilarious pieces of prose I have ever read. How that can be some reader may be able to explain. I cannot.

The playwright is still a poet

[1955]

Mr. William Shakespeare was—among other things—a good psychologist. But neither he nor his contemporaries ever heard the word, and there is a lesson in that for the playwright of today. I don't mean that this playwright should not know anything which the sixteenth century did not. I do mean that he ought to be a poet first and leave technicalities to those whose business they are. That is what Ibsen, for instance, did do, and Ibsen's plays have lasted a good deal better than those of his contemporaries who prided themselves on being up on the latest theories.

One of the most successful plays on Broadway this season is *The Bad Seed*. One of its premises is that criminality is hereditary, and most laymen as well as most professional psychologists now believe that it isn't. Perhaps the author would have been wiser not to commit himself on that subject. But it really doesn't make as much difference as many critics tend to assume. If the action is convincing, the rightness or wrongness of the scientific theory used to account for that action is not very important.

Not long ago, in the days of Lombroso and Zola, the newest and most fashionable "scientific" theory of human conduct laid great stress on the hereditary "criminal type." If *The Bad Seed* had been written then, it would have been praised especially for the very thing for which it is now blamed. But it would not have been any better as a play than it is now. So far as popular success is concerned, the fact that its science is old-fashioned obviously makes very little difference. *The Bad Seed* is doing very well indeed. Neither does it make very much difference in the artistic worth of the play. The latter wouldn't suddenly become much better if it were proved tomorrow that Lombroso was right after all, and that criminal tendencies really are handed down from parents to children.

I won't go so far as to say that the scientific soundness of *The Bad Seed* is as irrelevant as the question of the reality of ghosts is irrelevant to *Hamlet*. Perhaps the fact that *The Bad Seed* seems to make some slight pretense to being scientific alters the situation a little. But I will maintain that in any play on any level of artistic intention, the worth depends less upon the correctness of the technical assumptions than upon what the playwright has been able to achieve upon the basis of those assumptions; upon how persuasive he is and, especially, upon what truth he can present over, above, and beyond those alleged truths he has borrowed from philosophy, or religion, or science.

To the poet, theories are never more than a sort of prevailing mythology which he accepts as a skeleton, but which he clothes with the living flesh of the poetic imagination. If he forgets this and writes as though his only business were to expound or illustrate what philosophy, or religion, or science is teaching, then he writes plays essentially worthless in themselves and bound to be recognized as such when intellectual fashions change. Otherwise, how could it be true that great literature actually outlives the greatest philosophical, theological, or scientific treatises?

Shakespeare was instinctively so aware of this fact that, even today, scholars pretty generally admit that they don't know what his own convictions were on political or religious questions. In any play he seems to make whatever assumptions will best serve his intentions at that moment. On the other hand, his friend Ben Johnson was much more learned and scientific. His contemporaries and immediate successors praised him highly for this fact. If he were alive today he probably would be a well-read Freudian. At least he paraded his familiarity with what we should call the psychological theories of his day; he drew his comic characters in terms of the prevailing theory of the humors; and he wrote a famous prologue in which he set forth those theories—which is much as though a modern playwright were to publish a preface explaining what is meant by complex, inhibition, and fixation. But are his comic characters any better than Falstaff or Polonius? Haven't they ceased to be convincing just in so far as they were "scientifically" founded, and haven't they survived just in so far as they were true to a knowledge of human nature independent of scientific theory?

About a hundred years ago phrenology (or bump reading) was having a great vogue even in quite reputable circles. I shouldn't be at all surprised if it got onto the stage, though I must confess that I don't know any play which could then have been described as "a profound phrenological drama." Nearly every other science and pseudo science has been exploited—including hypnotism, Christian Science and whatever it was that *The Ladder* expounded. In *Damaged Goods* Brieux even wrote a syphilological drama. And of course the latest theories in economics, sociology, and psychology have been favorites.

During the early thirties nearly all "serious" playwrights became convinced that, even for poets, the study of Karl Marx was more important than the study of human nature. Yet there are few people today who believe that these plays were greatly improved by their authors' novel preoccupation. Does anybody doubt that Odets' *Awake and Sing* is better than his *Paradise Lost?* Conversion is nearly always bad for the writer of any form of fiction. Once he knows all the answers, he has nothing to give except those answers—which we already know from the philosophers and the scientists he got them from.

There was much wisdom in Ibsen's famous saying, "My business is to ask questions, not to answer them." The problem of why Hamlet behaves as he does is dramatically interesting. Try to explain it all by saying, "He had a mother complex," and only a very dull play remains. Most of Shakespeare's tragedies continue to be interesting because we can never quite make up our minds whether their heroes are destroyed by fate or whether their own characters and passions lead them to destruction.

Like nearly everybody else today, I believe that many of Freud's insights are valid, though I believe it less because of his arguments and his evidence than because these insights sharpen and confirm vaguer insights of my own. And that is the only reason why he is genuinely useful to playwrights. He himself was at least as much poet as scientist, and it is the poet who had contributed to literature. When writers try— as too often they have tried—to take his science instead of his poetry, the result is almost always unfortunate.

So far as I remember, the first mention of Freud's name in an American play was in George Cram Cook and Susan Gaspell's one-act *Suppressed Desires,* produced by the Washington Square Players just before our entry into World War I. Because it was satiric and farcical, it was legitimate. But many playwrights were soon seriously committing themselves to a kind of orthodoxy. Were Sidney Howard's *The Silver Cord* or Moss Hart's *Lady in the Dark* better or worse because of the extent to which each depended, not upon insights to which Freud might have helped the author, but upon technicalities, doctrines, and a jargon taken over from psychological textbooks? *Lady in the Dark* is interesting up to the moment when everything is "explained" in terms of a complex. But here, as always, when a dramatist "explains" anything in that cut-and-dried fashion, the drama as drama collapses—very much as the mystery-melodrama collapses when someone reveals just before the final curtain that it was a mad doctor disguised as the butler who hid corpses in the clothes closets. If, we say to ourselves, that is all there is to it, then who cares? As for *The Silver Cord* I can only repeat: *Hamlet* demonstrates that Shakespeare knew exactly enough—but not too much—about mother fixations, and he did not care to be dogmatic on the subject.

Of all the American plays exhibiting the influence of Freud, *Strange Interlude* is certainly the best. Is it not the best just because O'Neill did not write it to expound what he had just learned about Freudian doctrine, but used that doctrine much as Sophocles used Greek myth, simply as a scheme around which a dramatic story could be organized? If the time should ever come when we no longer believed in Freud, *Strange Interlude* will not be much more diminished by our loss of faith than *Oedipus Rex* is diminished because we no longer believe in Greek myths.

We can go even a step further and say that the very best Freudian plays and novels were written before Freud. Notoriously, Dostoevsky is full of Freudian insights. More to our purpose is the fact that Hedda Gabler is still the best— as she was also perhaps the first—example of The Neurotic as Hero, though we have had a lot of them since, goodness knows. Ibsen did not need any textbooks of abnormal psychology to teach him that neuroticism consists of the substitution of irrational ambitions, desires, and values for rational ones; or that seemingly unmotivated aggression is one of the symptoms of some neuroses. Hedda is, in some respects, a better study than Iago of gratuitous malice. It is better because of a deeper psychological insight. But Ibsen boasted truly that he read little current writing because, being a poet, he could get what his contemporaries were thinking "out of the air."

We might, indeed, go a great deal farther back than Ibsen for similar cases. Milton makes his just-created Eve fall in love with her own reflection, and he sends an angel to bid her look at Adam instead. Would the psychological truth of this incident have been improved if Milton could have told his readers that the incident is in conformity with the "psychological law" that narcissism precedes the ego's turning outward toward an external love object?

Am I saying that a playwright "oughtn't to know anything"; that he shouldn't "share the interests of the world he lives in"; or that he mustn't be "engaged"? Not quite. At least, not quite unless you think that Shakespeare and Ibsen "didn't know anything." What I am saying is that he should know most, and use most, of what he has learned from observation, from self-examination, and from imaginative insight, rather than what scientists have taught him; that if he uses science at all, he should use it only in so far as the scientists can supply hints which put him on the trail of things he can learn and know in his own way. As soon as he begins to rely upon what he knows only in the sense that it is what some scientist has told him, he ceases to be a playwright at all. Why should I or anybody else want to get our Freud or our Marx from a playwright when we can get it more authoritatively from Freud or Marx himself?

A certain professor of poetry at Oxford once remarked that the trouble with "didactic poetry" is that you can't learn anything from it. And that is exactly what is wrong with "scientific" plays. You can't learn anything from them—not any science because you know that already from a better source; not anything other than science because the playwright has surrendered the attempt to say anything as a playwright. What we really want of him is a poet's insight, not secondhand psychology, or economics, or sociology.

If this fact seems less and less recognized, perhaps it is because audiences and writers alike seem more and more inclined to the assumption that scientific knowledge is the only kind of knowledge there is. If that were true, if the writer could do no more than popularize such knowledge on a rather low level, then literature might as well shut up shop. That there are other kinds of knowledge is demonstrated by the fact that something is still to be learned from Sophocles or Shakespeare. Our playwrights would do well to try to find out what it is. But that is another story.

G.B.S. and intimations of immortality

[1961]

It is said that Bernard Shaw once refused the Order of Merit on the ground that he had long ago conferred that distinction upon himself. Such impudences he may have learned from his contemporary, Oscar Wilde, but he had more to back them up with, and lived long enough to know that the world had accepted him at his own valuation.

What had once seemed only his little jokes in more than questionable taste turned out to be merely sound prophecies. Nobody had believed him in the early dark days when he wrote Elisabeth Marbury that he would presently be enriched "by a dramatically regenerated public"—but he was. He may have gone a bit too far in the famous "Better than Shakespeare?" preface but he did, after all, only ask the question! And his prediction that he would, in any event, be read as long as any English literature endures seems less preposterous today than when he made the boast. He who, by his own confession, had been caviar to the general and a sure way to empty a theater is now something like an almost sure prescription for filling it. What had been caviar is now daily bread. Even his worst fear—that he might, like Shake-speare, be made an instrument of torture in the schools—has been realized.

"Pyrotechnic," he was usually called by his first grudging admirers, and even today "brilliant" is the almost inevitable adjective. But the true value of a brilliant object is notori-ously difficult to judge, and though some of his paradoxes have turned into the platitudes of "advanced" thought, it may be just possible that we are still too bedazzled to be quite sure what his absolute magnitude is.

Shaw made his case against Shakespeare—without much damaging the victim—and it would be easy to make a case against him. Despite the proudest of his boasts, "I invented my morality," it might be argued that he never had an orig-inal idea. His religion, "The Life Force," he confessedly took from Bergson; his economic theory from Marx, who, he said, "made a man of me." Ibsenism (considerably per-verted), Wagnerism (distorted beyond recognition), and Nietzscheism (tamed into a kindly respectability), he lifted out of context from their inventors. And as though all that borrowing were not enough, he got the lunatic fringe of his doctrine—anti-vaccinationism, vegetarianism, teetotalism, spelling reform, and the rest—from the assorted cranks among whom he spent his early years. Only Freud came too late to make any significant contribution to the potpourri that he managed by some adroit legerdemain to arrange into what purported to be a consistent philosophy—the most in-clusive since St. Thomas Aquinas.

One might go on to point out that what are ordinarily called "the passions" are so nearly absent from his plays that we willingly suspend our disbelief in puppets unlike any human being who ever lived (except possibly their creator) only because they are so lively, so articulate, and so entertaining. Endowed with ideas and convictions alone, they are never convincing psychologically, and they act only as logical abstractions might act, never as believable men and women. Any visitor from outer space who prepared himself for the adventure by reading Shaw's works would have a surprisingly complete knowledge of what arguments had been taking place on earth; but he would have formed a very wrong idea of the way in which human beings behave.

Yet, just as Shaw realized well enough that the greatness of Shakespeare is not to be disproved by the most convincing analysis of what he did not do, so we are similarly aware that in Shaw's case also what count are his qualities, not his limitations. If he did not invent a morality, he did invent a kind of play that had never existed before. No one else had ever written dramatic works like his in intention, in technique, or in effect. Neither had anyone ever exploited the possibilities of the English language in quite the same way. There is hardly a page in any one of his plays—hardly two successive sentences in his prefaces or his pamphlets— that is not immediately recognized as indubitably his by any moderately perceptive person.

That he was a master of language does not mean that he could use it for every purpose for which language has ever been used. Under certain circumstances Shakespeare might conceivably have written like Shaw. Shaw could never under any circumstances have written like Shakespeare. The virtues of his prose are never those that suggest anything *but* prose, and his only real failures are those in which he attempts an effect of which only poetry is capable.

The fact remains, nevertheless, that no one ever made pure prose more effective. He is economical, fluent, vigorous, and precise. His prose, rich in purely comic invention, is also full of sudden turns and delightful, unexpected extravagances. We understand so clearly and so readily what he means to say that for the moment, at least, we would not think of disagreeing with him, and he entertains us so lavishly that we have no desire to escape from his spell. So many dragons are slain on every page, and so many Goliaths are toppled by the missiles from his sling, that we feel quite capable of taking on a few dragons or giants ourselves. No one ever gave a better demonstration of what is called the battle of words, or made the joy of such a battle seem more real.

The chief virtue of the dramatic form he invented is simply that it gives full play to his gift for brilliant expository prose. His plots are almost invariably artificial, usually eventually farcical, and though he employs various theatrical tricks quite skillfully when he fears that without them the audience may begin, like Polonius, to call for "a jig, or a tale of bawdry," these theatrical devices are usually familiar ones. His characters may be passionless and curiously unaffected by recognizable human motives, but they are all endowed with his own gift for vivid, forceful, and humorous speech —much as Shakespeare's characters are all gifted with their creator's poetic powers. "I can explain anything to anybody," one of his characters exclaims, "and what is more I enjoy doing it." Such men are usually bores, but Shaw is one of the few to whom the astonished auditor is moved to reply, "Please do."

"Not all great writers are copious, but the very greatest usually have been. Shaw never runs short of ideas, of convictions, or quips—or of words, words, words. His abnormally long plays are preceded by prefaces that are often books in themselves. And to whom except Shaw would it have ever occurred that, having written, in *Man and Superman,* a comedy twice the usual length, and having given it a preface equally long, he might just as well also append to it the whole text of a book (*The Revolutionist's Handbook*) that one of the characters is supposed to have written?

At first it seems odd that there were no plays much like Shaw's in either form or tone before his, and that there have been no successful ones since. It is true that Oscar Wilde wrote comedies that depend almost entirely upon good talk, and also true that new plays are sometimes described by reviewers as "Shavian." But Wilde's are not at all like Shaw's, and "Shavian" usually means no more than an attempt to make entertaining a more or less paradoxical thesis. There are no truly Shavian plays except those Shaw himself wrote because there has never been anyone else who could talk so well in his characteristic way.

"Playboy and Prophet" was the subtitle Archibald Henderson gave to the 1932 version of the biography that Shaw himself authorized (the second of three major biographies of Shaw by Henderson), and it is singularly apt. Though Shaw may have been wholly sincere in his insistence that he was a fundamentally serious man, he was also congenitally a wit—a clown even—who fortunately could never resist an opportunity to be funny even if it meant a temporary derailment of his argument. Nothing exasperated his first audience more than this inveterate frivolity mixed in with his seriousness (and nothing pleases the audience of the present day more than the same mixture).

We are also much more aware than we once were of just how much his bark is worse than his bite. He clipped Nietzsche's claws so effectively that the cult of the Superman comes down to little more than a belief that the man of tomorrow should be gentler and more intelligent than the man of today. Even Karl Marx is so tamed that most of what he teaches is little more than the liberal wing of our own Republican party accepts, and the Revolution Shaw preaches turns out to mean only what can be accomplished at the ballot box. Genuinely puritanical in his insistence that life is real and life is earnest, also, in his distrust of self-indulgence and sensuality, Shaw is certainly one of the oddest of those recurrent cases of a moralist regarded by his contemporaries as dangerously immoral.

There is no other important dramatist from whose plays

sexual misconduct is almost completely absent. *Getting Married* launches a brilliant attack upon marriage, and then ends by defending it. His supposed rakes (as in *Heartbreak House*) usually turn out to be rigorously continent.

The only such paradox he never resolved was his unexpected and persistent defense of at least some aspects of fascism and Communism. That he was by nature a kindly man almost pathologically sensitive to the spectacle of either injustice or pain seems beyond dispute, and it is hard to understand how he could have brushed aside the brutalities of a Mussolini and a Stalin. Perhaps it was only a perverse refusal to agree with any majority at home. Or perhaps he was, for once, the victim of mere theories like those that, in nearly every other case, he rejected whenever they threatened to lead to any actual cruelty or injustice. But he never explained away his distressing tenderness toward two modern tyrannies.

Most popular and highly esteemed artists meet a severe test within one or two generations of their triumph. Just as an ornament or a piece of furniture must be outmoded for a while before it can become an antique, so a great writer often seems out of date before he is recognized as a classic. The first difficult period Shaw seems already to have passed successfully. His plays are revived by professionals and amateurs alike much more frequently than they were fifteen years ago. May he then be certified as "not for an age but for all time"?

Perhaps it is still too soon to say. But the augury is favorable. With the possible exception of Ibsen, no other playwright of the nineteenth or the twentieth century had an impact upon his contemporaries even remotely comparable. And while Shaw continues a vigorous life in the theater, even Ibsen tends to languish there, and most of the others who were once named with Shaw as the great figures in "The New Drama" are all but forgotten.

One question remains. Was he too much a journalist, a pamphleteer, and a preacher, and will he therefore survive only so long as the issues raised in his pamphleteering and his preaching remain alive? Most pamphlets are dull once their theses have been either completely accepted or completely dismissed.

One may cite his own pronouncements either for or against him. Literary works, he once said, may deal with manners, with morals, or with passions. Only the last change so little with the passing of time that they are never outmoded. Hence the enduring interest of the *Iliad* despite the fact that the manners of Homer's characters are unfamiliar and their moral ideas—so at least he contended—repulsive. But since Shaw's own plays deal almost exclusively with manners and, more especially, with morals, he seems to be hoist on his own petard and denied the possibility of that immortality he predicted for himself.

But there is another and more characteristic Shavian argument, and it points in the opposite direction. All great literature, he said, is journalism first, because only the timely has vitality enough to become timeless. Beauty in art and happiness in life are by-products of a commitment too passionately serious to pursue either beauty or happiness as ends in themselves.

To date, at least, it is that thesis, rather than the other, which seems to be justified by the example of his work.

Perhaps the final answer is even simpler. Of a once famous and popular dramatic satire it was said that "it has not wit enough to keep it sweet." But that, I suspect, is precisely what the plays of Shaw do have.

Why not "Methuselah"?

[1954]

No Shaw plays were produced on Broadway during the season just past. That was certainly not because he hasn't been popular in recent years and certainly not because there aren't half a dozen major works not seen here in a generation. The only problem is the problem of choice, and I have an idea that the best choice would be the one that sounds most improbable. Why doesn't some drama quartet—or sextet at most—try *Back to Methuselah?* It could easily be cut down to manageable size now that the old boy is no longer here to come up with his famous "No."

Most of the obvious objections vanish if you think of a reading instead of a conventional presentation. It is true that the Theatre Guild lost money on the first and only American production—unless you adopt the Shavian arithmetic which calculated that the Guild made a tidy profit because the red figure it ended up with was so much smaller than the one it had been prepared to accept. It is also true that Shaw was most uncharacteristically openhanded in the matter of assigning rights because, so he said, no one would ever be fool enough to produce it again. But that was before anyone had proposed to do "Don Juan in Hell" as chamber music. And there was certainly no money lost on that enterprise.

But why *Back to Methuselah?* It is one of the talkiest and one of the most relentlessly philosophical of all the plays. Moreover everybody admits that the middle section is so topical that many of the points have been lost. Who cares what the Garden of Eden was like or about that future which lies ahead "as far as thought can reach"? How relevant is all that?

The best answers to these questions are two others. First, have you read the play lately? Second, just which of Shaw's many plays have audiences found most interesting recently?

In a consideration of the second of these questions, the answer is pretty obvious. The most successful of recent productions have been those which presented Shaw the philosopher and Shaw the argufier, not Shaw the mere popular entertainer. *Man and Superman* had been neglected for more than a generation. Few living American playgoers had ever seen it performed before Maurice Evans brought it to Broadway. The Theatre Guild had persistently passed it over during the whole of its long and admirable career as producer of one Shaw play after another. And it had passed it over because, as one of the directors told me years ago, it was "too heavily loaded with doctrine." Yet the Evans production—minus the Hell scene—had the longest run any Shaw play had ever enjoyed in New York. Then the First Drama Quartet tackled the talkiest, most argumentative section of the whole work and so delighted audiences all over the country that it started the whole vogue of readings.

If that proves what I think it does, namely that there is now a larger audience than ever before for Shaw's philosophy —or for Shaw's notions, if you want to dismiss them as that —then why on earth stop with an exposition which he himself regarded as more or less out of date and as largely superseded by a newer version of the gospel according to St. Bernard?

Because Shaw was so suggestible and so enthusiastic, he gave his contemporaries the impression that he was always running off in several directions at once. Quite frequently he was. At different times he called Samuel Butler's common sense, Bunyan's puritanism, Marx's "dialectical materialism," and Bergson's "creative evolution" the dominant influence on his thought. But what was most original in him was his passionate determination to reconcile all these doctrines with one another and to get at some truth which would include them all. Nowadays our young intellectuals are fond of lamenting the failure of the modern mind to achieve a "synthesis" such as—to use their favorite example—the medieval synthesis of Dante. That was precisely what Shaw was seeking before most of them were born. As a matter of fact, whatever else you may say about *Back to Methuselah*, it manages to reconcile more different ideas than anything since Thomas Aquinas. And if Shaw's ideas really are interesting, it seems a pity to leave his most ambitious attempt to expound them on a shelf from which, I suspect, the work is not often taken down even for private reading.

To an American fundamentalist who once wrote to ask him why he didn't stop all his nonsense and "return to the Bible," Shaw replied by asking which Bible he meant. "I myself," he added, "have written several." Actually he wrote only two—of which *Man and Superman* is the first, *Back to Methuselah* the second.

What the First Drama Quartet gave us is now a half-century old—not very old for a Bible, to be sure, but nevertheless the work of a relatively young and very bumptious man. Until then Shaw had been trying to win an audience with entertaining plays loaded with just so much doctrine as he thought members of this audience would stand for. Now he felt confident enough to give them the works. But he was just emerging from the period during which it had seemed to him that Marx had most of the answers, and into the book which John Tanner is supposed to have written he put the simplest version of Marxism ever formulated: "The only

trouble with the poor is poverty." And yet he was already uncomfortable with the determinism of Marx as well as with
the determinism of Darwin, and uncomfortably convinced
that Man ought to do something for himself, not merely wait
for evolution and the dialectic of matter to do something for
him. Hence Tanner is a Marxian who is also, and somewhat
inconsistently, a believer in the Life Force as the prime
mover in Creative Evolution—meaning evolution with a purpose, with which man may cooperate, rather than evolution
blindly proceeding as it must. The purposefulness of the Life
Force is something which neither Darwin nor Marx had
taken into account, and Tanner had to descend into Hell to
understand it.

Brilliant as it is, "Don Juan in Hell" is nevertheless early
Shaw and early modern age. The man who wrote it had a
good deal of maturing still to do, and the audience for which
it was intended was still living in that almost forgotten Age
of Confidence before World War I. The work is cocky and
glib and less than perfectly clear because neither the preacher
nor his audience had any idea how acute their problems
really were. If "Don Juan in Hell" is interesting still, then
surely we ought to be interested in what twenty more years
of living in a disintegrating world did for the thinking of one
of the most active minds operating in our time.

None of this would mean much if the leading ideas in
Back to Methuselah were not brilliantly dramatized or if
the dialogue did not sparkle and the humor flash. Actually,
by any of these tests, the long section, which begins in the
Garden of Eden and ends when the sons of Adam have
established the main patterns of human behavior, is as brilliantly imagined and as brilliantly executed as anything
Shaw ever wrote. In *Man and Superman* the Don Juan legend
can hardly be twisted into the meaning he is determined to
give it. In *Back to Methuselah,* on the contrary, one of the
best stories in the world lends itself so perfectly to Shavian

reinterpretation that he seems almost to have invented it. Take for example the suggestion that the meaning of death has escaped all previous commentators because they have thought it lay in death itself when, in truth, people die only to make way for those who are to be born. This insistence that not the invention of death, but the invention of birth is the great event of the Garden is one of the finest of all the Shavian paradoxes. In all *Man and Superman* there is no speech so eloquent as that in *Methuselah* on the imagination and the role which it plays in changing the world. Tanner's declamation about the artist is amusing; what is said about the artist in the Garden of Eden is profound.

Saint Joan is the only one of the plays written subsequently in which the decline of Shaw's powers is not painfully evident. This work we have had several times and it is worth having at least that often. But it bears somewhat the same relation to *Methuselah* that *Major Barbara* does to *Man and Superman*—it is, in other words, not a "bible" but the development of one of the themes in the "bible" which preceded it. And for the understanding of Shaw's thought it is not so nearly indispensable.

The title page of *Back to Methuselah* bears the characteristically half-spoofing subtitle "A Metabiological Pentateuch." The adjective, to be found in no dictionary, is the key to the whole. If "metaphysical" means, as it did when Aristotle invented the word, "beyond physics," then "metabiological" means "beyond biology." Let us, says Shaw, not start as Darwin and Marx did, with the assumption that the only known facts are those which concern the behavior of material particles. When you do start with that assumption and explain everything else in terms of them, then you end up with the dismal science of Darwinian and Marxian determinism. Let us start instead with some other facts which we know—but which mechanists disregard—about living organisms. Let us assume that consciousness, imagination, will power, and the thirst after righteousness are the primary, self-evident facts which they really are. If we do start with them, we will emerge with a faith by which men may live instead of a despair by which they can only die. Man is not merely a product of the forces operating upon him. He has the gift of imagination and the gift of will. Thanks to them he can make a world—not merely submit to one.

It is true that Shaw borrowed this protest against Darwinism from Samuel Butler. It is also true that he bolstered it with references to Bergson, whom he seems to have cited more than he studied. But who now reads Butler's *Evolution Old and New?* Who outside professional circles reads Bergson? In more senses than one, Shaw dramatized their ideas. He dramatized them in the sense that he emphasized the difference they made in a thoughtful man's conception of himself and of his relation to the universe in which he lives. He dramatized them also in the more obvious sense that he told a story which conveyed his argument.

By now Shaw's Marxism is pretty platitudinous. By now there are few who haven't heard all his arguments and already accepted or rejected them. But determinism versus free will is a very live issue, even though most people seldom think of it in terms which sound so theological. It is what every disagreement about "what is bound to happen" to civilization, versus the choices which civilization might make, comes down to. It is also what people are really talking about when they argue the importance of "conditioning" versus "character" in determining whether a man will act decently or not. Every dispute between the democracies and the totalitarian states, between the would-be managers of men and the believers in freedom, really turns on that same question.

On the whole, psychology, sociology, and most physical science—at least up to the time of the "new physics"—have tended to support the determinist's position. So too did the naturalistic novel as represented, say, by Theodore Dreiser.

So too, for that matter, did Shaw when he wrote like a Marxian. But *Back to Methuselah* sets all his eloquence and passion and wit against it. My guess is that the contemporary audience which was interested in "Don Juan in Hell" would find Shaw's later version of the debate more exciting and more clearly relevant.

Back to Methuselah filled three whole evenings. But the entire middle section could well be dispensed with. The Old Testament scenes plus, by way of conclusion, just a glimpse into that odd Utopia which lies ahead "as far as thought can reach," would make a full evening. And a very exciting one too.

Will someone please try it?

The poet: Pillar of Ibsenism

[1956]

Just fifty years ago Henrik Ibsen died quietly in Christiania, six years after a stroke had rendered him mentally incompetent. A statue in his honor was standing in the public square, and he was certainly the most famous international man of letters alive at that moment. Birthdays are happier occasions than deathdays, and this year celebrates two—the hundredth anniversary of Bernard Shaw's coming into the world and the two hundredth of Wolfgang Mozart's. But 1956 should also remember a man whose greatness is seldom questioned, whose influence is admittedly immeasurably great, but who, after having been endlessly discussed for a generation, now figures surprisingly little in either the living theater or the discussions of it—at least in the United States.

Ibsen had come very slowly and a long way to the emi-nence, official and otherwise, which he finally reached. Born in a country whose language had no literary standing, and with only an elementary education, he began unpromisingly as a minor journalist and provincial theater director. More-over, his early writing gave little indication of the direction his genius was to take. He was already nearing forty when *Brand* and *Peer Gynt* first revealed something of his pow-ers, and they are not what we now think of as characteristic. He was fifty-one when *A Doll's House* first indicated clearly one aspect of his originality; fifty-three when *Ghosts* started him on the way to international notoriety; sixty-two when *Hedda Gabler,* perhaps his best play, was performed. The mere chronology is astonishing—especially to us Americans of today who have been so long accustomed to a succession of playwrights who do their best work in their twenties or early thirties and proceed, if at all, diminuendo.

Even more astonishing was the transformation of notoriety into fame. We are not wholly unfamiliar with the process; but it has seldom been exemplified in so extreme a form. When *Ghosts* was new, a typical Scandinavian critic apologized for the necessity of discussing so repulsive a work. A typical English one, after the play had had its first London perform-ance, called it "a dirty deed done in public." Of Ibsen it might be said as aptly as it was said of Wagner that he built his reputation out of the bricks thrown at him. But it is difficult to know just when or how the reputation was built. Perhaps the support of Georg Brandes in Scandinavia and of Bernard Shaw in England had something to do with it, though they cannot actually be responsible. Within about fifteen years after the dirty deed done in public, Ibsen was widely referred to even in the English press as an accepted modern classic, and before he died he was, in Norway, one of the chief objects of national pride, pointed out to tourists like an ancient building. Apropos of his state funeral, Alfred Kerr remarked shrewdly: "A demon lived among them but they have buried a grandee." The Enemy of the People had been turned into something which looked distressingly like a stuffed shirt.

Among many young people today, there is, I suspect, some tendency to think of him as precisely that. Historically important of course; but stiff, old-fashioned, perhaps a little dull, as those connected with dead controversies often are. He won the first decisive victory for realism in the drama; he was a liberal even if sometimes an ambiguous one; he brought "modern social problems" into the theater. No doubt, therefore, he deserves to be called The Father of the Modern Drama. But that was a long time ago. And how quaint his paradoxes now seem.

Nora announced that her first duty was not to her children but to herself; instead of returning to the protection of her husband, she went out to make her own way in the world, and, as was said, the slamming of the door behind her was heard round the world. Oswald Alving blasted the respectability of Parson Manders, and his mother proclaimed that "evils grow in the dark." Dr. Stockmann denounced the damn compact majority and announced that "He is strongest who is most alone." But these paradoxes have turned into platitudes. It was Dr. Stockmann himself who said: "Truths are by no means the wiry Methuselahs some people think them. A normally constituted truth lives—let us say—as a rule, seventeen or eighteen years; at the outside twenty; very seldom more. And truths so patriarchal as that are always shockingly emaciated." Just how much life can be expected to remain in the truths enunciated in *A Doll's House* and *Ghosts* some three-quarters of a century ago?

Such disparagements as these cannot be answered on the basis of the premises behind them. "Contemporary social problems," stated strictly in contemporary terms, and so limited by the literalness of the treatment to temporary circumstances that they are relevant only to the moment, cannot be expected to last. In so far as Ibsen's plays were merely pamphlets, they must share the fate of all pamphlets—which is to become uninteresting just to the extent that they successfully make their points. No writer continues to live just because he was so right or so effective. Such reasons may give "historical importance" but they cannot cause him to be read.

The "permanent Ibsen" must be sought somewhere else. To find it one must, I think, dig deep through several layers of reputation, and of these, the reputation as a propounder of certain social questions for his day is the first. What else may one say of him?

One may of course bring up the subject of his once famous technique, with its rejection (after *A Doll's House*) of the methods of "the well-made play" and its large dependence (as in *Ghosts*) upon progressive revelations of the past, so that the action seems to move simultaneously in two directions. We may also remind ourselves that almost alone—certainly more than any one man—he brought drama back into the literary and artistic world so that, for a time at least, those who lived in either world must pay to plays an attention they had not paid for several generations. But both of these considerations again suggest "historical importance." His technique has been learned and absorbed; many dramatists since his time have been taken seriously as literature and as thought. He can be neglected without bringing back either "the well-made play" (what Shaw called Sardoodledom) or the assumption that what is acted in the theater is necessarily remote from either profound thinking or literary merit.

One begins to get a little closer, I think, when one remembers that Ibsen himself was not an Ibsenite. His admirers tried to make him one even after he had slapped them down with the Ibsenite villain in *The Wild Duck*. They were always inquiring which side he was on in this or that controversy, and always getting some version of the famous answer, "My business is to ask questions, not to answer them." Shaw was perhaps the worst offender because his *Quintessence of Ibsenism* (which should have been called the Quintessence of Immature Shavianism) made Ibsen precisely what he was not—a man with a system to sell. Whatever else his refusal to abide his admirers' questions may have meant, it certainly meant that he persisted in thinking of himself as an artist rather than a teacher.

Of course he was "interested in ideas." But he always called himself "a poet," not "a thinker," and he once boasted that he did not have to read the works of his contemporaries because, as a poet, he had the poet's power of absorbing from the air the ideas afloat in the prevalent intellectual atmosphere. On the other hand he believed that there was something properly called "modernity," and that he was very much "a modern." As a matter of fact the tardy but decisive clarification of his intentions seems to have come when he read Brandes' *Main Currents of Nineteenth Century Literature*, of which the thesis was precisely that "modernism" was definable. He wrote Brandes an enthusiastic letter of congratulation expressing his firm agreement. And how many "modern ideas," less specific than the right of the individual to self-realization, the right of women to be persons, the need for frank discussion for forbidden subjects, his plays hold, as it were, in solution. Like Dostoevsky, he was a kind of Freudian—not because he had read Freud, but because, like Freud himself, he breathed an intellectual atsmophere which made Freudianism almost inevitable. Nora in *A Doll's House* has often been called the first classic embodiment of The New Woman, but it is probably more important that Hedda Gabler marks the first definite emergence of The Neurotic as Hero. Characteristically, however, an insight into the workings of the unconscious did not mean for Ibsen, as it did for Freud, a tight system of dogmas. It meant only a recognition of what is sometimes called The Irrational Element in human life, of that element which Strindberg was to exaggerate until it became the only significant element, and which has meant so much in the work of, say, Eugene O'Neill and Tennessee Williams.

Moreover, and perhaps most important of all, Ibsen was always a heretic because he believed that a perpetual proliferation of heresies—rather, heresy which becomes orthodoxy—was the essence of modernity. Freud might turn his heresy into a dogma and, less spectacularly, "liberals" might work toward the establishment of those liberal platitudes which are so tiresomely prevalent today, both in and out of literature. But Ibsen, though he inspired other prophets of modernity, set himself at most crucial points against the orthodoxy into which modernism was tending to develop. Thus he distrusted democracy without, like Shaw, leaning toward any sort of totalitarianism. What is perhaps more important, he remained to the end essentially a moralist, not an economist or a believer in the sole responsibility of society for the state of man. He was a "social critic" only in the sense that he criticized the society which men made, not in that he criticized society for making men what they are. In *Ghosts* the final responsibility is charged, not against the hypocritical respectability of the community in which Mrs. Alving lived, but to Mrs. Alving herself, who lacked until too late the moral courage to disregard the false ideals of the community. And in *Rosmersholm* he faced, as few conventional liberals ever have faced, the question of whether or not it is possible to repudiate the moral absolutes of Western society without, like Rebecca West, embracing the ruthlessness of an unrelieved egotism. He anticipated Freud; he also asked whether or not Nietzsche was inevitable.

If Ibsen was not the propounder of a set of doctrines,

then what was he? A naturalist? Certainly not; for he put on record his contempt for Zola. What then? Why, as he himself always insisted, a poet; a poet whose chief task and most influential achievement was to destroy in the theater one kind of poetry and then to create another.

The curve of his career illustrates how consistently, though perhaps at first unconsciously, he went about his task. He began very conventionally as a romantic nationalist whose announced intention it was to revive the legendary past of his race. *Brand, Peer Gynt,* and *Emperor and Galilean* move away from that juvenile ideal but still carry with them too much suggestive of a convention which Ibsen felt had outlived its usefulness. Verse had to be discarded along with everything which suggests romanticism. And after several half-successful attempts, he achieved in *A Doll's House* a play which seemed stripped of everything except prose, contemporaneity, and a characteristic social situation. But no sooner had he got rid of everything which "poetic" suggests, than he began to enlarge his themes and to give his plays a kind of resonance which *A Doll's House* does not have.

Externally this means the use of symbols, like the burning of the orphanage in *Ghosts.* More important, it means the continual suggestion of implications beyond the specific situation, and the gradual disappearance of anything which could be reduced to a simple "thesis" or be called merely "realistic." *A Doll's House* means just what it says and no more. *Ghosts* suggests as well as says. *The Wild Duck* has become what the French have always considered it, not a realistic play or a social play, but "symbolist drama." *Hedda Gabler* is essentially character study of a new kind, and the subsequent plays come to rely so completely upon symbols and suggestions as sometimes to defeat their purpose.

If there is a permanent Ibsen (and I think there is), it is Ibsen the dramatist who passed through realism to achieve a new kind of poetry for the theater. And is it not precisely this new kind of poetry which the most interesting contemporary dramatists are still trying to find?

O'Neill the inevitable

[1954]

There are, of course, some things which only time can tell. But time cannot change one fact: O'Neill is the only man without whose name playwriting in twentieth-century America cannot possibly be discussed.

Half a dozen other dramatic writers may seem to most people "important." Several of them may seem to certain persons "better." But even among such there is no general agreement *which* was better or whether any given one actually was. Moreover, O'Neill is the inevitable writer with whom the other must be compared.

You may cite him to prove how good or how bad his own work is; you may cite him to illustrate how good or how bad American playwriting has been. But you cannot leave him out, and there is no one of his contemporaries of which the same can be said. He imposes himself upon even the most unwilling. Eric Bentley, for example, does not admire him, but in his most recent book Bentley finds it necessary to devote a chapter to explaining why he does not. And there is no other American playwright who creates that same obligation. Old-fashioned dramatists used to talk about "the obligatory scene." For critics O'Neill is the obligatory subject.

I happen to believe, and have from the very beginning,

that the absolute merits are very considerable—specifically that in certain of his plays he has at least come closer than any other American, closer perhaps than any contemporary European, to recapturing for a modern audience what, for want of a more precise term, we have to call the Tragic Sense. I believe also that he was able to do this partly because— unlike Ibsen or Shaw, greater though they were in certain respects—he was able to communicate the Tragic Sense with emotional directness rather than via the bypaths of intellectual analysis and sociological preachment.

Even so, I still prefer to assert his right to a preeminent position in American drama on the basis of facts more objectively demonstrable. He was the first native playwright to win from any large general public a recognition of his right to be as serious, as bold, and as ambitious as he felt the desire to be; to say to that public, "There is nothing absurd in the fact that one of your contemporary fellow countrymen is frankly asking you to take him as seriously as any playwright of any time was ever taken."

Every American dramatist since owes to him the fact that the right to make a similar demand is recognized. And whatever else one of them may or may not owe him, to whatever extent he may or may not be "influenced" by O'Neill, he has open a path which O'Neill first cleared. It was O'Neill who wrote and who successfully demanded recognition for the American playwright's declaration of independence and charter of liberty.

Genius is better than talent

[1954]

The two paradoxes of Eugene O'Neill are the almost unbelievable difference in quality between individual plays, and a certain technical clumsiness in even the best of them. If you judge him by the average of his achievement or if you value at too high a rate mere deftness of construction and smoothness of dialogue, you are bound to underestimate him as many of this generation do. He had, as I have never doubted, a measure of real genius, but he was curiously devoid of talent—if by that you mean the kind of workman's competence which very small as well as very great artists sometimes are blessed with, along with their genius. Bernard Shaw once called him "a banshee Shakespeare," and there is a kind of unfair truth in the phrase. But genius can get along without talent, desirable as talent may be even for a genius, and O'Neill did get along without it.

Both of these paradoxes are glaringly illustrated in *A Moon for the Misbegotten,* which is scheduled to have its first New York production this season by a new repertory group, The Ensemble, after being withdrawn following a Midwestern tryout in 1947. It has a few powerful scenes and a few flashes of memorable dialogue. But it is certainly not one of his best plays, and the over-all execution is cruder than in some quite early works like *Desire Under the Elms* (which is one of the best) or *The Hairy Ape* (which is prentice work). Though *A Moon for the Misbegotten* was completed at least eleven years ago, and therefore at a time when the illness which gradually incapacitated him may have begun to have its effect, there is no real reason for invoking that explanation. Throughout his career O'Neill alternated fine plays with vastly inferior ones. *Dynamo* was produced between *Strange Interlude* and *Mourning Becomes Electra*. And though he was always too passionately absorbed in whatever he was doing at the moment to be capable of self-judgment, he usually accepted the public's reaction and, when it was unfavorable, turned without rancor to something else. Had life and health been granted him, he might well have gone on to write something greater than he had ever written before. But it would be a mistake to claim that this most recent of all his plays accessible in any form to the public will add much to his reputation.

The story, hardly more than an anecdote, is one of the least complicated in its action that he ever used. The central character, a rebellious, passionate Irish girl so scornful of her own lack of feminine charm that she gives herself promiscuously to men whom she despises, attracts the attention of a debauched neighbor who is financially, if not socially, far above her. To her father's suggestion that she trap him into a marriage, she seems to agree. But her real, only half-acknowledged hope is that they will discover in one another something worth having at the bottom of that abyss into which both fell long ago. She keeps with him a rendezvous on her moonlit porch to which he comes drunk from a bar. All he really wants from her is the illusion that he has found that "purity" which, in his maudlin state, he thinks he wants. She lets him sleep out his drunken sleep on her breast and in the morning contemptuously sends him away. It is too late for either to find salvation in one another or, for that matter, anywhere else.

In many respects this is merely *Anna Christie* with an unhappy ending instead of a happy one. And, again like *Anna Christie*, it is one of the few O'Neill plays in which the emphasis is on the story of the individual characters rather than upon the large general implications of that story. But the milieu, the atmosphere, the themes, the motives, and the psychological determinants are all familiar parts of O'Neill's world. The action takes place not in the lower but in the very lowest depths, the contemplation of which seems—as in *The Iceman Cometh*—to have fascinated O'Neill even more in later life than it had at the beginning of his career. When the girl says of her grotesque lover, "He only acts like he's hard and shameless to get back at life when it's tormenting him," she is saying precisely what Dion Anthony in *The Great God Brown* said of himself, and what was said or implied of many another O'Neill character. When the lover in the course of his drunken maunderings reveals his overmastering sense of guilt, which has come to center itself around his memory of the night when he caroused with a slut on the train carrying his mother's corpse home to burial, we are again in a familiar world. And as in so many of the other plays, the more or less Freudian explaining away of remorse and guilt is less significant than the fact that the remorse and guilt are so strong and so destructive. For all his professed scorn of the Puritan sense of sin, O'Neill himself was obviously ridden by it.

Over and over again his characters dream of some pagan innocence and of idyllic sensuality uncorrupted by either prohibitions or inhibitions. But they find only depravity, and in the midst of that depravity they begin to be obsessed by an ideal of purity which is based not upon innocence but upon the self-denial that appears also as a form of corruption. As far back as *Diff'rent*, written in 1920, the returned seaman who had visited Paradise in the South Seas shocks his betrothed, who then pays the penalty of her squeamishness by being compelled to cheapen herself in vain when she tries to captivate a coarse and brutal youth. O'Neill's New Englanders can never bring the islands back with them, can neither find nor cease to desire what those islands stand for in their imaginations.

Nearly everything in *A Moon for the Misbegotten* which approaches the best of which O'Neill is capable is concentrated in the very short last act. It is morning on the porch. The father, come to see how his scheme has worked, enters. "The two make a strangely tragic picture in the wan dawn light—this big sorrowful woman hugging a haggard-faced, middle-aged drunkard against her breast, as if he were a sick child." There is nothing, the girl tells her father, to see. "Nothing at all. Except a great miracle they'd never believe, or you either . . . a virgin who bears a dead child in the night, and the dawn finds her still a virgin. If that isn't a miracle, what is?" And this ending is probably truer than the ending of *Anna Christie*. As the girl herself realizes, it is far, far too late to redeem her lover. "It was my mistake. I thought there was still hope. I did not know that he'd died already—that it was a damned soul coming to me in the moonlight, to confess and be forgiven and find peace for a night." There follows a passage in which the father curses the drunken suitor and then, speaking for all O'Neill characters, says: "I didn't mean it. . . . It was life I was cursing." The daughter, ready to begin with a certain cheerfulness to get her father his breakfast, turns back to the still sleeping lover with this final speech: "May you have your wish and die in your sleep soon, Jim, darling. May you rest forever in forgiveness and peace."

No doubt there are those who will feel that even in this scene, as in so many others, O'Neill overdoes the violence of the contrast between the seeming depravity of his characters and the perverted nobility which he finds in them; that the tragedy would be more effective if that nobility were more easily perceived by the ordinary eye. Perhaps they are right. But there is no use asking of O'Neill a moderation of which he was not capable, and when he is at his best we accept his premises because we must. If all of *A Moon for the Misbegotten* were as good as this last scene, the play would be worthy to stand among his best. Unfortunately and for a number of reasons, it is not.

One cause for the weakness of the whole may be simply that the story as plotted is hardly long enough for a full-length play. A great deal of time is taken up with somewhat repetitious exposition and byplay between father and daughter which does not succeed too well in justifying the only excuse which could be made for it, namely, the establishment of atmosphere. O'Neill is decidedly not one of those writers who can kill time gracefully, and there are many passages which seem no more than quite inexpert padding. Unquestionably a good many of them could be simply struck out in an acting script, but unfortunately, not a little of the necessary exposition is surprisingly clumsy, very amateurish in its obviousness. Even in the next to the last act, which is already building toward the achieved climax of the last scene, O'Neill is capable of the banality of "You'd hate me and yourself" put into the mouth of the reluctant lover. And there are scenes in which father and daughter tell one another things they already know almost as brazenly as such characters used to in the old melodramas. Professor Baker's famous course is sometimes given credit for O'Neill's success, but it is obvious that while his virtues are those which can never be learned, he never learned at college or anywhere else the things which can be taught.

Many years ago Mark Van Doren wrote an essay—often quoted since—in which he defended the paradox that The Poet is a man not more but less sensitive than his fellows. Emotions overwhelm the ordinary man into inarticulateness, but The Poet, feeling less intensely than he, can order and express his emotions, give shape to his discourse, and seek the right word. Perhaps the paradox of O'Neill is to be resolved in a similar way; perhaps that is why he seems to have a kind of genius while he is devoid of the talent so many lesser men are blessed with.

No one who ever knew him failed to have personal acquaintance confirm what his plays suggest; namely, the fact that he was obsessed, dominated, tormented, and hag-ridden by the passions which he tried to express in his plays. The vulture tore at his liver, and playwriting was less a career than a desperate necessity. He never had peace enough to learn very well even the tricks of the trade, much less to practice the art of meticulous revision. To say this is not to claim that his faults are virtues. But it is enough to suggest how it can be that the faults are not fatal. A score of recent American playwrights know how to avoid his crudities. Not one can produce the impact which his sincerity produces. And if you can't have both, genius is better than talent.

Eugene O'Neill's claim to greatness: A review of "A Touch of the Poet"

[1957]

Bernard Shaw once called Eugene O'Neill "a banshee Shakespeare." And that, as the historically minded will remember, is precisely what Voltaire called Shakespeare. Moreover Shaw's remark was not intended to be entirely uncomplimentary and neither, for that matter, was Voltaire's. A banshee Shakespeare is still some kind of Shakespeare and "a barbarian genius" (Voltaire's phrase) is still some kind of genius.

Certain American critics, on the other hand, have hurled the insult without the qualifying compliment. Eric Bentley, after calling O'Neill "the Broadway intelligentsia's patron saint" and after explaining how hard he has tried to like him, winds up by saying that O'Neill cannot write and cannot think. To Mary McCarthy his "lack of verbal gift was a personal affliction that became a curse to the American stage" and the most important conclusion to be drawn from *The Iceman Cometh* is that "you cannot write a Platonic dialogue in the style of 'Casey at the Bat.' "

Obviously, then, O'Neill, if not witty himself, is, like Falstaff, the occasion of wit in others. And Edwin Engle, whose *The Haunted Heroes of Eugene O'Neill* is the only recent book-length study concludes: "O'Neill's style remained not only strained and turgid, but awkward, inarticulate, banal."

Of Theodore Dreiser's "style" much the same sort of things have been said, but among critics of general literature there has been, for some reason, more readiness to forgive in him what only those specifically concerned with the theater have excused in O'Neill. And the reply of the former has been usually that his defenders were, in Miss McCarthy's phrase, "propagating the theory that a playwright was not subject to the same standards as other writers, the theory, in other words, that the theater is an inferior art."

It is true that Mr. Bentley goes so far as to admit that an O'Neill play "comes out of a bigger head" than that of certain other contemporary playwrights and that Miss McCarthy speaks grudgingly of "the element of transcendence jutting up woodenly—like a great homemade Trojan horse." But the conclusion of both can be summed up in Miss McCarthy's words: "O'Neill belongs to that group of American authors, which includes Farrell and Dreiser, whose choice of vocation was a kind of triumph and catastrophe; none of these men possessed the slightest ear for the word, the sentence, the speech, the paragraph . . . how is one to judge the great logical symphony of a tone-deaf musician?"

In the case of Shakespeare the final answer to Voltaire was given by that consensus of opinion which alone is capable of giving a final answer in artistic matters. Audiences are often wrong for a time. They often fail to appreciate novel excellences and they are often misled by mere fashion. But in the long run they are right—if only because, as some say, there is no other definition of what being right means. And it may be that the astonishingly vigorous O'Neill revival now in progress is posterity giving its decision. At least, if this seems a premature conclusion, it is a demonstration of O'Neill's power to interest a new audience which is far more significant than his first success for the simple reason that it demonstrates his ability to gain a second hearing in the contemporary theater, where second hearings are extremely rare. Has any other American playwright ever enjoyed anything comparable to the present revival?

To suggest that posterity may even now be proving wrong those critics who have been saying "This will never do" is not to suggest that posterity will call O'Neill a great stylist or list verbal felicity among his virtues. It is to say only that it may well recognize his continued triumph over the defects which his recent critics have exaggerated into intolerability.

As a matter of fact his most ardent admirers have, from the beginning, not only recognized but stressed them. Reviewing the first production of *Mourning Becomes Electra,* the present writer made this comment:

> The one thing missing is language . . . Take, for example, the scene in which Orin stands beside the bier of his father . . . What one longs for with an almost agonizing longing is something not merely good but magnificent, something like "Tomorrow, and Tomorrow and Tomorrow" or "I could a tale unfold whose lightest word" . . . But no such language does come and *Mourning Becomes Electra* remains, therefore, only the best tragedy in English which the present century has pro-

duced. This is the penalty we pay for living in an age whose most powerful dramatist cannot rise above prose.

Or consider the parody written by Lee Simonson who designed some of the sets for O'Neill's plays, was one of the directors of the Theater Guild, and, what is more important, an admirer and personal friend. In his book *The Stage is Set* he published this version of a Hamlet soliloquy as he imagined that O'Neill might write it:

> God! If I could only kill myself—get away from it all. There's nothing to live for. I'm afraid! Afraid to do anything. Afraid of death. Spooks. What they told me when I was a kid. (*Looking at the snowman*) I'm just so much mush—mush like you. . . . If I could only thaw with you tomorrow—thaw, just dissolve, trickle into the earth—run off into the sewer.

This is the kind of parody which one conventionally calls "deadly." It is no more unjust than parody has a right to be. But Mr. Simonson did not think that it was deadly and he certainly did not want it to be. "Parody," as Oscar Wilde replied to Gilbert's *Patience*, "is the tribute which mediocrity pays to genius." It takes no great gifts to see what is wrong with O'Neill. But not all the witty are clever enough to recognize sufficiently, as Simonson also did, what is right with him. In the classroom I used always to read this parody and it never failed to get its laugh. But I never knew any student to dismiss O'Neill because of it.

On occasion he can write almost as badly as his detractors say. Not always of course and he has passages powerful simply as writing, though even in them one does not think primarily of writing in the technical sense. And the case for him is best made by admitting his defects. He used dialect a great deal and he had so little ear for it that good actors always made it better than he had written it. There are seldom any subtle overtones, never that kind of ambiguity now so much admired. And it is, I think, worth noting that with

the exception of the not especially notable "That old debbel
sea" he invented no phrase which passed into current speech,
even temporarily or even derisorially. Though I think he is
likely to be longer remembered than, say, Tennessee Williams he had nothing comparable to the Williams gift
(shared by Erskine Caldwell) for the vocabulary, the syntax,
and the rhythm of Southern speech.

Why then does a new generation brought up in the theater
on the neurotic subtlety of Williams turn appreciatively
again to O'Neill? What quality has he that is lacking in, to
take another example, the whole contemporary French school
of which Jean Anouilh is the best known representative? Like
Williams the members of that school are, in a sense, tragic
writers and certainly writers of a more sophisticated sort. Perhaps this is, in itself, one of the answers. In Anouilh the subtlety, the wit, and the gift for words are astonishing. So too are
the endless involutions of a mind always turning back upon itself and, as it were, dying in convulsions. The subtlety is self-
destructive, leaving nothing except emptiness when the last
ingenious twist has been performed. His plays seem to hope
for nothing more than a display of the author's skill at playing
an intellectual game. And perhaps Americans are essentially
too serious (too unsophisticated if you insist) to accept the conclusion that the Pursuit of Truth is no more than a game.
They are unwilling to look for the black cat in the dark cellar
unless they believe that it may just possibly be there. O'Neill
can be deeply involved in genuine passion because he is not
merely playing a game which exhibits his skill. He can be
black enough at times and on occasion actually tumble into
the nihilism against which he perpetually struggled. Though
there may be more faith in honest doubt, etc., "honest doubt"
is never complacent doubt. And O'Neill is never complacent,
never other than deeply involved. Man emerges from the
bludgeoning he receives in the plays with his essential dignity
intact. He is a creature worthy of respect. That can hardly be

said of the plays of either Williams or Anouilh. And it may be that the present generation has found him stimulating for precisely that reason.

Mere sincerity of intention is, of course, not enough. As one of Shaw's characters remarks, "Behind every bad poem lies a perfectly genuine emotion." Bentley has the same thing in mind when he jibes at the "recent rehabilitator" of O'Neill which is "taking the will for the deed" and "applauding O'Neill for strengthening the pavement of hell." But there is a fallacy in the argument or at least in its application. It is not merely a question of high intention versus lesser achievement. The crucial question is "To what extent and in what way is one aware of good intentions, of that genuine emotion behind a less than perfect poem. Is it merely that the author *says* he has high intentions, that he tells you *about* them? Or is it that you actually perceive them in the work itself? If the second is true then more than merely the intention is present. I have read no detraction of O'Neill whose author did not seem slightly uneasy, who did not somewhere concede more than he safely could. O'Neill's first audiences did a great deal more than concede and so do the new audiences to many of whom he is a new discovery. Whatever his other limitations as a writer he had the writer's one indispensable gift. He "communicated"—the situation, the characters, and above all the depth of his concern with them. That is not everything but it is enough.

Somerset Maugham once declared that all the great novelists—Balzac, Dickens, and Dostoevsky, for example—"wrote badly." He did not say that the novels were great because they were badly written or that no writer is both a great stylist and great in other ways besides. He did suggest that, as novelists, his favorites were superior to the Flauberts and the Jameses whom another school admires so much more because Balzac and Dickens and Dostoevsky had important virtues that Flaubert and James lacked and that, instead of torturing themselves in the vain attempt to "get a style," they wrote what they had it in them to write. An O'Neill who wrote better could have been a better O'Neill. But he will last longer and mean more than many who can, in any ordinary sense, write rings around him.

Long day's journey into greatness: A review of "O'Neill" by Arthur and Barbara Gelb

[1962]

This is a giant of a book—almost a thousand pages of fact, opinion, anecdote, and quotation. It is the product of an enormous assiduity, but also of a remarkable gift for organization. What might have been an indigestible mass is a coherent narrative giving a clear picture of the often confused career of a confused man who happened to be also a genius.

Arthur Gelb, a drama reporter for the *Times,* and his wife Barbara spent six years in the preparation of this new O'Neill biography and interviewed some four hundred persons who had direct or indirect connection with the playwright, his family, his friends, or his associates. They have also consulted all the available documents, searched magazines and newspapers, analyzed the plays and traced the history of their production and of the various critical judgments passed upon them. No other American playwright—few if any other American writers of any kind—have had their whole careers so thoroughly explored. Had the authors not begun as they did, just in the nick of time, much that they learned would have been lost forever. The mystery of personality and of talent must, of course, remain somewhat mysterious, but it is not likely that we shall ever know much more than we do now of what is knowable about Eugene O'Neill. And it is fortunate that he happens to have been a man whose story is a fascinating, if often painful, one.

Another reason why this book is so absorbing is the completeness with which it pictures the various milieus in which its hero acted out his role: the theatrical world of his famous father, the actor, James O'Neill; his own exploration of the various lower depths he persistently sought out; and, of course, the world which he somewhat reluctantly entered when he became the most famous and successful of our playwrights.

The cast of characters is enormous and many of them are sharply drawn. Some are totally unknown to fame; some are Bohemian figures whose once shadowy notoriety has almost evaporated, while others have had subsequent histories of their own worth remembering. Here, for instance, are such minor denizens of the Greenwich Village Bohemia as Polly Holliday and Frank Shay; writers who belong in a way to history like Alfred Kreymborg and Mike Gold; other men like John Reed and George Bellows, who are still vividly remembered. Here also are the dazzling Louise Bryant, the spectacular Mabel Dodge and Dorothy Day, who abandoned Bohemia to become the present head of the Catholic Worker Movement. Nearly all of those who survived also contribute something to the portrait of a man who somehow impressed everyone he met, even in the days when he seemed determined to die in the gutter.

Before the publication of the confessedly autobiographical *Long Day's Journey Into Night,* it was already generally recognized that there were autobiographical elements in certain of O'Neill's plays. One of the many contributions of the critical portions of the Gelbs' book is the convincing demonstration that even those plays which seem to be remote in theme—even *All God's Chillun Got Wings,* for example—were often related to personal experiences. Few men have ever been more deeply involved in the passions their works depict.

Some vulture was perpetually tearing at Eugene O'Neill's vitals. It drove him into adolescent debauchery far more serious than that customarily achieved by "wild" youths. It motivated his various flights and pursued him into the oblivion which he sought for years in drink, promiscuity, and the companionship of the most completely lost souls he could find in such abodes of the damned as the appropriately named Hell Hole Saloon. What was this vulture? How did it most improbably happen that he saved himself from the early death which seemed inevitable, and instead successfully resolved to create rather than destroy?

O'Neill was never psychoanalyzed "in depth." He did, however, have a brief session with one analyst—and other psychiatrists have offered psychological interpretations that the authors of this book quote. Yet the Gelbs themselves wisely refrain from glib explanations, and what the professionals have to offer amounts to little more than easy references to "the death wish," "the love-hate relationship," and so forth. It has been said, for instance, that O'Neill suffered a trauma from which he never recovered when, as a child, he was suddenly removed from the warmth of a family life to a boarding school where he was unhappy. But thousands of children have undergone a similar painful experience without becoming either debauchees or geniuses, and there remains at least the question why, in this case, the wound was so deep.

O'Neill himself seems to have laid the blame on his father's selfishness, his mother's weakness, and the corrupt influence of his brother, Jamie. Perhaps all these things were factors. The Gelbs, however, make clear that the picture of the father in *Long Day's Journey Into Night* is less than fair and that Eugene himself was not free from precisely the defects for which he bitterly reproached James O'Neill. The latter may have been somewhat less than lavish in supplying his son with money, but he did take him back into favor again and again long after the patience of many fathers would have been exhausted. Eugene, too, was extravagant at times, rather close at others; and no one could have called him a conspicuously "good father" to the three children of whom he saw little and of whose behavior he was far from tolerant. His daughter he disowned when she made what he regarded as an unsuitable marriage with Charlie Chaplin; the eldest of his children, Eugene, Jr., killed himself.

A family doomed, like members of the House of Atreus, is a theme which appears again and again in O'Neill's plays. Perhaps that is an explanation as satisfactory and as unsatisfactory as any. But the greatest mystery of all is that of this doomed family only one was doomed to greatness.

That he loved and hated the same things, that he aspired to and fled from the same convictions and ideals is obvious enough. He adored women and despised them; he longed for purity and sought defilement; he loved life and hated it; he sought God and blasphemed. Yet it seems oversimple to be content, as one psychiatrist was, to reduce all this to the single fact that he both loved and hated his father. The unresolved ambivalences were everywhere. And it seems to me that even the Gelbs do not stress sufficiently the significance of the fact that this man who so persistently sought out and so persistently romanticized the lower depths nevertheless found the only woman whom he could endure for long in a wife who came from the world of wealth and elegance, whose tastes were not only respectable but aristocratic, and who induced him to lead an orderly, even a physically lavish life. His favorite characters were prostitutes and derelicts, but the woman to whom he stayed married had played in *The Hairy Ape* the role of the elegant passenger who represented everything his hero despised.

None of these facts and theories would be of more than curious interest if O'Neill had not been an extraordinarily powerful writer, despite all the limitations that finicky critics have emphasized. What kind of powerful writer was he? One is tempted, of course, to put him in that convenient category occupied by the *poet maudite* but he does not fit quite comfortably there. Despite all his interest in the rebel, the outcast, and the derelict, he never quite succeeded in equating good and evil. There is not much of sheer perversity in his work. He undertook no radical transvaluation of values; though he sometimes fell into a nihilistic despair, he never rested there for long. He was a perpetual seeker after what he could not find and what, at times, he denied the reality of.

It is such facts as these which make O'Neill neither a "decadent" nor fit company for the Becketts, the Ionescos, or even the Tennessee Williamses of today's theater. Quite properly, the Gelbs balance their account of both the disorder of his early life and the gloom of his plays with statements of his own and opinions of some of those who knew him. To Dorothy Day it seemed that the love which he failed to find, and for which he longed, was not the love of his father, but the love of God. What he feared, she said, was death; and he feared that because he could not believe that it was not final. And he himself, in explicit statements, attributed the "sickness of today" to an absence of belief in God.

Strindberg and Nietzsche were two of the most powerful influences upon him and in denying, as he always did, that he was a hater or denier of life, O'Neill always fell back

upon some version or other of the thesis, "Life is good because it is painful." As early as 1923, he wrote to the nurse
who had cared for him during his bout with tuberculosis:

> I know you're impervious to what they are pleased to call my
> pessimism. I mean, that you can see behind that superficial as-
> pect of my work to the truth. I'm far from being a pessimist. I
> see life as a gorgeously ironical, beautifully indifferent, splen-
> didly suffering bit of chaos, the tragedy of which gives Man a
> tremendous significance, while without his losing fight with fate
> he would be a tepid, silly animal. I say "losing fight" only sym-
> bolically, for the brave individual always wins. Fate can never
> conquer his—or her—spirit. So you see, I'm no pessimist. On
> the contrary, in spite of my scars, I'm tickled to death with life.

If it is a fact that O'Neill was not a decadent and that he
would have refused to accept the fashionable existentialist
pronouncement that life is merely "absurd," it is that fact
which also makes him in certain other respects more a con-
tinuer of the classic tradition of tragedy than a forerunner
of the contemporary school of existential surrealism. It is
because of the same fact that some younger writers find him
old-fashioned—even though Tennessee Williams, for example, has praised him as the founder of serious American
drama.

Fortunately, it is not necessary to "understand" O'Neill's
character or indeed even to "understand" his plays in order
to be moved by them. He is one of those writers whose greatness does not depend upon the correctness, or, for that matter, upon the consistency of his ideas, but upon his power
to project images and to communicate emotions.

In their book, the Gelbs quote from my review (which
I had quite forgotten) for *The Nation* of the first performance of *Desire Under the Elms*. I shall repeat a few lines of
it here since they seem to me to sum up as well as anything
what little of significance I can say concerning the nature of
O'Neill's greatness:

In this age of intellectualized art, there is an inevitable but unfortunate tendency to assume of Eugene O'Neill . . . that his greatness must lie somehow in the greatness or the charity of his thought; to seek in *All God's Chillun* some solution of the problem of race, or in *The Hairy Ape* some attitude toward society. . . . The meaning and unity of his work lies not in any controlling intellectual idea and certainly not in a "message," but merely in the fact that each play is an experience of extraordinary intensity.

And now—"Hughie"

[1959]

Hughie (Yale University Press $3) is another heretofore unpublished—and, until recently, unsuspected—play by Eugene O'Neill. Its all-round excellence is also another gratifying surprise. Because it is only a longish one-act and also on a more restricted theme, it cannot have the importance of *Long Day's Journey Into Night*. But it is again a real addition to the canon.

Posthumous works are rather rarely that. Usually they are either something written after the powers of their authors had begun to decline or early works that the authors wisely withheld. Those who take advantage of a writer's death in such cases often do him a disfavor. It was Meredith, I think, who dreaded what "the ghouls" would dig up when he was no longer there to stop them, and Max Beerbohm once wondered at the mental processes of collectors who loved nothing so much as books of which they could say,

"These are the very pages which The Master hoped no one would ever see." But *Long Day's Journey* added substantially to O'Neill's reputation and helped turn the tide that had been running against his reputation. *Hughie,* relatively slight though it is, will stand high among his short works.

The brief, tight-lipped note on the jacket says only: *"Hughie,* the only surviving manuscript from a series of eight one-act monologue plays that O'Neill planned in 1940, was completed in 1941. Its world premiere at the Royal Dramatic Theatre in Stockholm, on September 18, 1958, was highly praised by Sweden's leading drama critic, Ebbe Linde, who wrote of it, 'We have watched a performance of O'Neill's finest short play.' " Probably we shall not have to wait long for a New York production, and it is a little difficult to understand why O'Neill himself did not release the play. There are no obvious personal reasons like those that explain his unwillingness to make *Long Day's Journey* public. The central character may have been based to some extent upon his brother Jamie. He calls delirium tremens "the Brooklyn Boys," and we know that was Jamie's phrase. But there is no obvious biographical or autobiographical element.

The time is between 3 and 4 A.M. in the summer of 1928. The scene is the lobby of one of those shabby and dubious small hotels on a West Side street in mid-town New York, not far from Broadway. The only two characters are the bored and hopeless night clerk who has never been anything else, and a very seedy, very small-time horse player—a minor, unsuccessful chiseler who knows in his heart that he is not the glamorous wise guy he would like to persuade someone that he is.

The first few minutes of the play are pure genre: a vivid and economically established atmosphere created by the so immediately recognizable hotel, the sleepy clerk who neither wants nor hopes for anything except to be left in dreary peace, the jumpy wise guy who cannot face either himself or the empty squalor of his room until he has strutted for a few minutes in his role in front of someone who will at least pretend to believe that it is not a role but the truth.

Then a small story begins to emerge. The clerk is a new one, taking the place of the wise guy's old audience, the recently deceased Hughie, who for years had been the necessary ear. Gradually one becomes aware that the binge from which the gambler is just recovering was not set off by bad luck that is becoming chronic, nor by his fear of the tough customers to whom he owes money that he knows he cannot pay. It was set off by Hughie's death and the realization that he had lost the only person who would believe his lies and thereby enable him to do without the respect for himself that he lost long ago. Can the new clerk be cajoled or hypnotized into a reliable performer of the same function?

The situation looks far from hopeful. In many respects the new clerk is much like his predecessor; he even looks much like Hughie. But he has sunk even deeper into apathy. He is obviously not even listening most of the time. Brought almost to desperation, the gambler begins to tell something like the truth. His winnings—even when occasionally real— were not the big winnings Hughie gladly believed in. The "dolls" with whom he spent the night were not beauties from the *Follies* but tramps who demanded ten dollars and usually got two dollars. Fortunately the clerk is not paying much more attention to these confessions than he had paid to earlier boasts. And then a spark is struck. The clerk does have a hero, and he reveals the hero's identity in a reference to a famous gambler: "Do you know Arnold Rothstein?" The gambler in the play almost misses the opening. Just in time he sees it. Five minutes later he is saved. The clerk has become another Hughie. The act has again the believing audience without which the player cannot survive.

Obviously this is another version of one of O'Neill's

favorite themes, the Life Illusion. His gambler would have been quite at home in the saloon of *The Iceman Cometh*. And yet *Hughie* is novel in treatment if not in theme. For one thing, it is more restrained, more compact, without the repetitiousness of *The Iceman*. In fact, I doubt that any other O'Neill play makes its points as effectively with so little lost motion. One does not usually speak of his craftsmanship in any ordinary sense; indeed, one hardly notices the fact that it is often rather clumsy. But *Hughie* is well made in every respect, including even the handling of the dialogue of illiterate speakers, and that is something O'Neill seldom did very well, so far as the printed page is concerned. More important and more striking is the fact that the difficult task of sustaining interest and belief through thirty pages in which only two characters appear is very successfully accomplished. And though the clerk has relatively little to say, he emerges as a solid character and by no means a mere feeder.

If, as the jacket says, *Hughie* was completed in 1941, that would place it as exactly contemporaneous with *Long Day's Journey*, whose dedication is dated July 22, 1941. During his lifetime O'Neill was to have only one more play produced on Broadway (*The Iceman Cometh*); yet, from the evidence of the two works completed in 1941, it may be suspected that he was actually just reaching the maturity of his powers. Or at least that he was mastering the techniques of playwriting to a degree he had never attained before.

It is no doubt profitless to guess what he might have done had his health not given way, but certainly these two plays do not suggest that the work of which he might have been capable was all accomplished. It is also tempting to speculate on the possible meaning of the fact that both *Hughie* and *Long Day's Journey* are (except for the unusual length of the second) essentially conventional in method and seem to suggest that, though O'Neill had experimented with so many unconventional theatrical devices, he might have begun to feel that he had mastered his art to the extent that he no longer needed them. There have always been those to maintain—Bernard Shaw was one of them—that, though "experimental" techniques are perfectly legitimate when the playwright does not know how to do without them, the fact nevertheless remains that the maturest works of the greatest dramatists suggest that the classic forms are the best when the knowledge of how to use them fully has been acquired.

We should be grateful to the Yale Press for giving us the posthumous plays in handsome form. But one little complaint may be permitted. Were we not told that *Long Day's Journey* was the only hitherto unknown play available? Was it not then whispered that another was scheduled for production in Sweden? Now here is *Hughie*. Is the Press discovering things it did not know, or is it simply playing its cards very close to the chest? If so, that seems hardly fair to a public with an eager and legitimate interest in O'Neill. Is *Hughie* really "the only surviving manuscript from a series of eight one-act monologue plays"?

IV

THE WORLD WE DIDN'T MAKE

Miracles to show your child

[1962]

Dear Suburbanite,

You have taken your children out of the city; but have you taken them into anything else?

What interests and opportunities and experiences do they have that the urban child is denied? Do they know that the world of nature is at their doorstep? Have they established any contact with it, or do they lead a merely city life outside the legal limits of the city?

Jokers twit you with having escaped from one rat race only to get into another. The suburban cocktail party and the suburban P.T.A. aren't, so they say, so very different from the metropolitan. Your reply is that at least the children have advantages. How many of them do they really get?

By nature and by instinct the child's earliest interests are in the earth and its living creatures. He reaches out his arms toward the moon, and he clutches the woolly bear we give him in his cradle. He cries out with delight at the first sight of a dog or a cat because he recognizes that this is the world into which he was born and of which he is a part. Unfortunately his joy is one from which the busy and demanding world will try to wean him. He may or he may not recover it—as some do—and he may as an adult find in it his deepest satisfactions and consolations. But there is no reason why he should ever lose it at all, and of the advantages which we are so anxious to give our children none is more valuable than a chance to let its love of nature grow instead of wither.

For both good and ill this is an age of science and technology. We boast of the extent to which we have learned nature's laws and how she may be manipulated and conquered. This is the business of the biologist and the physicist. But for those of us who are neither, "knowledge about" the natural world is less important than appreciation of its beauties and its wonders. The only soil out of which such an appreciation can grow is love. That is what the infant is prepared to give when he clutches his teddy bear. It is also what I would advise any parent to encourage first, and that kind of interest in nature is likely to begin with a pet and most likely to become a joy and consolation.

Into the smallest child's room I would put at least a goldfish in a bowl or a parakeet in a cage, and I would remember that no child is afraid of any animal unless he has learned the fear from an adult. Don't recoil from a harmless garter snake, and don't say "ugh" when you see a toad. If you do you may predispose him to grow up into one of those unfortunates who pick their way timidly through the world and are uncomfortable even on a picnic because they don't know what terrible things may be hidden in the grass.

I would give the child no pet he can touch until he is old enough to realize that to be alive means to be capable of pain as well as of pleasure, and I would see to it that he not only knows but realizes this fact. "A cat," said the mad poet, Christopher Smart, "is an instrument for children to learn benevolence upon." But if they learn cruelty instead it will be a curse to them as well as to those who suffer from it. A dog is a better first pet than a cat because it is tougher, but cats come next.

From pets I would lead the child—and he will be easily led—to the creatures living their own lives close at hand—

the bird that comes to the window tray to feed or the rabbit that must be reluctantly discouraged from too close attention to your flower bed. Going for a walk to see what one can see rather than merely to get somewhere is the first step in the education of a naturalist. But never let your child feel that since the dandelion and the rabbit are not immediately useful to you they are therefore to be classed as vermin or weed. The dandelion and the rabbit may be out of place but we would miss them nevertheless.

Take the child to a zoo, of course. Someday you may take him also to a National Park or, if you are up to it, camping in the woods. But don't forget that even in the city, to say nothing of the suburb, there is enough to keep a naturalist busy. Thoreau "traveled extensively in Concord" and, any child, or for that matter an adult, can travel extensively in his own back yard. Two of nature's greatest marvels—the butterfly and the tadpole—are accessible in any suburb.

Today as never before any bookstore can supply dozens of good books covering every aspect of natural history and adapted to every age. But to begin with, no elaborate directions are necessary. I distrust youthful experiments which involve drastic interference with nature's own processes, and I prefer those activities which involve a maximum of observation and a minimum of manipulation. Nevertheless, the child who sees what can be seen on a country walk will want to bring some of it into the house with him. One never knows what will suddenly strike an imagination, but whatever it is, that is the thing to be pursued. I think it was a bean sprouting in sawdust between two pieces of glass which first made me feel the wonder of plant life, and I have never gotten so much excitement from any subsequent garden as I did when, as a child, the notion came to plant all sorts of things I had never seen growing—unroasted peanuts from the candy store, flaxseed from the medicine chest, cotton from I do not remember where, etc., etc.

There is really no wrong place to begin so long as the child thinks it is the right place. But I have one suggestion which will bring delighted wonder—not to every child, perhaps—but to all those who will later develop a taste for the small miracles of nature.

If milkweed grows in your neighborhood, keep an eye on two or three of those green and black striped caterpillars which feed upon it, and when they have reached maximum size, put one in a box with an upright twig and a daily supply of fresh milkweed leaves to feed upon. Very soon it will grow sluggish and crawl up the twig. There it will fasten itself and, if you are lucky, you may see it suddenly drop its skin to reveal perfectly formed and exquisitely shaped a decorated urn—"the green coffin with the golden nails." What we call ugliness has suddenly become a thing of beauty; but that is only the beginning.

In surprisingly few days the coffin will break open and out of it will crawl a crumpled and seemingly deformed Monarch butterfly. Gradually the crumpled wings will spread in all their rich brown beauty. Now move the twig gently out-of-doors, and presently the wings will give a preliminary flutter and then the butterfly will sail away. (You may watch the same miracle as it is performed by the smaller caterpillar with the huge, false eyes which you can find on spicebush or by the huge "worm" which is eating up your tomato plants—though in the case of the latter it will want to prepare for transformation under some dry leaves instead of attached to a twig.)

Few children who have ever seen this miracle will ever forget it. Many may want to read in some book just how it all happened—how the caterpillar formed the green coffin just below its skin—how the substance of its body dissolved almost into an egg again, and then was incredibly reorganized—or was born again—as a creature in every respect new and different. But the miracle itself is enough in itself. Life will remain forever after something miraculous and beautiful no matter how much physiology or biochemistry we may learn. And I think that is something very important in an increasingly mechanized world.

If you think that things like this are too messy and too much trouble, please stop and consider. A tadpole in the cellar is not as messy as too many mechanical toys scattered over the living room. As for trouble, a busy child never demands as much attention as an idle one. The budding naturalist is not likely to whine "What can I do now?" You will spend a lot less time chauffering him about from one "organized recreation" to another.

Of course, you can also participate as much as you like. The manufacturers of small arms recommend fathers to go hunting with their sons as a healthy form of "togetherness." But why take a gun? There are rather too many of the latter on TV already. You can get as much exercise and as much fresh air observing (and photographing, if you like) as you can killing something which would prefer to be alive and is, besides, a good deal more interesting alive than dead.

One of the best all-around naturalists I know, Louis Wayne Walker, formerly of the American Museum of Natural History in New York and now of the Arizona-Sonora Desert Museum in Tucson, was a bad boy, especially prone to playing hooky from school. Then a wise principal found out that he was spending his illegitimate holidays in the woods and suggested that he create a natural history museum for the school. The problem was solved.

Your children may not be a problem and you may not want them to become professional naturalists, but there is no better hobby—either casual or serious—than the natural world. It makes every expedition from the Sunday stroll to the around the world tour an absorbing adventure. Guy Emerson, one of the high officers of the Bankers Trust Company of New York, is an eminent ornithologist, and Crawford Gruenwald, president of the Du Pont Company, has recently published a stunning book about humming-birds. It does not appear that in either case their hobby has interfered with "the serious business of life."

Schools sometimes help and sometimes they do not. Some have excellent nature study programs and provide field trips. Others offer courses suitable only to those who are going to be doctors or professional biologists. They seat students permanently on stools in a basement laboratory and begin with the dismal routine of dissecting earthworms and cockroaches, from which they proceed ultimately to the investigation of the inner organs of cats preserved in formaldehyde. "Experiments" are increasingly popular, and it is quite possible that your teen-age son or daughter is learning how to produce cancer in baby chicks or how to starve captive rats by omitting certain elements from their diet. He may even be encouraged to invent interesting types of vivisection, and his instructors may be boasting (as one recently did in print) that students are sternly forbidden to take any personal interest in the creatures they are maltreating.

All this is said to come under the head of avoiding sentimentality and encouraging a truly scientific attitude. We do have to keep up with Russia, you know. But it is hardly likely to develop that kind of interest and attitude which will enrich the life of the nonprofessional and which, therefore, should be a part of a liberal education. Cruelty to animals, as St. Thomas Aquinas pointed out almost a thousand years ago, leads easily to cruelty to other human beings. And you would do well to inquire at the next P.T.A. meeting whether the nature study courses in your school are teaching compassion or brutality.

> He prayeth best who loveth best
> All things both great and small.

So wrote Coleridge at the end of the *Ancient Mariner,* which your child may have been required to read on the same day that he was given his very own rat to starve. No doubt our world needs to learn more facts. But it looks as though it might collapse less because of the facts it does not know than because it has forgotten how to pray and love.

On being an amateur naturalist*

[1962]

This is an age of specialists and I am by nature as well as habit an amateur. That is a dangerous thing to confess because specialists are likely to turn up their noses. "What you really mean is," they say, "a dilettante—a sort of playboy of the arts and sciences." You may have a smattering of this or that but you can't be a real authority on anything at all, and I'm afraid they are at least partly right. Not long ago my publisher asked me for a sentence or two to put on a book jacket, which would explain what he called "my claim to fame." And the best I could come up with was this: "I think I know more about plant life than any other drama critic and more about the theater than any botanist."

That sort of thing was once quite respectable. You could, like Francis Bacon, take all knowledge for your province. But there is just too much of it today. One has to choose between knowing more and more about less and less or doing what the specialist contemptuously calls "spreading yourself thin."

Now I could put up some sort of solemn defense of the

* TV program. Printed by permission of National Education Television.

fellow who chooses to interest himself in a lot of things and gets a general view of the world he lives in. After all, "amateur" means literally "lover" and an amateur of, say natural history, very often loves the wonderful world of nature in a way that the specialist in, say, the classification of garter snakes, probably did when he was young, but long ago forgot all about while dissecting specimens preserved in formaldehyde. Plato and Aristotle called themselves, not sophists or wise men, but philosophers and lovers of wisdom. The important thing is that the amateur is a lover of whatever he is an amateur of.

At least that is the excuse I give to myself. I think what I have wanted most out of life is to find living itself rewarding. I'm sure that I have wanted that more than I wanted wealth or fame. As Thoreau said, I don't want to feel when I come to die that I have never lived. Like Thoreau again, I am inclined to say that I came into this world not primarily to make it a better place to live in, but to live in it be it good or bad. And that is part of the amateur spirit. I haven't always been happy—who has—but I have usually been interested.

Another of the advantages of being an amateur in natural history or anything else is that there are certain unconvincing poses you don't have to take. Consider for example the case of the professional who has wangled a place on an expedition to Timbuktu or the Solomon Islands. Convention demands that he tell everybody that he is making a sacrifice to that stern master called Science. When he writes the nearly inevitable book he will stress the discomforts and dangers of his exploits: the terrible heat (or cold), the dreadful roads, the nauseating food, the exhaustion, and the narrow escape from wild beasts or wilder men. Still, he is glad to have suffered all this because it has enabled him to Make His Small Contribution to the Sum of Human Knowledge. What he may possibly not know but what all his readers do know is that nine times out of ten this is pure eye-wash. What he really wanted was the somewhat masochistic pleasure of going to the Solomons or some other outlandish place while the benefits to that abstraction called Science are just a *good* reason, not the *real* reason, for going.

Your unashamed amateur, on the other hand, is not obliged to practice any of this hypocrisy. When he gets a chance to go somewhere he is perfectly free to tell the truth. My *excuse,* he can say, is to add a new bird to my life list or to photograph a something-or-other in its native habitat.

Practically in my back yard are some of the most beautiful as well as some of the strangest of plants and flowers. There are also enough mysteries unsolved by science to keep an investigator busy through a whole life without having to go anywhere, as Henri Fabre kept busy studying the insects found on an acre or two in southern France.

Yet instead of staying in my back yard I have, during the last four years, made some fourteen or fifteen expeditions in the company of respectable scientists to the astonishingly primitive area of Mexico known as Baja California, which is not as far away as Timbuktu or the Solomons, but is, I imagine, almost as strange and remote from what we call the comforts of civilization. My *excuse* was, among other things, to see in its only home a certain giant treelike monstrosity so grotesque that only a botanist could love it. The Mexicans call it a *cirio,* the professionals give it the resounding name *Idria columnaris,* but a generation ago when the first American botanist saw it in its native land, he opened his eyes in a wild surmise and exclaimed: "There ain't no such animal. It's a Boojum!"—and that name, borrowed from the author of *Alice in Wonderland,* has stuck.

This I say was my excuse. The real reason for going was that I expected to enjoy myself; and I did.

Traveling with assorted specialists, I have come to realize that some—and by no means the least competent—are specialists in one thing and amateurs in all the others. But some, on the other hand, are profoundly uninterested in everything except their specialty—like one I knew who attended nothing except water beetles and, since there isn't much water in Baja California, this was the next best thing to being a specialist on the snakes of Ireland.

Your amateur, on the other hand, is delightfully, if perhaps almost sinfully, free of responsibility and can spread himself as thin as he likes over the vast field of nature. There are few places not covered with concrete or trod into dust where he does not find something to look at. Best of all, perhaps, is the fact that he feels no pressing obligation to "add something to the sum of human knowledge." He is quite satisfied when he adds something to his knowledge. And if he keeps his field wide enough he will remain so ignorant that he may do exactly that at intervals very gratifyingly short. A professional field botanist, for instance, has done very well if in the course of a lifetime he adds a dozen new species to the flora of the region he is studying. Even a hitherto unrecognized variety is enough to make a red-letter day. But to the amateur, any flower he has never seen before is a new species so far as he is concerned and on a short trip into a new area he can easily find a dozen "new species."

Of course he is well and somewhat guiltily aware that he could not have all this fun if the more responsible specialists had not provided him with the treatises and the handbooks which answer his questions and reduce what he has seen to some sort of order. More relevant is the further fact that if the specialist did not go on field trips, the amateur would never be fortunate enough to be allowed to go along with him.

Another advantage of accepting an amateur standing—and it's the last I am going to mention—is this: It permits one to speculate freely and to get "further out" than a specialist fearful of his responsibility dares to go. And it sometimes happens that a free speculation will suggest to the specialists an attempt to put props under it. That is what happened in the case of evolution. Several early amateurs indulged in the wild surmise that man and the ape might be related. It's quite possible that the idea would never have occurred to Darwin if they hadn't. After all, one of the speculators was his own grandfather.

Now let me give an example from my own experience: Not very long ago I had the privilege of accompanying a group of biologists who were dredging up marine organisms in Mexico's Gulf of California. Every now and then a haul would include a small bag of rather leathery jelly whose only conspicuous feature was two open tubes communicating with the water around it. Even I did not have to be told that this was a sea squirt, famous in biology as one of the two most primitive surviving organisms which possesses that ancestor of the vertebrate column known as a notochord. What makes it even more remarkable than Amphioxus, the other primitive possessor of this fateful gadget, is this: in the case of the sea squirt, the notochord is present only during the creature's embryonic stage and it disappears as the sea squirt grows up. This must mean, so the biologists say, that sometime, many millions of years ago, it abandoned instead of following up the possibilities which the notochord opened to the living organism. It rejected Progress. Instead of evolving, it devolved. The fruit of my observation of the sea squirt is a very short fable.

Once upon a time an unusually bright little sea squirt invented for itself a notochord. "This," it muttered, "will make me more fit to survive and, as even a sea squirt knows, only the fittest do." Unfortunately his thinking did not stop there. "In some millions of years," he said, "I will become a true vertebrate—first a fish, then an amphibian, then a reptile, then a small mammal, then an anthropoid, and ultimately Man Himself. Having reached that exalted state, I will be able to take evolution into my own hands, I will invent the wheel, the steam engine, the dynamo, and even the hydrogen bomb. . . . I will . . . but shucks, do I really want to do all that? Maybe it would be wiser, maybe I would survive longer (and survival is the only objectively demonstrable good), if I just went back to being an old-fashioned instead of a new-fashioned sea squirt." Thanks to that decision he has survived longer than most of the organic forms which succeed him and may quite possibly survive all those now alive, including Man himself.

I am still not sure whether to call this little fable "The Road Not Taken" (with apologies to Robert Frost) or, more colloquially, "The Little Squirt Who Wouldn't."

At any rate, I think there is a moral somewhere.

Man's ancient, powerful link to nature—A source of fear and joy

[1961]

What is "nature"? One standard reference devotes five columns to fifteen different and legitimate definitions of the word. But for the purposes of this article the meaning is simple. Nature is that part of the world which man did not make and which has not been fundamentally changed by him. It is the mountains, the woods, the rivers, the trees, the plants, and the animals which have continued to be very much what they would have been had he never existed.

In another sense man is, of course, himself a part of nature. But he is also in so many ways so unique that it is convenient to speak of man *and* nature, especially of man's relation to the rest of this nature of which he is also a part.

The relationship is something which he can never forget; but he responds to it in the most diverse ways. He regards nature sometimes as a friend and sometimes as an enemy. He loves it and he fears it. He uses it and destroys it. Nature is what he tries to get away from and then something he wishes to keep. He replaces it with his homes and factories, then wishes to return to it. He tries to impose on it human order and civilization, and then suddenly finds himself dreaming of a golden age when man and nature were one.

This paradox is as old as civilization itself. Though it is true that man never admired the more savage aspects of nature until life had become comparatively safe, it is equally true that he had scarcely built the first cities before he began to try to get away from them. In ancient Greece poets idealized the shepherd's life, and in imperial Rome the literary cult of the simple life had already reached the point where satirists ridiculed it. In our modern world the engineer, the industrialist, and the builder of skyscrapers moves his family to a country house in the suburbs. He plants trees and cultivates a garden. He acquires animals as pets, and perhaps he takes up bird watching—all of which reveals his unwillingness to let go of what, in theory at least, he has not valued.

Ancient as these paradoxes and conflicts are, there is today one supremely important respect in which they pose a problem that never existed in so acute a form before: now for the first time man can effectively act out his impulses and his decisions. He can, if he so desires, all but banish nature and the natural from the earth he has come to rule.

Until a few centuries ago man was not even a very numerous species. It has been an even shorter time since his technology became advanced to the point where he could upset seriously the ancient balances of the natural world. Formerly he might love nature or hate her, might attempt to preserve her or destroy her; but she was more powerful than he. Except over relatively small areas she remained in control. Now the balance has shifted. Man controls forces which at least rival and seem on the point of surpassing hers. He can decide as never before what part, if any, of the natural world will be permitted to exist. Thus the question "What is man's place in nature and what ought to be his relation to her?" is fateful as it never was before.

In its most abstract form this fundamental question was asked and opposing answers were given by the ancient religions. In the Hebraic tradition man was the child of God, and God was separate from, rather than a part of, nature. Greek paganism, on the other hand, worshiped gods who were themselves aspects of nature and it taught man to think of himself also as part of her. These gods were more at home in the woods and streams and mountains than in the temples built for them. Nature was the source of health, beauty, and joy, and to live in accord with nature's laws was wisdom. The Great God Pan, or nature god, was one of the most ancient and powerful of deities, so much so indeed that an early Christian tradition made the exclamation "Great Pan is dead" a cry of victory announcing the triumph for the new faith; and many centuries later, the neopagan poet Swinburne could turn it into a lament to Christ Himself: "Thou hast conquered, O pale Galilean; the world has grown grey from thy breath."

To Noah, unloading his animals after the flood, Jehovah said, "And the fear of you and the dread of you shall be upon every beast of the earth, and upon every fowl of the air, upon all that moveth upon the earth, and upon all the fishes of the sea; into your hand are they delivered." Throughout the Greek and Roman ascendencies and all through the Middle Ages the most admired aspects of nature were those which man had tamed, at least to a degree. It has often been said that the fourteenth-century Italian scholar Petrarch was the first man who ever confessed to climbing a mountain just for the sake of the view, and it is not so often added that, at the end of his description, he apologized for this eccentricity.

The conflicting attitudes which even today somehow relate "the natural" to "the divine" began to emerge some three centuries ago. The first great English biologist, the pious John Ray, in his enormously popular *The Wisdom of God Manifested in the Works of the Creation* (1691), maintained that God did not create the living world exclusively for man's use but that, on the contrary, He "takes pleasure that all His creatures enjoy themselves." And Ray urged that men should study nature as well as books because it was by such study that the greatness and goodness of God was most clearly revealed.

A bare generation later Alexander Pope, the most read English poet except Shakespeare, could put the same thing in epigrammatic couplets:

Has God, thou fool! work'd solely for thy good,
Thy joy, thy pastime, thy attire, thy food? . . .
Is it for thee the lark ascends and sings?
Joy tunes his voice, joy elevates his wings.
Is it for thee the linnet pours his throat?
Loves of his own and raptures swell
    the note. . . .
Know Nature's children all divide her care;
The fur that warms a monarch warm'd a bear.

Already we were halfway to Wordsworth's "the meanest flower that blows can give/Thoughts that do often lie too deep for tears" or Blake's "Kill not the moth nor butterfly/ For the Last Judgment draweth nigh."

Out of such attitudes emerged the whole romantic glorification of nature which blossomed in the eighteenth century and continued almost unchecked to the middle of the nine-

teenth, when scientific objectivity began to struggle against
it. By that time life had become comparatively secure and
men increasingly were finding the somewhat terrifying spectacle of nature's savage grandeur thrillingly beautiful. Mountains, as modern scholarship has pointed out, were almost
always called "sublime." The philosopher-statesman Edmund
Burke devoted one of his earliest writings to distinguishing
between "The Beautiful" (that which is soothing and re-
assuring) and "The Sublime" (that which strikes us with
awe and with something almost like terror). Everywhere
men were beginning to exclaim over thunderstorms, lashing
seas, and icy peaks—over whatever suggested something
grander and less comfortable than their own cities or, even,
their own lawns and gardens.

In this period also the cult of nature as "the kind mother"
or, in the words of Goethe, as "the living garment of God"
grew. This wildly unrealistic view attributed to nature below
the human level a consistent kindliness and benevolence
which man himself to this day has by no means achieved.
Nature is not always a kind mother; she is as often a stern,
and sometimes a brutal one. Yet Burns spoke of "Man's in-
humanity to man" and contrasted it with "Nature's social
union" which, he said, man had so cruelly disturbed. Wordsworth's God had his dwelling in "the light of setting suns,"
and "Nature," he proclaimed, "never did betray the heart
that loved her."

It was against such romantic idealism that the nineteenth
century gradually rebelled until, just after the mid-century,
Charles Darwin took a position at the opposite extreme and
drew his picture of a natural world which assumed its form
through the operation of mechanical processes, and which
was devoid of anything which could be called moral values.

If few today doubt that Darwin's theory of "natural selection through the struggle for survival" explains much, there

are many who insist that it does not explain everything. Some of the most primitive organisms have survived for many millions of years—far longer than other more advanced organisms and possibly longer than man himself will prevail. If only "the fittest survive," then the sea squirt is fitter than any mammal—including, perhaps, man. And "natural selection" cannot account for the intensification of man's consciousness or the value which he puts upon such ideals as justice, fair play and benevolence. It cannot account for them inasmuch as creatures in which these traits are not conspicuous are at least as successful in the "struggle for survival" as he is.

If nature herself has exhibited a tendency, if she seems to "want" anything, it is not merely to survive. She has tended to realize more and more completely the potentialities of protoplasm, and these include much that has no demonstrable "survival value." Evolution itself has spread before us the story of a striving toward "the higher," not merely toward that which enables an organism to survive.

If the romantic view of nature was mere wishful thinking, merely the projection upon nature of our own fully developed desires and ideals, then Darwinism generated a romanticism in reverse in which all is conflict, violence, and blood. But the fact is that animals do not spend all their time fighting for survival, though for the sake of excitement anti-romantic popular books and films do strive to give that impression. Animals also give tender love to their offspring as well as, sometimes, to their mates and the fellow members of their group. Those theories of human society which propose ruthless, devil-take-the-hindermost political and social systems sometimes claim that they are in accord with the laws of nature, but they are not.

There was a time not too long ago when orthodox science talked only of instincts, behavior patterns, chemical drives, and the like, while any tendency to see in the animal even faint analogies to the conscious processes, the intelligence, or the emotions of man was ridiculed as sentimental and "anthropomorphic"—*i.e.*, stated in terms appropriate to man only. But the tide has turned. So notable a student of animal behavior as Konrad Lorenz has protested against what he named "mechanomorphism"—the interpretation of animal behavior exclusively in terms of the mechanical—which he calls an error no less grave than anthropomorphism. Animals are not men, but neither are they machines. If they cannot think as man does in terms of abstract concepts, neither are they controlled entirely by push-button reflexes. To some extent they exhibit the beginnings of "the human." They can sometimes take in a situation and modify their behavior in the light of circumstances. They have individuality also; one does not behave exactly like another. Even insects, once thought to be the most automatic and invariable of creatures, seem to be able sometimes to change purposely the pattern of their conduct.

As a matter of fact, the life of the senses in some of the higher animals is possibly more vivid than ours, and in some of them the emotions may be more powerful also. As Sir Julian Huxley, one of the greatest living authorities on evolution, has said of the birds he has observed with scientific exactitude: "Their lives are often emotional, and their emotions are richly and finely expressed. . . . In birds the advance on the intellectual side has been less, on the emotional side greater: so that we can study in them a part of the single stream of life where emotion, untrammeled by much reason, has the upper hand."

Thus all the strange powers and potentialities of the living thing are diffused throughout animate nature—which remains mysterious, and our relation to it no less so. The universe is not the mere machine which early Darwinians tended to make it. The man who thinks of his dog as another human being is wrong, but no more so perhaps than his opposite who refuses to acknowledge any kinship. Yet an appreciation of this truth still leaves unanswered the question of man's own position. To what extent is he unique; to what extent is he not only "higher" than any other animal, but also radically different from, and discontinuous with, that great chain which connects by close links the humblest one-celled animal with the most intelligent of the apes?

The traditional answer, given by some philosophers and theologians, is that man is an animal to which something (a soul, if you like) has been added and that this something distinguishes him absolutely from all other living creatures. This answer is at least logically tenable, whether you accept it or not. If, on the other hand, you say, as some old-fashioned biologists did, that though man has "evolved" by purely natural process, he is nevertheless endowed with capacities of which not a trace is to be found in any other animal, that is not logically tenable. "Evolution" implies the growing complexity of things previously existing in simpler form. Hence man's consciousness, thought, and sense of purpose must either have been added to his natural endowment by something outside nature, or they must have truly evolved from something in the "lower" forms of life.

William Morton Wheeler, the late great student of the social insects, once wrote that we can only guess why animals are as they are and can never know except very imperfectly how they came to be what they are. Nevertheless, he added, "[the fact] that organisms are as they are, that apart from members of our own species they are our only companions in an infinite and unsympathetic waste of electrons, planets, nebulae and stars, is a perennial joy and consolation." It is upon this "perennial joy and consolation" that the deepest and most rewarding "love of nature" must rest.

Even to say that we can and should know this joy and consolation is not to answer all the questions. How far should we not only enjoy nature but also follow her; to what extent should we take our cue, as it were, from the natural world? We are something more than merely part of it. However we came to be where we are, our position is, as an eighteenth-century poet put it, "on the isthmus of a middle state." We face back toward our primitive ancestors, perhaps even to the ape; but we also look forward to we know not what.

To what extent then should man, to what extent dare he, renounce nature; take over the management of the earth he lives on; and use it exclusively for what he sometimes regards as his higher purposes?

Extremists give and have always given extreme answers. Let us, say some, "return to nature," lead the simple life, try to become again that figment of the romantic imagination, "the noble savage." Henry David Thoreau, the greatest of American "nature lovers," is sometimes accused of having advocated just that. But he did not do so; he advocated only that we should live more simply and more aware of the earth which, he said with characteristic exaggeration, "is more wonderful than it is convenient; more beautiful than it is useful; it is more to be admired and enjoyed than used."

Others suggest a different extreme. They talk about "the biosphere" (loosely, that which has been here defined as the natural world) as contrasted with "the noosphere" (translated as that portion of the earth upon which man has imposed his own will so successfully that whatever conditions prevail there do so because of his will). It appears that civilization, according to this notion, is to be completed only when the noosphere is the whole earth and the biosphere is completely subordinated to the human will.

Within the last one hundred years we have approached faster and closer to that condition than in all the preceding centuries of civilization. But would man, whose roots go so deep into nature, be happy should he achieve such a situation?

Certainly he would become a creature very different from what he is, and the experience of living would be equally different from what it has always been. He would, indeed, have justified his boast that he can "conquer nature" but he would also have destroyed it. He would have used every spot of earth for homes, factories, and farms, or perhaps got rid of farms entirely, because by then he could synthesize food in the laboratory. But he would have no different companions in the adventures of living. The emotions which have inspired much of all poetry, music, and art would no longer be comprehensible. He would have all his dealings with things he alone has made. Would we then be, as some would imagine, men like gods? Or would we be only men like ants?

That we would not be satisfied with such a world is sufficiently evidenced by the fact that, to date at least, few do not want their country house, their country vacation, their camping or their fishing trip—even their seat in the park and their visit to the zoo. We need some contact with the things we spring from. We need nature at least as a part of the context of our lives. Though we are not satisfied with nature, neither are we happy without her. Without cities we cannot be civilized. Without nature, without wilderness even, we are compelled to renounce an important part of our heritage.

The late Aldo Leopold, who spent his life in forestry and conservation, once wrote: "For us of the minority, the opportunity to see geese is more important than television, and the chance to see a pasqueflower is a right as inalienable as free speech."

Many of us who share this conviction came to it only gradually. On some summer vacation or some country weekend we realize that what we are experiencing is more than merely a relief from the pressures of city life; that we have not merely escaped *from* something but also *into* something; that we have joined the greatest of all communities, which is not that of men alone but of everything which shares with us the great adventure of being alive.

This sense, mystical though it may seem, is no delusion. Throughout history some have felt it and many have found an explanation of it in their conviction that it arises out of the fact that all things owe their gift of life to God. But there is no reason why the most rationalistic of evolutionists should not find it equally inevitable. If man is only the most recent and the most complex of nature's children, then he must feel his kinship with them. If even his highest powers of consciousness, intellect, and conscience were evolved from simpler forms of the same realities, then his kinship with those who took the earlier steps is real and compelling. If nature produced him, and if she may someday produce something far less imperfect, then he may well hesitate to declare that she has done all she can for him and that henceforth he will renounce her to direct his own destiny.

In some ways man may seem wiser than she is, but it is not certain that he is wiser in all ways. He dare not trust her blindly, but neither does he dare turn his back upon her. He is in danger of relying too exclusively upon his own thoughts, to the entire neglect of her instincts; upon the dead machine he creates, while disregarding the living things of whose adventure he is a part.

We have heard much about "our natural resources" and of the necessity for conserving them, but these "resources" are not merely materially useful. They are also a great reservoir of the life from which we evolved, and they have both consolation to offer and lessons to each which are not alone those the biologist strives to learn. In their presence many of us experience a lifting of the heart for which mere fresh air and sunshine is not sufficient to account. We feel surging up in us the exuberant, vital urge which has kept evolution going but which tends to falter amid the complexities of a too civilized life. In our rise to the human state we have lost something, despite all we have gained.

Is it merely a sentimental delusion, a "pathetic fallacy," to think that one sees in the animal a capacity for joy which man himself is tending to lose? We have invented exercise, recreation, pleasure, amusement, and the rest. To "have fun" is a desire often expressed by those who live in this age of anxiety and most of us have at times actually "had fun." But recreation, pleasure, amusement, fun, and all the rest are poor substitutes for joy; and joy, I am convinced, has its roots in something from which civilization tends to cut us off.

Are at least some animals capable of teaching us this lesson of joy? Some biologists—but by no means all and by no means the best—deny categorically that animals feel it. The gift for real happiness and joy is not always proportionate to intelligence, as we understand it, even among the animals. As Professor N. J. Berrill has put it, "To be a bird is to be alive more intensively than any other living creature. . . . [Birds] live in a world that is always in the present, mostly full of joy." Similarly Sir Julian Huxley, no mere sentimental nature lover, wrote after watching the love play of herons: "I can only say that it seemed to bring such a pitch of emotion that I could have wished to be a Heron that I might experience it."

This does not mean that Sir Julian would desire, any more than you or I, to be permanently a bird. Perhaps some capacity for joy has been, must be, and should be sacrificed to other capacities. But some awareness of the world outside of man must exist if one is to experience the happiness and solace which some of us find in an awareness of nature and in our love for her manifestations.

Those who have never found either joy or solace in nature might begin by looking not for the *joy they can get,* but for the *joy that is there* amid those portions of the earth man has not yet entirely pre-empted for his own use. And perhaps when they have become aware of joy in other creatures they will achieve joy themselves, by sharing in it.

Now the animal world goes to sleep

[1959]

To Thoreau it was "that grand old poem called winter," but neither writers nor the general public usually speak so well of it. The ski enthusiasts excepted, few ever exclaim "Winter has come!" in the tone of voice they reserve for the more popular seasons and Shelley couldn't think of anything more favorable to say than that spring could not be far behind.

Snow, ice, and bitter winds seem to fall upon the living world like some irretrievable calamity and to leave nothing but ruin where trees had rustled and flowers bloomed. Even those to whom the love of nature is a dominant passion sometimes speak of "the dead of winter" and a winter landscape can indeed look like a lunar one—as though forever silent and never to live again.

But of course "the dead of winter" is wrong. Even "Sleep of Winter" doesn't cover everything but it does cover a great deal more. Though a few of the animals such as the fox, the rabbit, and the winter birds are wide awake, most of them are, like most of the plants, more or less quiescent—some lying motionless but awake; some in the half-sleep of the bear whose young are born while their mother dozes; some in that deep sleep called hibernation; many more locked in the deathlike suspension of all visible activity characteristic of the wintering egg, seed, chrysalis, or cocoon.

Even for the proudly technological human being, survival is to some extent a problem and there are few if any animals who do not either withdraw in one way or another from winter or face an intensified struggle for existence. The chickadees who come in from the woods where they have summered and the juncos who come down from the north may sometimes seem positively to enjoy a good blizzard but they are cheerful rather than safe, for a drenching rain followed by a hard freeze will take a heavy toll, of the chickadees especially.

Obviously all the various devices by which winter is eluded or made endurable have been learned in the course of time. At least all the higher animals and plants must have got their start in regions where winter never came and, if the evolutionists are right, must have slowly worked out their astonishingly varied techniques for surviving gradually increasing rigors. What is true of the animals is true of the plants too—but with differences. And if we leave the plants aside for the moment to consider only that half of animate creation with which we are closely allied, we may be humiliated to discover how little man himself has added to the techniques invented by his humble cousins. One of them—hibernation—he has abandoned and one—the great, Promethean discovery that fire can be started and controlled—is his alone. Otherwise he does only what other animals were doing many millennia before his appearance—building shelters, getting heavier clothing, storing food, or simply going away to some region where it doesn't get too cold.

This last maneuver is called "taking a winter vacation" when men perform it and "migration" in animals. Many of the latter make minor shifts from a cooler spot to a warmer, but on any large scale migration is practiced almost exclusively by the hoofed animals (like the caribou of the north) and, preeminently of course, by the birds. Some of them, the chickadee for instance, are found the year around in the same regions; others, like the robin, may move a short distance;

many others, like the oriole and the tiny hummingbird, go all the way to Central or South America, while one frantic world traveler, the arctic tern, spends the northern summer in the arctic and the southern summer in the antarctic.

Why do they do it and how do they do it? No problem of animal behavior has been more discussed or still involves more mysteries. What is south for one bird is north for another. In New England, for instance, your oriole moves out and your junco comes in but all birds nest in the most northerly part of their range, principally perhaps because the summer days are longest there and afford more daylight hours in which to hunt food for the voracious young. Why can a chickadee stand a New England winter while an oriole cannot? At least this much may be said: it is not exclusively a matter of resistance to cold. The chickadee can find seeds, insect eggs, and scraps in winter; most of the flying insect eaters must go where insects are active the year around. How, having no calendars, do birds know when to take off? Experiments seem to prove pretty conclusively that the lengthening and shortening of daylight rather than any change in temperature is the signal. How do they find their way? Well, that is still largely a disputed question. As late as the eighteenth century an educated man could still believe that swallows spent the winter beneath the mud of pond bottoms. And what they do do is no less remarkable. Our chimney swifts, as has only rather recently been discovered, seem to go one and all to Peru. Why Peru? Well, perhaps only for the same reason that some human beings always vacation in the same spot. "Our family has been going there for years."

But what of the many kinds of animals which, like most human beings, cannot manage a winter vacation? Most of the mammals are active. Deer, foxes, weasels, rabbits, and wildcats store no food, and some of them—deer especially—may have a pretty hard time living upon what they can find by scraping away the snow. In the water under the ice muskrats find food the year around and the prudent squirrels and field mice lay up winter stores. The field mouse also supplements the store by foraging under the snow as he makes his way along the tunnels he digs through the snow. Gray squirrels too are equally active, though in really inclement weather they may remain for days curled up snugly in their leaf-houses high in some tree.

If all these animals as well as the wintering birds "can take it," why can't others not too distantly related? Why is it that the flying squirrel is active all winter while the eastern chipmunk retires in autumn to a well-stored burrow and stays there almost continuously, even, in colder climates, sinking into a more or less complete dormancy? And why do the woodchucks, the raccoons, and the brown bats fall into complete hibernation?

No animal habit is stranger, for hibernation is not the same as sleep, no matter how deep. It seems halfway to death and one wonders if it could have arisen first in animals which barely escaped death in the course of increasingly rigorous winters. Men on the point of freezing are said to grow drowsy and that is exactly what happens to the hibernators as the cold comes on. The process begins at about fifty degrees. They grow sleepier and sleepier and their body temperature drops because the success of the maneuver depends upon the fact that they cease to be "warm-blooded." Thus the temperature of a hibernating woodchuck may fall to about thirty-seven degrees; his rate of breathing declines from a normal of thirty times a minute to as little as once in five minutes. His heart may beat only four or five times per minute and he may remain completely motionless for days on end. Violent wakening is likely to kill him but wakening at the normal time is rapid. Metabolism which was very low rises to a fever pitch and before long the woodchuck which was hardly alive is again as good as new.

It used to be said that no bird ever hibernates—perhaps

because he knows the better trick of going south if necessary. But only a few years ago it was discovered that at least one bird does, namely a southwestern relative of the eastern whippoorwill who tucks himself into a cranny and stays there in the deep sleep of real hibernation. Truly a most unbird-like habit.

Warm blood kept at a constant temperature by a sort of internal thermostat which opens the metabolic draft when necessary is a characteristic of the mammals and birds alone. Its obvious advantage is that it enables the animal to be as lively in cold weather as in warm whereas the cold-blooded reptiles and amphibians move and indeed live at a variable rate which grows more and more sluggish as the temperature falls. The same is true of many insects and you may, if so inclined, tell the summer evening temperature by the common green tree cricket, who chirps at a rate which a simple formula will translate into degrees Fahrenheit.

But warm-bloodedness has its disadvantages too, of which the most obvious is that cold can reach a point where the blood temperature cannot any longer be maintained and the animal will die unless he either migrates to a warmer place or, like the few hibernators, has learned the trick of becoming temporarily a cold-blooded instead of a warm-blooded animal. For the normally cold-blooded it is all very much simpler. Expose a man or any warm-blooded animal continuously to a very low temperature and he will die. But a frog may be frozen solid in a cake of ice for weeks at a time and come back to life when the ice thaws out.

That is an extreme case but many of the humbler creatures who disappear from the scene in autumn or winter are simply somewhere out of sight sleeping the inclement season away. Of those insects who pass the winter in the adult stage, millions are tucked away in crannies, in or under the bark of trees, and millions more below the ground cover of dead leaves; and to them a snow blanket is so great a help that where the surface of the bare ground is nearly zero two inches of soft snow may keep the temperature a few inches below ground just a bit above freezing. Some frogs and toads pass the winter quiescent in the mud of pond bottoms, but the little spring peeper who will somewhat prematurely announce the end of winter around the middle of a New England March sleeps the worst of the weather away under the frozen leaves near the pond to which he will return to breed and sing as soon as a little relaxing of the winter's cold makes him active again.

"Not dead but sleeping" is, then, the most fitting epitaph to write over the tomb of a winter landscape. But of course some do die in their sleep and there are other species to whom the end of summer is, for the individual, always the end of the world. That is true of a great many, but by no means all, insects, some of which have come to the end of their life span and would not live very much longer even if kept artificially warm. The female lays her eggs and dies, much as an annual plant produces its seed before it withers and the seeds of plant and animal alike survive. Even more curious are the in-betweens, especially the moths and the butterflies, who are caterpillars first, then chrysalises or cocoons, and finally the beautifully winged insects. Perhaps just to show that there is more than one way of doing a thing some species winter as adults, some as eggs, and some in the cocoon where the caterpillar has all but returned to the egg in order to be born again—and born better.

Most people probably know rather more about plants in winter than they do about animals. Even nongardeners are aware that some are annuals which would live for but one summer whether winter ever came or not and that others are perennial, some evergreen during the fiercest blizzards, others merely losing their leaves like many trees and shrubs, and still others retiring underground to a sort of hibernation in root or tuber.

Superficially these seem roughly analogous to the various methods adopted by animals but the reason why many plants must take some defensive measures is not the same. They are not warm-blooded or cold-blooded. They are, indeed, not blooded at all and while they have many different reactions to changes of temperature the most obvious cause of death when freezing sets in is the simple fact that ice crystals forming inside the leaves penetrate like needles the living cells and so destroy them. Woody plants can meet that problem by sacrificing the leaves and exposing to the air only the dead covering of bark; herbaceous plants by dying down to the protected root. But why, then, can the evergreens keep their leaves; why do some that are not evergreen droop at the first breath of chill while the skunk cabbage often starts its growth in marshes still rimmed with ice? Two of the many answers to that are that winter-resistant leaves are tougher in texture and also that in winter many of them contain less water to freeze and expand. But the subject is so very complicated that some readers will prefer to say merely "the nature of the beast" and let it go at that.

Perhaps the most striking difference between plant and animal adaptation to winter is that to far more plants than animals winter is not merely something to be endured but something which is absolutely necessary. A woodchuck kept awake in warm quarters all winter will not die because he did not get his accustomed sleep. On the other hand many perennial plants must go into winter dormancy or they will die. Also, many seeds will not germinate unless they have been frozen at least once. And many buds formed in the late summer or autumn will not unfold in spring unless they too have been frozen. Bring the bare branches of your forsythia into the house in autumn and the buds will never open. Bring them in in January or February after they have been well frozen and they will—long before spring has come. Many of the animals active in winter deserve your pity. But don't pity the sleeping plants!

Winter is as good a time as spring to observe the ingenuity of nature and to marvel at the many different ways—sometimes one is tempted to say all the possible ways—in which a given problem is solved. Why have some plants and animals chosen one and some another? Evolution gives part of the answer when it stresses adaptation. But why, in a given instance, this adaptation rather than another? It can hardly be just to make the world more interesting. But at least that is exactly what it does do.

The miracle of grass

[1962]

Of all the green things which make up what Goethe called "the living garment of God," grass is one of the humblest, the most nearly omnipresent, and the most stupidly taken for granted—a miracle so common that we no longer regard it as miraculous.

To some (poor things) it is merely what you try to keep the dandelions out of, or what you strike a golf ball across. But even such are paying some tribute to it. To those of us a little more aware of the great mystery of which we are a part, its going and its coming, its flourishing and its withering, are a sort of soft ostinato accompaniment in the great symphony of the seasons.

Even in the arid Southwest it springs up bravely for a few short weeks. In California the brown hills turn to emerald almost overnight. And in the gentler, more circumspect East, one hardly knows when the great awakening took place. So imperceptible, but ineluctable, is its progress that those of us who watch for it never quite catch the very moment when the transformation occurs. While our backs are turned it is alive again, and no other phenomenon of spring is at once so quiet and so all-enveloping. If there are astronomers on Mars peering at us as our astronomers are peering at their planet, they must see, much more dramatically, what is usually observed there by earthly astronomers. Martian vegetation is perhaps only a dry lichen much like what we see clinging on the bare rocks near the summits of our highest mountains. But ours is a green carpet, soft to the feet, restful to the eye, and announcing to all living things that spring is here again.

What is this thing called grass? "Why," says the botanist, "that is a question easy to answer. Grass, properly so-called, is any one of the numerous genera and species which compose that family of monocotyledonous flowering plants long known as the Gramineae. Unfortunately, its early evolutionary history (like that of all the flowering plants) is obscure since the fossil record is scanty. But at least we can say with reasonable certainty that no grass carpeted the earth in that long ago when the first air-breathing animals crawled out of the water. Also that it was not until the cool weather of the Miocene (say a mere forty million or so years ago) that it became a dominant plant and thus made possible the flourishing of the herbivorous mammals over a more peaceful earth where the bellowing of the dinosaurs had given way to the lowing of herds. Then, only yesterday as world history goes, grass conferred upon our own species that tremendous blessing called wheat.

For a less dusty question and answer we must turn to the poets, many of whom have had their say, though only Walt Whitman put grass at the center of a magnum opus.

A child said, "What is the grass?" fetching it to
    me with full hands;

I guess it must be the flag of my disposition, out
    of hopeful green stuff woven.
Or I guess it is the handkerchief of the Lord,
A scented gift that Remembrancer designedly dropped,
Bearing the owner's name some where in the corners,
    that we may see and remark, and say, "whose?"

Few today have time for such meditations or for such quiet pleasures. Most of us are too desperately busy seeking recreation, entertainment, and amusement ever to experience that joy for which all the other things are but disappointing substitutes—as essentially ersatz as plastic for china, neon lights for dawn and sunset, or the corner grocer's cottony horror offered us in place of that other great gift of grass called bread.

"Joy be with you," people used to say when parting from a friend. Now the modish farewell is, "Have fun!" Sometimes those thus sped away actually do have fun; often they do not; and even the most successful in this enterprise are not too much to be envied. Those of us who want something more than fun, whether it be the exaltation of great art or the mystical experience of "belonging" to something greater than one's self, are a little afraid of being called highbrows or "nature lovers" because neither grass nor Wordsworth's meanest flower that blows are what we call "fun things." They can be something much more rewarding, nevertheless.

Henry David Thoreau once explained that he did not drink wine because he was afraid it might "spoil his taste for water." Henry loved to shock by "going too far" in defending what he wanted to defend, and perhaps he was going too far when he said that. If ours were an age tending toward the puritanical and the ascetic, he might be a dangerous influence, persuading us to surrender in the name of simplicity things much worth having. But since our manners and our morals are not, whatever else they may be, puritanical or ascetic, his voice is more worth hearing than that of those who call for more complexity, for madder music, and for stronger wine. Both of these last pay diminishing returns.

We boast that this is the age of abundance, and the proudest achievement of our best-intentioned men is that, for the first time in history, abundance has been democratized or, to put it somewhat sourly, that now as never before nearly everybody can have rather too much of many things not worth having. Deprivation can kill joy, but so, almost as certainly, can superfluity, for though we always want more, the limiting factor is ultimately what we can take in. More toys than he can play with are a burden not a blessing to any child be he five or fifty. It is disastrous to own more of anything than you can possess, and it is one of the most fundamental laws of human nature that our power actually to possess is limited.

In 1689 Louis XIV ordered the following for his garden at Versailles: 87,000 tulips, 800 tuberoses, 400 lilies, and 83,000 narcissus. In this egalitarian age there are not very many individuals likely to be able to be quite that absurd. But there are many who can and do make the same mistake for the same reason. You just can't take in or possess that many tulips, and if you are foolish enough to try, you will miss the violet by the mossy stone, and even more surely the "thought too deep for tears" which one violet or one tulip might inspire.

"The happiness of the great," wrote Francis Bacon, "consists only in thinking how happy others must suppose them to be." In Bacon's time the term "status," so beloved of present-day sociologists, had not yet been invented, but Bacon had grasped the concept behind it. The desire for status is the same desire to be envied which Bacon had in mind, and it was what Louis XIV also was aiming at. "It will be evident to all," so he said to himself, "that no one else in all the world can have as many tulips as I can, and they will envy me—though, God knows, the whole eighty-seven thousand of them look dull enough to me."

When grass becomes merely "a lawn," it is in danger of becoming what that sour economic Puritan Thorstein Veblen said it always was, namely, a"status symbol," a display of conspicuous expenditure meant to demonstrate that its owner can afford to waste in mere display what might be used to produce wheat or vegetables. Veblen was wrong, because a lawn can also demonstrate a great truth which economists are prone to forget, namely, that beauty may be its own excuse for being. But a lawn *can* be what he called it, and there is no greater paradox than this transformation of the humblest and most unshowy of green things into a status symbol. Of course, neither your lawn nor mine (when in Connecticut I had one) is that. But just to be sure that it isn't, a salutary experience can be had if we ask ourselves from time to time what our real reasons for having it is.

If we have any doubts an experiment might be worth while. Lie down upon your lawn to see what happens. And while I would not advise that all lawns be surrendered to dandelions, I would suggest that you ask yourself, when one of these gay little miracles raises its flower toward the sun, whether you reach for the weed killer without first remembering Whitman's tribute:

> Simple and fresh and fair from winter's clothes
> emerging,
> As if no artifice of fashion, business, politics,
> had ever been,
> Forth from its sunny nook of sheltered grass—
> innocent, golden, calm as the dawn,
> The spring's first dandelion shows its trustful
> face.

"All flesh is grass." For once the apostle and the scientist seem to be in agreement though they were not saying the same thing. To St. Peter all flesh is grass because man, too, "witherith and the flower thereof falleth away." To the biologist all flesh is grass in a more literal sense. No animal, man included, could exist if it were not for the fact that green plants mediate between him and the inanimate materials of the earth. They alone have the power of rising by one step the relative simplicity of the mineral to the complexity of the proteins indispensable to him. Where they leave off his mysterious metabolism takes over. What was mineral but became protein now becomes that even more mysterious thing called protoplasm. And protoplasm is the base of all man's life, thought, imagination, and ideals.

In time, a man passes away, he also withers and the flower thereof falls away, protoplasm descends the scale again to the merely mineral, and grass picks it up once more to repeat the cycle. The process began some billions of years ago and must continue as long as life lasts.

Which of the two truths is the most profound and the most important? The moral truth of the apostle, or the strange, inhuman truth of the biologist. One is as old as civilization, the other almost as new as yesterday. And perhaps just because it is uniquely ours we tend to value it most highly. But we may be wrong. Many civilizations, some of them glorious, were created and then destroyed by men who were innocent of chemistry. But they could not have been what they were had they not known what Peter and what Whitman knew. It is just possible that our civilization will fail because we do know one kind of truth and, in our pride, forget the other.

> And now it seems to me the beautiful uncut hair
> of graves.
> It may be you transpire from the best of young
> men,
> It may be if I had known them I would have loved
> them.
> It may be you are from old people, or from offspring
> taken soon out of their mother's laps,

And here you are the mother's laps.
This grass is very dark to be from the white heads
   of old mothers,
Darker than the colorless beards of old men,
Dark to come from under the faint red roofs of
   mouths.

Man's mark on the desert

[1962]

Like many another I came to the desert primarily to live
in it rather than to make a living out of it. Like most of us
I was, nevertheless, obliged to do both, but I was fortunate
in that I was a writer who did the desert no harm even when
it was the subject of my writing. Physically, I have left it no
less beautiful than it was.

   Not everyone who wants, or for some reason is compelled,
to live here can make his living without to some extent
changing the environment in which he lives. The more our
population increases the more obviously this is true. To suppose that our deserts can remain everywhere as open and as
spacious as they once were is impossible. To some extent it
is inevitable that they will be used for something besides
the study, the contemplation, and the admiration of their
unique beauties.

   But there are suitable and unsuitable ways of "using"
and even of "exploiting" a given environment; and the tragedy is that the Southwestern environment is being increas-

ingly used and exploited in ways peculiarly unsuited to, and sometimes completely destructive of, its unique character. People with no sense of its special opportunities and attractions, with no appreciation of them and no desire that they should be preserved, come among us to build factories and even to raise unwanted cotton. Thus they create problems as well as destroy beauties in a region where industry and some kinds of agriculture are impossible without the permanent depletion of underground water.

In our most selfish moments some of us wish that no more people would come here or, perhaps, less drastically, that no one would come except those who would like, and are able, to make their living in ways which do not destroy the special advantages and pleasure of desert living. If even this is too much to hope for (or even wish), then could we not try to persuade communities not actively to promote "development" and "progress" of the most unsuitable kinds?

Tucson is no longer recognizable as the town I came to live in some dozen years ago. Large areas of what were then open deserts have been stripped of their natural growth, covered with hastily built houses crowded one upon another and, at best, now surrounded by struggling grass plots which not only require the expenditure of precious water but are aesthetically unsatisfying because they simply do not fit the landscape. Twelve years ago the Catalina Mountains, ten miles from my front porch, stood out in clear bold outline made changingly beautiful with each shift of shadows from sunrise to sunset. Today it is rare to see them not blurred by haze, and from the summit one looks down upon a pall of smoke and dust which lies like an ugly lake over the town. Newcomers are quite right to ask me where are the clean pure air and the sparkling night skies which I described so enthusiastically in my first book about the desert. "Progress" has taken away from me both my invigorating air and my brilliant stars.

No doubt some of all this is an inevitable result of the exploding population of the United States. But the major effort of the community has been not to mitigate but increase it. Many of those who first came here because Tucson was what it then was have most illogically done all they could to turn it into something else. "We mustn't," they say, "stagnate." . . . But why was it necessary to "promote" the community by making it their chief effort to destroy its uniqueness and to "bring industry" to a region which should never be industrialized? Why could they not have invited especially those people and encouraged especially those activities for which this region is suited? I have sometimes been asked ironically if my own books had not encouraged in a small way the influx of population which I deplore. But at least, so I think, if it brought anyone here it was the kind of person who would appreciate what I tried to describe rather than the kind which would destroy it.

Recently the climax of absurdity was reached when the Mayor and the Chamber of Commerce bestirred themselves as they never have in the interests of preserving any desirable feature of the region as a place to live. And for what? To make sure that the Armed Forces would ring the city with Titan missile bases, thus making Tucson (so we are told by responsible authorities) one of the most dangerous places in the United States to live should war break out. Why? Because it is a patriotic duty? Not at all. Because it will bring more people and more money to our town.

When it was definitely announced that the boon would be conferred upon us, the city fathers rejoiced publicly— though I suspect that by now they are beginning to doubt whether, even from the promoter's standpoint, the bases are an advantage.

Some people at least do not choose the slopes of a volcano as an ideal place to live. And unfortunately those who are attracted only by the commercial opportunities provided by a multimillion-dollar enterprise are precisely the kind most likely to be completely indifferent to what the Southwest alone has to offer.

A few years ago I was put in a position where it was difficult to refuse an invitation from the Rotary Club to speak briefly at one of its luncheons on the subject, "Tucson as a Place for Writers." I decided that, instead of being politic and polite, I would let myself go. It was still, I said, a fairly good place. But it was a much less good one than it had been when I had come not long before. And it was becoming decreasingly so with every passing day. "Whenever I see one of those posters which reads 'Help Tucson Grow,' I say to myself, 'God forbid.' I suggest that the Rotary Club adopt a new motto: 'Keep Tucson Small'!"

Next day the brief item in the local newspaper said: "Most of the audience assumed that Dr. Krutch had a tongue in his cheek." But why should they have supposed anything of the sort? Only because they found it impossible to imagine that anyone would put a healthy, pleasant, and beautiful environment before such things as the possibility of making a good profit in a real estate deal. Still, such people do exist and they are the kind who first chose to live in Tucson.

An "inquiring reporter" on the same newspaper told me that he stopped a number of people on the street, asked the following questions and got, almost invariably, the following answers:

"Do you like to see more industry brought to Tucson?"

"Yes."

"Do you think that would make our city a pleasanter place to live?"

"No."

"Then why do you want industry brought here?"

"Well, you can't oppose Progress, can you?"

Nothing could illustrate more simply what is perhaps the most fundamental and dangerous error of our civilization:

the tendency to make size, wealth, and power as the highest goods to which both the spiritual and the physical health of human beings must be sacrificed. We no longer ask "What is a Good Life?"; but only what is a "prosperous" one.

Not even the most simple and obvious steps are taken to preserve the special amenities of desert living. Even the zoning laws which were supposed to do just that have become a farce. When I acquired my few acres, the regulations forbade more than one house per two acres. Now I am within the city limits and four houses per acre is the permissible number. When an area is zoned as for residence only, that means merely that you can't put a commercial building there —until someone wants to. Then the zoning will be changed. Who wants such changes? Not usually the people who hoped to continue to live under the conditions which led them to build a house there in the first place, but rather those who want to move out and make a profit.

Does all this mean that the desert, with all it has meant to many of us and might mean to generations still to come, is doomed to disappear in the not too distant future—unless indeed a fundamental change of heart should take place in the majority of the citizens who direct our destinies? Perhaps. Perhaps, on the other hand, there is a partial solution— namely the preservation of some sections of it as public land explicitly reserved in Parks, Monuments, and Wilderness Areas. It is far more rewarding to be able to *live* in the desert than merely to visit it. But that is at least better than nothing and the recognition of "wilderness areas" (including desert wildernesses) as having a value for and in themselves is a step forward.

Even that is being strenuously opposed. Against it two arguments are raised. One is that we simply cannot afford to withdraw from possible "use" any more of our country. The other argument is that comparatively few will visit genuine wilderness areas as distinguished from "developed" National Parks, and that it is therefore "undemocratic" to set them aside.

But to these two arguments there are two good answers. One is that the minority which would visit the wildernesses is not an insignificant one, and that respect for minority rights is the reverse of "undemocratic." The other is that the mere knowledge that areas of unspoiled nature do exist can mean something even to those who never visit them. The old frontier has affected the imagination of millions of Americans who never saw it. They knew that it was there and that they could reach it if they wished. So too, the wilderness, whether of forest or desert, is still a home of the imagination. It is something to be dreamed about and read about, something still there, not something lost forever.

Should I ever be compelled to live elsewhere, and know that I should never see the desert again, it would still be some consolation to realize that it still existed to comfort and delight others.

We have reached another crisis similar to that successfully passed in the days of Theodore Roosevelt when the cry "conservation" was first raised. The problem is more difficult now than it was then for the simple reason that available areas have shrunk at the same time that more of them are being claimed as indispensable to the practical needs of a fast growing nation. We shall certainly not reach a solution unless we want to, unless a sufficient number of us are convinced that nature has something to say to man's mind, to his spirit, and to his aesthetic sense which technology with all its wonders and all its benefits cannot supply the lack of.

Secretary of the Interior Stewart Udall has recently suggested that 2 per cent of the area of our country be reserved in the form of areas where nature holds sway and creates the beauties which only she can create. Some—many I fear— see no good reason why we should do anything of the sort. But can anyone sincerely maintain that we "cannot afford"

2 per cent of this great continent for any purpose regarded even by a minority as useful? We are not that poor in either land or resources.

Wilderness as more than a tonic

[1963]

In 1962 the Sierra Club of California published a magnificent book of seventy-two large color photographs by Eliot Porter. Though I wrote a brief introduction for it, this is not a plug. As a matter of fact my subject did not begin to worry me until the introduction was in type and I learned for the first time that the title of the book was to be *In Wilderness Is the Preservation of the World*.

"Oh dear," I said to myself, "that is a foolish title." Nature lover though I am, this is going too far. "Wildness is a tonic and a refreshment. I think we are losing something as it disappears from our environment. But to call it 'the preservation of the world' is pretty farfetched." True, I doubt that we can be saved by increased production or by trips to the moon. In fact, I sometimes doubt that we can be saved at all. But wildness! Now really!

Another shock came when I learned that the phrase is a quotation from Henry David Thoreau. Henry, I know, confessed his love of exaggeration and once said his only fear was the fear he might not be extravagant enough. But he rarely said anything really foolish. I thought I had better look up the context. And not to keep the reader in suspense (if I may flatter myself that I have generated any) I must confess that I have come to the conclusion that what Henry said is neither foolish nor an exaggeration. It is a truth almost as obvious as "the mass of men lead lives of quiet desperation."

Here is the context: "The West of which I speak is but another name for the Wild, and what I have been preparing to say is, that in Wildness is the preservation of the World. Every tree sends its fibers forth in search of the Wild. The cities import it at any price. Men plow and sail for it. From the forests and wilderness come the tonics and barks which brace mankind."

What is this wildness Thoreau is talking about? It is not D. H. Lawrence's Dark Gods and neither is it the mindless anarchy of some current anti-intellectuals. Those are destructive forces. Thoreau's wildness is, on the other hand, something more nearly akin to Bernard Shaw's Life Force— it is that something prehuman which generated humanity. From it came a magnificent complex of living things long, long before we were here to be aware of them, and still longer before we, in our arrogance, began to boast that we were now ready to take over completely; that henceforth we in our greater wisdom would plan and manage everything, even, as we sometimes say, direct the course of evolution itself. Yet if—as seems not unlikely—we should manage or mismanage to the point of self-destruction, wildness alone will survive to make a new world.

Like so much that Thoreau wrote, this appeal to wildness as the ultimate hope for survival is more relevant and comprehensible in the context of our world than it was in his. A few of his contemporaries—Melville and Hawthorne, for instance—may have already begun to question the success of the human enterprise and the inevitability of progress. But life as it is managed by man was becoming increasingly comfortable and seemingly secure. Men were often anxious (or as Thoreau said "desperate") concerning their individual lives. But few doubted that mankind *as a whole* was on the right track. Theirs was not yet an age of public, over-all anxiety. That mankind might plan itself into suicide occurred to nobody. Yet, though few today put such hopes as they have managed to maintain in anything except the completer dependence upon human institutions and inventions, the possibility that we have too little faith in "wildness" is not quite so preposterous a suspicion as it seemed then.

In a world which sits, not on a powder keg, but on a hydrogen bomb, one begins to suspect that the technician who rules our world is not the master magician he thinks he is but only a sorcerer's apprentice who does not know how to turn off what he turned on—or even how to avoid blowing himself up.

Should that be what he at last succeeds in doing, it would be a relatively small disaster compared with the possibility that he might destroy at the same time all that "wildness" which generated him and might generate in time something better. Perhaps there is life (or shall we call it "wildness") on other planets, but I hope it will remain on ours also. "Pile up your books, the records of sadness, your saws and your laws. Nature is glad outside, and her merry worms will ere long topple them down."

This wildness may often be red in tooth and claw. It may be shockingly careful of the type but careless of the single life. In this and in many other respects we are unwilling to submit to it. But somehow it did, in the end, create the very creatures who now criticize and reject it. Nor can we be so certain as we once were that we can successfully substitute entirely our competence for nature's. Nature is, after all, the great reservoir of energy, of confidence, of endless hope, and of that joy not wholly subdued by the pale cast of thought but which seems to be disappearing from our human world. Rough and brutal though she sometimes seems in her far from simple plan, it did work, and it is not certain that our own plans will.

A very popular concept today is embodied in the magic work cybernetic—or self-regulating. "Feedback" is the secret of our most astonishing machines. But the famous balance of nature is the most extraordinary of all cybernetic systems. Left to itself it is always self-regulated. The society we have created is not, on the other hand, cybernetic at all. The wisest and most benevolent of our plannings requires constant attention. We must pass this or that law or regulation, then we must redress this balance of production and distribution, taking care that encouraging one thing does not discourage something else. The society we have created puts us in constant danger lest we ultimately find ourselves unable to direct the more and more complicated apparatus we have devised.

A really healthy society, so Thoreau once wrote, would be like a healthy body which functions perfectly without our being aware of it. We, on the other hand, are coming more and more to assume that the healthiest society is one in which all citizens devote so much of their time to arguing, weighing, investigating, voting, propagandizing, and signing protests in a constant effort to kep a valetudinarian body politic functioning in some sort of pseudo-health that they have none of that margin for mere living which Thoreau thought important. It's no wonder that such a situation generated beatniks by way of a reaction.

Many will no doubt reply that Thoreau's ideal sounds too close to that of the classical economists who trusted the cybernetic free competition of Herbert Spencer *et al.* and that it just doesn't work. But is it certain that our own contrary system is working very well when it produces, on the one hand, a more or less successful welfare state and, on the other, an international situation which threatens not only welfare but human existence itself?

Should the human being turn out to be the failure some began a generation or more ago to call him, then all is not necessarily lost. Unless life itself is extinguished nature may begin where she began so long ago and struggle upward again. When we dream of a possible superman we almost invariably think of him as a direct descendant of ourselves. But he might be the flower and the fruit of some branch of the tree of life now represented only by one of the "lower" (and not necessarily anthropoid) animals.

When I recommend that we have a little more faith in the ultimate wisdom of nature, I am not suggesting that national parks, camping trips, and better bird-watching are the last best hope of mankind. But I do believe them useful reminders that we did not make the world we live in and that its beauty and joy, as well as its enormous potentialities, do not depend entirely on us. "Communion with nature" is not merely an empty phrase. It is the best corrective for that hubris from which the race of men increasingly suffers. Gerard Manley-Hopkins, unwavering Catholic Christian though he was, could write:

> What would the world be, once bereft
> Of wet and wildness? Let them be left,
> O let them be left, wildness and wet;
> Long live the weeds and the wilderness yet.

The modern intellectual feels very superior when he contemplates the cosmology unquestioningly accepted by his ancestors. Their view of the universe was always so quaintly homocentric. Everything must find its ultimate explanation in man's needs. There was only God's Will on the one hand and the natural world which He created for man's convenience on the other. But we have only exchanged one kind of homocentric cosmology for another. For God's Will we have, to be sure, substituted the mindless mechanism of Darwinian evolution and assumed that a mere accident put us in a position to take advantage of what chance created. But in at least one respect we have only arrived by a different route at the same conclusion as our benighted ancestors: Only we count. Only we have minds. Only we can escape from absurdity. Only we, lifting ourselves by our own bootstraps, can save ourselves.

Pure Darwinism insists that we were elevated to what we regard as our exalted state by sheer accident followed by ineluctable necessity and that if nature seems to have been wise that is sheer illusion. But perhaps there was some wisdom as well as blank necessity in her processes. Man needs a context for his life larger than himself; he needs it so desperately that all modern despairs go back to the fact that he has rejected the only context which the loss of his traditional gods has left accessible. If there is any "somehow good" it must reside in nature herself. Yet the first item of our creed is a rejection of just that possibility.

"Nature books" generally get kindly reviews even from those who regard them as no more than the eccentric outpourings of harmless hobbyists. For that reason it was a salutary shock to come across in the admirable but not sufficiently well-known magazine *Landscape* an excoriation of the whole tribe of nature writers in a review by Professor Joseph Slate of a book to which I had contributed a chapter. Its author calls us for the most part mere triflers in the genteel tradition, too devoted to the gentler pages of Thoreau and Muir, too little aware of the Dark Gods.

He has, to put it mildly, a point. We do not dig deep enough. We slip too easily into a spinsterish concern with the pretty instead of the beautiful. We tend to get only just far enough away from the "cute" to think of the natural world as primarily a gentle consolation instead of a great force, and we are content to experience it only superficially.

He is also quite right when he accuses us of quoting too seldom those passages of Thoreau which face, as we hesitate to face, things dark enough in one way if not exactly in the way which D. H. Lawrence celebrated.

Consider, for example, the passage from *Walden* which begins: "We can never have enough of nature." Stop there and you might conclude that he was about to embark upon just the kind of discourse Professor Slade finds so objectionable. But read on and you will come in the next sentence to wildness at its most wild:

> We can never have enough of nature. We must be refreshed by the sight of inexhaustible vigor, vast and titanic features, the sea coast with its wrecks, the wilderness with its living and its decayed trees, the thunder cloud, and the rain which lasts three weeks and produces freshets. We need to witness our own limits transgressed, and some life pasturing freely where we never wander. . . . I love to see that nature is so rife with life that myriads can be afforded to be sacrificed and suffered to prey on one another; that tender organizations can be so serenely squashed out of existence like pulp,—tadpoles which herons gobble up, and tortoises and toads run over in the road; and that sometimes it has rained flesh and blood! . . . Poison is not poisonous after all, nor are any wounds fatal.

This is not the world we made and it is not the world we hope for. Neither is it the one where Thoreau himself most often felt at home. But it is at least an all but inexhaustible potentiality. Powerful as our weapons are, vast as is the destruction we are capable of, there is something still more powerful than we. That something is in part the least amiable but also the oldest and most enduring aspect of what Thoreau called "wildness" and it may survive when we have destroyed the better order we tried to make. To remind ourselves of its existence is only one (but not the least important) of the rewards for those who "in the love of Nature hold communion with her visible forms."

Thoreau was not a pessimist. He had faith in man's potentialities though little respect for the small extent to which man had realized them. He did not believe, as some do to-day, that man was a failure beyond redemption—he believed only that his contemporaries were failures because the true way had been lost a long time ago and primitive man (still a savage even if a noble one) had taken the wrong road toward what he mistakenly believed to be wisdom and happiness. Thoreau's return to nature was a return to the fatal fork, to a road not taken, along which he hoped that he and others after him might proceed to a better future.

Please note that he called "wildness" merely the "preservation" not the "redemption" or the "salvation" of the world. It may well be that its redemption may depend upon aspects of nature almost exclusively human. But man of the present day is more and more inclined to feel that mere survival or preservation is all he can hope for in the immediate future. If he is indeed granted a second chance to discover a genuinely good life, it may require him to go far back to that point where the road not taken branched off from the dubious road we have been following for so long and which we more and more stubbornly insist is the only right one because it takes us further and further away from the nature out of which we arose.

How far back would we have to go to find that road not taken? Could we, even supposing that we wanted to find it, reverse the direction in which our civilization is moving; or are the Marxians right and man is not a free agent but inevitably the captive of evolving technology that carries him along with it willy-nilly.

Thoreau thought he had an answer: "Simplify!" We get what we want and if things are in the saddle it is because we have put them there. And I have no doubt that he would say, "If you have hydrogen bombs that you are beginning to suspect you don't really want, it is because you have for too long believed that power was the greatest of goods and did not realize soon enough that it would become, as it now has, a nemesis."

Perhaps he was right and perhaps if we don't have a change of heart, if we don't voluntarily simplify, we and our civilization will be simplified for us in a grand catastrophe. That would take us a good deal further back than is necessary to find the road not taken.

If you don't mind my saying so . . . [XI]

[1960]

Thanks to a gift from a generous foundation, the University of Arizona recently has been able to buy an electron microscope. A number of institutions now have them; and wherever one is put into operation scientists working in many different fields queue up, waiting their turn to give the camera a peek at something so inconceivably small that no one has ever been able to see it, even indirectly, before.

More than half a century ago the optical microscope was perfected to the point that it had actually reached the theoretical limit of resolution set by the wave length of light. It was commonly assumed that we should never be able to see or to photograph anything that a magnification of something like two thousand diameters was not sufficient to make visible to the eye. Now beautiful, sharp photographs more than a hundred thousand times larger than life are routine; and, although the theoretical limits have not yet been reached, the difference between what the best an optical microscope can do and what the electron microscope is theoretically capable of is as great as the difference between the naked eye and the best "old-fashioned" microscope. Atoms are still too small to be seen, but many molecules are not. The flu virus, which a few years ago was something that could only be inferred, can now have its picture taken: it turns out to be a homely, harmless-looking sphere, with a curious tail two or three times the length of the sphere's diameter. Its innocent appearance is no great surprise, for the relatively gigantic bacillus of Asiatic cholera looks no more alarming.

All this interests me somewhat more than it does most other laymen simply because I have never entirely given up the habit acquired in boyhood of spending a few hours every now and then with an optical microscope as good as I have any business owning. I am unlikely to change over to the electron because the technique is for specialists only and also because the instruments come rather high—forty or fifty thousand dollars for a reasonably good one, I am told. There is, moreover, a theoretical aspect of the whole business that interests me even more because it relates to a situation I find myself pondering from time to time, and was called to mind again by a few sentences in the introduction to a recent book entitled *The World of the Electron Microscope* (Yale University Press) by Ralph W. G. Wyckoff, one of the great technical experts.

The scientist has, he points out, come to be more and more dependent upon instruments that enable him to deal with things inaccessible to any of the five senses. Until quite recently the most important of such instruments—notably the telescope and the microscope—merely extended the *range* of sight, giving us what are, in effect, merely better eyes. The world which they reveal is the same world we see with our own visual sense and is apprehended in the same way. Moreover, this is almost equally true of the electron microscope. Although it is, like the great telescopes, most effective when used to take photographs that the eye then examines, the photographs are recognizable images like those formed by the eye itself.

On the other hand, most of the other new instruments upon which the scientist has been compelled to depend in his efforts to penetrate deeper and deeper into the secrets of the physical universe are of a different kind. The cloud chamber and even the Geiger counter do no more than enable the physicist to *infer* the existence of the particles with which they deal. The traces left on a photographic plate by cosmic rays are not images of the particles responsible for them but merely tracks. And because we are getting so far from what can be seen, touched, or smelled, it becomes increasingly difficult for the physicist to construct, on the basis of his inferences, even a theoretical model understandable in visual or tactile terms. Light is a wave, or a particle, or neither, or both. In despair he may be driven to say, as some have said, that reality is simply incomprehensible and unimaginable —which may, in part, mean that it can only be inferred from, never really perceived by, the senses that our minds must use to form even a mental image.

It is something of this kind, I think, that Wyckoff has in mind when he contrasts the electron microscope with other recent instruments. "The world of invisible radiations revealed is an enlargement of the world our eyes actually see and not a fundamentally different one; and we can interpret what they show in long-familiar ways without the possibilities of error that are always present with those more elegant forms of experimentation where the observation is several intellectual steps removed from the explanatory picture to which it points."

It may seem to be stretching a point to speak of photographic images of a virus magnified seventy thousand times or of a group of protein molecules magnified one hundred and ten thousand times as part of the common-sense world.

But what Wyckoff is saying is that, in actual fact, they are much nearer to this common-sense world than much with which the modern physicist finds himself compelled to deal and, sometimes, to attempt to explain to the layman who is now becoming more thoroughly convinced than at any time since the supernatural went out of fashion that things are far from being what they seem.

I do not think it is an overinterpretation to say that Wyckoff finds reassurance in the common-sense aspect of the electron microscope in an age that finds itself compelled to attach less and less importance to what it can see, hear, or feel. Moreover, it is upon this lessening importance of the world of sense and of some of the consequences of it that I find myself often speculating.

The human mind, imagination, and spirit did, after all, develop in a world of consciousness generated by our senses where what things *seem* is much more important than what they *are*. Even today we lead our ordinary lives in accord with the assumption of what Santayana called "animal faith"; and animal faith is, essentially, the assumption that things are what they seem. Our most intimate and personal decisions and actions are directed by, and our most vivid emotional experiences (including the aesthetic) are based upon, an acceptance of it. Yet while this continues to be true, we are increasingly aware that animal faith is almost wholly a delusion—at least in the opinion of what seem to be the profoundest intellects of our time. We "know" that the sun doesn't rise, that roses are not really red, and that solid objects are not solid. Nevertheless, the rising sun, the red rose, and the solid earth we tread have been, at least until now, the most real parts of our actual experience.

According to one theory of history, the degree to which a civilization may be called "advanced" is measured by the amount of power it has at its disposal. Although we command power to an extent that would have been unimaginable at any previous time, we summon it by the exercise of abstract thought, and it appears (or rather doesn't actually "appear" at all) in the form of invisible forces and fluids. We used to see the water wheel working until we exchanged it for the somewhat less obvious steam engine, and then exchanged the steam engine for the electric motor that goes round and round for no visible reason. The vacuum tube in which almost nothing seems to be happening gives way to the transistor that performs its miracles soundlessly, without motion or any visible or audible activity. So far as any naïve observer can see, it is pure hocus-pocus—not technology but mere magic. To most of those who snap switches and push buttons it is all as mysterious as it would be if they were summoning genii by rubbing a lamp. Even the engineer or the theoretical physicist lives in a world which is retreating further and further from the reach of the five senses that remain useful chiefly, not to make any direct contact with his world, but merely to read the instruments by means of which that world may be inferred.

A Helen Keller, blind and deaf, learned to infer what the world of the normal human being is like from signals reaching her consciousness from the blankness of a space without light or sound; and so far as what we now believe "reality" to be we are all in a somewhat similar situation, clutching at such tenuous data as the streaks left by a particle on a photographic plate or inferring from the slight displacement of the red band in a spectroscope that nebulae a billion light years away are rushing farther onward at some meaningless speed.

Moreover, our increasing willingness to assume that things are very different from what they seem is not confined to the nature of the physical universe. Animal faith assures us, for example, that we know our own minds and that our consciousness is the most real and most trustworthy part of ourselves. But we are told, are coming to believe, and are trying more and more to act upon the contrary assumption: namely, that our unconsciousness is a larger and often a more important part of ourselves; that our decisions are not made for the reasons we think we make them; that our desires are not what we believe them to be; and that our likes or dislikes are not based upon the rational sense of value by which they seem to us to be justified.

What the more sociological aspects of "the science of man" tell us about ourselves is almost equally at variance with what seems to be. The uniqueness that is so important to us, and that we think we recognize only somewhat less vividly in others, is declared to be also largely an illusion. We and they are said to think and feel and want in accordance with the patterns of our class. Our sense of what is right and proper, good taste and bad, is the prejudice of our culture. And yet, so far as our conscious life is concerned, the reverse is true. We feel that we have the power of choice, that we are virtuous or wicked, refined or coarse. And the more we accept the statement that all this is a delusion, the greater the conflict between animal faith and intellectual conviction. Our consciousness, so we are asked to believe, is as misleading as our senses, and what the mind seems to be is as different as physical reality from what the one and the other really are. Yet it is even more difficult to accept wholly and without conflict the substitution of this view of "things as they really are" for our animal faith in things as they seem than it is to agree wholly and without conflict with the physicists who tell us that our senses have misled us absurdly when we accept the version of physical reality that these senses have foisted upon us.

In some respects our situation is rather like that of the men who lived in "the age of faith" when they also were told and they tried to believe that they too ought to live, not by animal faith in the reality of things as they seem, but by a religious faith in the unseen drama of God versus the Devil, and the claims of this world versus the claims of the next. Yet their example affords but dubious assistance since history suggests that, a few holy men excepted, they acted most of the time as though they did not really believe what they professed. Can we or should we attempt to do more? What sort of adjustment will we ultimately make?

One possible answer is "Let us cultivate our garden"—in a sense more far-reaching than Voltaire had in mind. Let us, in other words, live our lives, cultivate our emotions, and make our value judgments in terms of the world as our sense-limited minds and imaginations present it to us. If that world is more real to us than the world of things-as-they-are, then we can live most successfully in that less real world which is also the world of many of the most resplendent creators and teachers civilization has ever known.

So far as our own inner experience and much of our relationship with other human beings is concerned, this is a practical solution, and it has had some support from some of the leading philosopher-scientists of the present day. At least it is, I take it, something like what is in the minds of James B. Conant and P. W. Bridgman. Speaking of the attempt to unify physical science, biology, psychology, sociology, and ethics, Conant once said, "My preference would be for more adequate exploration of limited areas of experience." More recently Bridgman, in his subtle and far-ranging book *The Way Things Are,* seems to reach much the same conclusion when he suggests that psychology and sociology have failed (and probably always will fail) in their attempt to achieve the kind of objectivity that would make them analagous to the physical sciences; that they fail just because we cannot deal with man without recognizing the importance of man-as-he-seems to himself, however different we may believe that to be from man as merely a part of some total physical reality.

Such answers as these to one aspect of the question leave

even those willing to accept them still faced with the other
aspect of the question, namely, that of how to live philo-
sophically as well as practically with the unthinkable physical universe of the physicists. And to that question an answer
diametrically opposite to "Let us cultivate our garden" is
sometimes given. "Let us," say those who give it, "cease cher-
ishing a nostalgia for the garden from which we have been
exiled and which was, after all, something less than a paradise." Man's intellect, they go on, is greater than either his
senses or his emotions. Why should he not be glad to live
more and more in it and to welcome increasing abstraction
if it leads him into a clearer, purer reality than that of the
Platonic cave to which he has always been confined? Pure
intellect works even in technology; and the time may come
when supermen, freed from sense and passion, have become
indeed like gods who need no longer disturb their contemplation of the ineffable even to the extent of pushing a but-
ton, for by then they will be capable of merely thinking
into action whatever apparatus may still be necessary to
supply any residual physical needs.

Something like this seems to have been Bernard Shaw's
vision at the end of *Back to Methuselah*. If I ask, by way of
objection, who really wants to be a Shavian Ancient, I suppose I might be met with the counter question, "What ape, if
asked, would have said that he wanted to be a man?" To that
I know no fully satisfactory reply, although I still feel that
my proper home is under the dome of many-colored glass
rather than where I should be dazzled by the white radiance
of eternity. There is too much of the past and present of
man I should hate to give up. And if that is merely a an-
ticipatory nostalgia for the cave, I can say only that I feel
already the nostalgic twinge.

If you don't mind my saying so . . . [XII]

[1959]

The year 1956 marked two centenaries, oddly assorted but not without connection. After all, Mozart and Shaw both made Don Juan a hero, and the second thought so highly of the first that he called Sarastro's arias "the only music ever written which would not be out of place in the mouth of God."

This year again offers two centenaries, again one hundred years apart and even odder in conjunction: *Rasselas* and *The Origin of the Species*. Still, in this case also, it is not too farfetched to note one similarity. Both are moral works in intention as well as in effect, for however "pure" Darwin's original intention may have been, one need only read the concluding paragraphs of *The Origin of the Species* to realize that he foresaw and approved what so many were soon to accept as a death blow to theism in any significant form.

Huxley may have more carefully dotted the *i*'s and crossed the *t*'s, but the tinge of wishful thinking is plain in both. Both had been understandably irritated by the obscurantist meddling of theologians in scientific discussion—and both felt that the surest way to get rid of this once and for all was to strike at the root. As Darwin wrote in a suppressed but recently recovered passage from his autobiographical sketch, he could not understand how anyone could want Christianity to be true.

Rasselas proclaims a mystery at the heart of man and the universe: "Every beast that strays beside me has the same corporeal necessities with myself: he is hungry and crops the

grass, he is thirsty and drinks the stream; his thirst and hunger are appeased, he is satisfied and sleeps, he arises again
and is hungry; he is again fed and is at rest. I am hungry and
thirsty like him, but when thirst and hunger cease I am not
at rest; I am like him pained with want, but am not like him
satisfied with fulness. . . . Man surely has some latent sense
for which this place affords no gratification. . . ."

Darwin, instead of proclaiming and accepting a mystery,
announced the end of one. The Middle Ages had believed
that logic and metaphysics demonstrated the existence of
God; the eighteenth century, including the author of *Rasselas,* believed that the strongest argument was the historical
one embodied in the vast literature of Christian evidences.
But by the nineteenth century, metaphysics was distrusted
and Christian evidences had been eroded away by historical
criticism. Nothing substantial seemed to remain except the
"argument from design." "The existence of a watch presup-
poses the existence of a watchmaker. And how much more
intricate is living nature than any watch!" But living nature,
said Darwin, can do what a watch cannot. It can make itself,
and the grand theory of natural selection shows how. The
necessity for a watchmaker remains; the necessity for a creator directly responsible for man has faded away. Man is an
animal who became what he now is because it was inevitable;
because, for clearly demonstrable reasons, he could not help
doing so. The universe runs itself. Newton had shown how
the inanimate part of it could do just that; Darwin, so at
least he thought, had shown how the animate could do the
same.

Neither Newton nor Darwin saw any logical necessity for
denying the possible existence of an aboriginal creator. Newton, of course, spoke of him with genuine faith; Darwin with
what may or may not have been merely a willingness to
make a conventional concession when he wrote in the very
last sentence of the *Origin:* "There is grandeur in this view

of life, with its several powers, having been originally breathed by the Creator into a few forms, or into one; and that, whilst this planet has gone cycling on according to the fixed law of gravity, from so simple a beginning endless forms most beautiful and most wonderful have been, and are being evolved." But a creator who thus completely retired from the universe billions of years ago and, if he still exists, exists only in some Lucretian isolation and indifference, is no longer of any importance. As for what Johnson called "some latent sense for which this place affords no gratification," man simply could not possibly be cursed with anything of the sort because utility is the sole criterion recognized in the course of natural selection, and a desire for which there is no possible gratification cannot be useful.

If the author of *The Origin of the Species* ever expressed any opinion of Johnson or of *Rasselas,* I do not know of it; but by a curious coincidence Johnson dismissed Darwin in advance. Although he had died too soon to have heard much, if anything, of even Charles Darwin's evolutionist grandfather Erasmus, he was acutely and scornfully aware of Lord Monboddo's hope that, sooner or later, a race of human beings still equipped with tails might turn up. And upon Monboddo he made one of his most rotund pronouncements: "Sir, it is all conjecture about a thing useless, even were it known to be true. Knowledge of all kinds is good. Conjecture, as to things useful is good; but conjecture as to what would be useless to know, such as whether men went upon all fours, is very idle."

But *The Origin of the Species* had an effect that neither Monboddo nor grandfather Erasmus could have had, just because it was presented not as speculation, but as truth very persuasively demonstrated. And the effect has been, in the long run, perhaps greater than that of any theory promulgated since Copernican astronomy.

As late as Monboddo's time the most often read book on the subject of man's place in nature was still the century-old *The Wisdom of God Manifested in the Works of the Creation* by the first great English biologist, John Ray. Now Darwin banished from the universe not only God responsible for these works, but also all wisdom of any sort, whether immanent or transcendent. And along with it went any possible meaning for such concepts as "purpose" and "meaning"— to say nothing of justice or virtue. Mere survival was left as the only conceivable *summum bonum,* the only criterion for any value judgment.

For more than a century the discovery and the contemplation of God's wisdom as manifest in the work of his creation had been the most generally proposed aim or justification for the study of nature. Neither this aim nor this justification any longer existed, and the only justification necessarily became the pursuit of a greater and more intimate familiarity with that unvarnished truth which, unpalatable though it might be, was supposed to be capable of setting men free from false hopes. Not only Darwin, of course, but Huxley also had moments of trying, in one way or another, to mitigate this bleak view. Both men were aware of the problem of values in an inhuman universe. Huxley could, on occasion, take refuge in the "I don't know" of his convenient new word "agnostic." But it is the bleakness that has triumphed. And it is a strange paradox that Darwin, who had, in his early days at least, so much of the loving warmth that was characteristic of the old naturalists, should have been responsible for the coldness that has seemed to so many biologists since his time the only respectable attitude.

Perhaps the modern view of the universe as no more than a battlefield upon which a struggle for survival is going on between a thousand different kinds of organisms, each mechanically perfecting itself as it perseveres in its attempt to eat while remaining uneaten as long as possible, actually is a tenable one. Perhaps nothing unifies the animate world except the universality of the struggle; and perhaps, therefore, nothing that could be called a general, over-all plan or tendency is present. But if this is true, then the modern concept strikes me as curiously similar to a very primitive one.

In the late Robert Marshall's *Arctic Wilderness* I happen to have read very recently his brief account of the Eskimo "world view" as it was explained to him by an old-timer. "Tobuk told me about the 'dooneraks' who were something like spirits, but a little less personal, and who were responsible for everything. . . . There were thousands and thousands of dooneraks, each with different ideas and objectives, often thoroughly antagonistic, and the happenings of the world represented the balance between their innumerable objectives.

Substitute for dooneraks the isolated wills to live of innumerable species, and the mere melee that results is very similar to Darwin's world. Moreover, if the Darwinian balance of nature is much like the balance achieved by the dooneraks, the two systems are also similar in the extent to which man may intervene and in the methods he must use to do so. Tobuk further confided to Mr. Marshall that "some order was brought among their chaotic competition through medicine men whose accomplishments always came through the dooneraks whom they controlled." Substitute for medicine men, controlling few or many dooneraks, biologists who know more or less about "the control of nature through a knowledge of nature's laws," and the general concept is much the same. Medicine man and biologist both play God in the absence of any God to play Himself. The chief difference between the two systems is that Tobuk would never have supposed that the anarchy of the dooneraks would somehow result in a steady progress toward perfection!

"It is the customary fate of new truths to begin as heresies and to end as superstitions." Thus said Thomas Henry Huxley himself. Has the theory of natural selection as the one and only truth about the nature of things come at length to illustrate that very dictum? Many, probably most, contemporary biologists reply with a firm "No." We have learned, they say, much more than Darwin knew. He believed some things that are not true—notably that acquired characteristics were inheritable—and he was ignorant of much, especially of the importance of mutations and the whole subsequent science of genetics. But new knowledge only confirms the all-sufficiency of his central contribution: natural selection is the sole and completely adequate explanation of evolution from protozoa to philosopher.

Yet even among scientists there are some who confess a certain degree of skepticism—not a doubt that natural selection operates and is important, but that it explains everything. Working hypotheses do not have to embody the whole truth in order to be exceedingly useful. It is obvious enough that the theory of natural selection served as a master key that opened the door upon innumerable secrets. But the time often comes when the working hypothesis bars the door to still further discoveries, as at last did the Newtonian hypothesis that every particle of matter in the universe behaves exactly like every other particle. Modern physics would be impossible if that once useful hypothesis had not been recognized as requiring qualification. And it is possible that too stubborn a faith in the adequacy of natural selection now stands in the way of new knowledge about the processes of life.

If one dared to go into metaphysics, difficulties of another sort might be raised. If nature knows no purposes and makes no value judgments, and if, at the same time, man is himself a part of nature, then from whence came his concepts of purpose and value? If they came from nature, then they are part of nature. If they do not come from nature, then man himself is touched by something outside nature's realm. The concept of purpose must be either immanent or transcendent.

This is an argument hardly to be entered upon lightly, and it would be better perhaps to turn instead to Dr. Johnson again as an illustration of a very fundamental premise so different from that of most modern men as to explain a great deal about the difference between the world of Darwin and the world in which Johnson lived: "The truth is that knowledge of external nature, and the sciences which that knowledge requires or includes, are not the great or the frequent business of the human mind. Whether we provide for action or conversation, whether we wish to be useful or pleasing, the first requisite is the religious and moral knowledge of right and wrong, the next is an acquaintance with the history of mankind, and with those examples which may be said to embody truth, and prove by events the reasonableness of opinions. Prudence and Justice are virtues and excellences of all times and of all places; we are perpetually moralists, but we are geometricians only by chance."

Today the vast majority of thinking men assume without argument that "knowledge of external nature" is the great, the frequent, and almost the only legitimate business of men. It is, they think, upon such knowledge of external nature that both our safety and the prosperity by which we set so much store depend. We are not perpetually moralists and geometricians only by chance. We have become geometers perpetually and moralists only by chance—if at all.

The most obvious result of the decision to consider knowledge of external nature the greatest, the most frequent, and perhaps the exclusive business of the human mind—actually quite well formulated before Johnson's time—is the physical world in which we live with all its wealth, power, and convenience, as well as its perhaps illusory security. The second most obvious result is the loss of Johnson's faith that "Prudence and Justice are virtues and excellences of all times and all places," with the substitution for it of the various relativisms which have persuaded us to believe that prudence and justice are merely the traditions of a given society and that a moralist is merely a man who has not yet learned that morals are only mores.

Although Johnson was no doubt thinking only of physical sciences, Darwinism is merely an extension of them. One more result of the conviction that "knowledge of external nature" is, in fact, "the great and exclusive business of the human mind" is the Darwinian world in which man is merely an animal, and the animal merely a machine.

Between the two centenaries to be celebrated in 1959, there yawns a gulf that we may or may not someday cross again.

An open letter to George Bernard Shaw

[1956]

Grand Canyon, Ariz.

Dear Mr. Shaw,

I never met you quite face to face though I did glimpse you once at Cap d'Antibes—where you were very much the great man surrounded by a solicitous court. At that very minute I had in my pocket a letter of introduction which I did not deliver for the same reason I had not delivered a similar one in London a few years before. When the time came I couldn't quite imagine what I would say to you and I was a bit afraid of what you might say to me. For a moment at least you had once been aware of my name because in a Malvern program you had accused me (a horrible charge) of having "an insufficient respect for the Apocalypse"— which meant in this case that I had doubted the significance of some vatic utterances in one of your later plays.

Now that I am safe on the opposite side of the line which separates time from eternity I dare congratulate you on the hundredth anniversary which you almost made in this same world with me and to say that no other man ever had on the course of my life the influence you had. As an undergraduate who believed himself destined to be a mathematician I happened upon *Man and Superman* and as I read it at a library table I felt like Saul of Tarsus when the light broke. "If literature," I said to myself, "can be like this then literature is the stuff for me." And to this day I never see a differential equation written out without breathing a prayer of thanks.

I realize now that you were not quite the all-wise and all-eloquent superman I thought you then. You once said that Marx "made a man of you," but I am not sure that this same Marx should not be blamed instead for the grand inconsistency which makes it impossible to reconcile your materialistic determinism with the mystical creed which at profounder moments you preach. What would Marx have thought of the Life Force? Wouldn't he have called it an opium for the people? I realize also that your style, for all its vigor and wit, does not, as I thought then, embody every virtue a style can have. It has all the efficiency of the most smoothly operating machine. But sometimes it makes you seem what Macaulay was called, "a steam engine in trousers"—or rather a jet engine dressed up like a man. There isn't much charm in that. There is wit, and fun, and most of all the exhilaration of conscious power. But there isn't much gaiety of a more relaxed sort, and when one is tired of being jet-propelled one misses in your writing that touch of nature which would make us feel you one of us. Yeats was more than half right when he accused you of being the inventor of the only truly modern style—one whose principal excellence is the utilitarian virtue of saying what it wants to say with a single-minded efficiency as devoid of poetical suggestiveness as though no such thing had ever existed in literature. In one contemporary theory, wit and poetry are very closely alike, but your kind of wit is poetry's opposite.

Despite all this, however, I back your candidacy for what is somewhat exaggeratedly called "immortality." If only one writer of the first half of this century is read a hundred years from now I think it will be you. And I am not forgetting the incredulous protest the Joyceans would make to any such prophecy. I will rest my case on Dr. Johnson's dictum: "Nothing that is odd will do for long." Our descendants will at least know what you are talking about and they may very well think *Ulysses* as well as *Finnegans Wake* decidedly odd.

You will like to have it remembered that your centenary is also the centenary of Mozart—of whom you said that what he wrote for Sarastro to sing was "the only music ever written which would not be out of place in the mouth of God." Of course, you claimed to have improved *Don Giovanni* when you rewrote it as *Man and Superman*. Of course, you talked nonsense about the moonshine of Mozart as contrasted with the "simple realism" (!) of Wagner. But you knew the answer to all that as well as you knew the answer to your more famous question "Better than Shakespeare?" You knew that a *Don Giovanni* without music, figuratively as well as literally, could not be an improved version. But this is not a musical age and you did what you could—admitting by your tributes and to your great honor the worth of what you could not do.

You will notice that this letter is dated at a place from

which not many letters on literary subjects have ever come. This morning, when I did not yet know that I would be invited to send you a greeting, I spent with my wife sitting at the canyon's edge about twenty miles from the tourists' hotel where we were so utterly alone (except for the swallows dipping above and below us) that there was nowhere any reminder of any of the things which have been done in (and to) the world during the last few thousand years. It would have neither looked nor been any different if Newton and Watt and Faraday, to say nothing of Mozart and you, had never lived.

The first part of the morning I spent in looking for and finding a scrap of conglomerate stone from the age of the dinosaurs which is said to survive in the canyon only in small pieces and only at this secluded spot; to be also the very youngest rock found there because all that was formed during the millions of years since has been eroded away. The rest of the morning I spent distinguishing from afar the successive layers of stone whose age goes backward further and further until one comes to those tortured rocks of the inner gorge which are among the oldest exposed anywhere on the face of the earth, though they are said to be themselves only the roots of mountains worn away at a time far further removed from the age of the dinosaurs than that age is removed from ours. You yourself, Mr. Shaw, liked to talk about what the earth would be in a future which lies ahead "as far as thought can reach." What say you of the equally long prospect in the opposite direction? What sort of perspective is this in which to talk about "lasting values" and "literary immortality"?

Sometimes you talked as though nothing but recent man was worth a thought; sometimes as though what went on at a Borough Council meeting was more important than all the speculation ever indulged in or all the plays ever written. Sometimes, in other words, you pretended that only the here and now was worth thinking about. "Beware," you said, "of the man whose god is in the sky." But what of the message you sent when Lawrence Langner told you that O'Neill was anxious about the state of the world? "Tell him not to worry. If, as I believe, man is about to destroy himself he will be replaced by something better." Wasn't that taking a very long view indeed? Isn't it in a truly geological perspective? Wasn't it very much like what one dinosaur might have said to another (or, for that matter, one trilobite to another) when either dinosaur or trilobite realized that his day was over even though the day of both had lasted a great deal longer than that of man seems likely to last?

Had you been with me this morning I think you would have forgotten the Borough Council for a time and would have asked again what you asked so eloquently in *Back to Methuselah* and in more than one preface: "How did all of this come about?" And you would again have ranged yourself with Alfred Wallace against his triumphant collaborator-opponent Darwin. Forgetting Marx as well as orthodox biology, you would have insisted again that it did not happen because it could not help happening, that it was not merely the result of the dialectic of matter. You would have proclaimed again that the great dynamic forces of evolution are two: the Imagination which can see what might be and the Will which can bring the might-be about. You would have added that neither Imagination nor Will originated with man and it may be that none of the thousands of positions you so positively took up involves an issue more important.

With the deepest admiration and respect I am your reader from way back,

(signed) Joseph Wood Krutch.

If you don't mind my saying so . . . [XIII]

[1963]

I don't suppose many people today read that late eighteenth-century "must," Bishop William Paley's *Natural Theology*. I never expected to and I haven't really read it. But I did have occasion to take it down from a library shelf and dis-cover that it begins with the once unanswerable "argument from design" and presents it on the very first page via the classic watch-and-watchmaker routine. A watch is too intricate and purposeful to have merely happened. But the world—especially the world of living things—is far more intricate and more elaborately adapted to its needs. If the presence of a watch implies a watchmaker, how much more inevitably does a world imply a world-maker?

How the Bishop got from this to the Thirty-nine Articles or whether, indeed, he attempted to do so, I do not know. But the argument for some sort of theism must have seemed irrefutable and it is sufficient to explain why few of even the hardiest skeptics then believed less than what Deism pro-claimed. Lucretius' chance meeting of atoms was simply too farfetched even for those "who could believe anything pro-vided only it was not in the Bible."

Bishop Paley's contemporary, Lord Monboddo, was al-ready insisting that the orangutan was a close relative of man and another contemporary, Erasmus Darwin, was already pro-claiming: "The Great Creator of All things has infinitely developed the works of his hands, but has at the same time stamped a certain similitude on the features of nature that demonstrates to us, that the whole is one family of one parent." But although such hardy speculations might encourage certain doubts about the Garden of Eden they left untouched the argument for theism based on the watch and the watchmaker.

The last of the eight lavishly endowed *Bridgewater Treatises* on "the Goodness of God as manifested in the Creation," appeared in 1840 or less than twenty years before Charles Darwin was supposed to have knocked the props from under that and all similar enterprises, making "the argument from design" as irrelevant as Ptolemaic astronomy. What Darwin was undertaking to prove was nothing less than simply this: A watch cannot make itself but, given time enough, organisms have performed a similar although far more astonishing feat. He made complete atheism seem for the first time a tenable creed. Add natural selection to Lucretius' chance encounter of atoms and you had something that could, in a pinch at least, be believed.

Although there were always a few, even within the ranks of official science, who remained just outside the new orthodoxy (Alfred Russel Wallace himself was one), the overwhelming majority of competent scientific men merely shrugged them off as victims of an absurd residue of irrationality and took it as proved beyond dispute that the living world did indeed "just happen." Even the Deists' vague deity tended to vanish because there seemed no function left for him to perform and with him went the whole of the somewhat distantly related concept of Purpose. Evolution, so it was said, had a *tendency* toward greater elaboration. The fish *tended* to become the philosopher. But nothing *intended* anything.

I have read a good deal of popular and semi-popular natural history and biology and I think it clear that a certain vague dissatisfaction with the complete and all-inclusive explaining away of the wonders of the living watch is commoner in respectable quarters today than it was even a generation ago. The clear demonstration of what natural selection can do, apparently all by itself, involves rather simple things like protective coloration. It is a long way from them to any one of the hundreds of all but incredible organs, instincts, and behavior patterns and there seems to be an increasing tendency to doubt modestly and in a largely negative fashion that the whole process really is understood.

Those who share these modest doubts are often accused of mere wishful thinking, of merely wanting to find some hint of an escape from the blind, purposeless, and meaningless universe of strict Darwinism. Perhaps I share that wish but I do not believe it is the only reason why I often find myself thinking of the problem or why that thinking has led me to the conclusion that the whole phenomenon of evolution becomes easier to credit if the process is assumed to have involved certain forces the reality of which there is far more reason (on the basis of evidence) to believe in than to reject. These processes involve that concept of Purpose (or intention) which, so it seems to me, is so often rejected out of hand because it actually is not clearly defined. There is (to put it more modishly although not necessarily more clearly) a semantic confusion. To say that Purpose may have been involved in the process of evolution may be to say any one of at least three quite different things.

The first, oldest, and most common meaning of such a statement implies a transcendental power, usually personal, which is outside of and beyond everything else that exists and which directs the universe it created. This is quite precisely the watchmaker and the watch he made. A second possible meaning implies immanence rather than transcendence. The purpose assumed to exist is not outside of but inherent in the natural world; is indeed a natural, primordial part of it which has existed as long as anything has existed and is simply part of things as they are. In a sense the watch still makes itself but not so mechanically or so blindly as strict Darwinism implies. The first of these hypotheses is the one that orthodox science most vehemently repudiates and it is only slightly more tolerant of the second which it is likely to regard as little more than a second line of defense desperately constructed by a rear guard attempting to cover the rout of the superstitions before the advancing army of rationalism.

There is, however, a third possible sense in which Purpose may have played a part in evolution and it is one that seems to me to have been largely overlooked despite the fact that even the most mechanical theories of evolution would seem to suggest it. That man himself is capable of purpose in the simplest sense of the word, that he can, that is to say, adopt a means toward an end, is certainly not doubted by anyone who is not—as most orthodox evolutionists are not—wholly committed to the narrowest possible interpretation of a kind of dialectic materialism. But if man, who is himself an animal, is capable of effective intentions, why should one suppose that this is something entirely new in the universe rather than that it has always been to some extent, however slight, characteristic of living things?

Take the case of the tool that illustrates concretely the simplest form of purposefulness. It is true that there does not seem to be any exception to the oft-repeated statement that man is the only animal who *makes* tools. But other animals do *use* those that they find ready-made. Many of the primates use natural objects as instruments or weapons and tool-using is demonstrable much lower in the hierarchy, as in the two notable cases of the wasp that uses a pebble to tamp down the earth over the concealed opening of its nesting burrow and the comic pseudo-woodpecker (actually a finch) that digs insects from bark crevices with a twig just because, for some unknown reason, natural selection failed to provide him with the long slender bill characteristic of the true woodpeckers.

One may readily grant that the step from tool-using to toolmaking is a very important one. But is there any reason for supposing that there is an absolute discontinuity between the processes involved? In both cases a means to an end is adopted and there seems to be no reason for the categorical statement that purposefulness in the simple sense of an effective intention exists in the case of one and not in the other.

Yes, reply the stubborn, there is a reason. Tool-using arose as the result of random motions and the survival value of certain chance discoveries enabled natural selection to pick them out and to fix them as instincts. But again one must ask is there any compelling reason why this should be categorically asserted? Mere trial and error plays a certain part even in the new inventions of the most advanced technology and no doubt played a larger one in the earliest stages of man's toolmaking. Does not the whole concept of evolution incline one to the assumption that intention has played an increasingly important role rather than that it appeared suddenly in a world where everything else was evolving from simpler forms as the result of purely mechanical processes? The difference between the degree of intention that existed in the wasp or the finch may be as great as the difference between their brain and the human brain. But the one was nevertheless evolved from the other.

To me it seems exceedingly odd (and exceedingly inconsistent) that the more dogmatic the evolutionist the more strongly he insists upon the absolute uniqueness of man's mind while, at the same time, he indignantly rejects Alfred Wallace's stubborn insistence that this very uniqueness disproves the theory that the mind has been mechanically evolved from the mind of one of the lower animals. Only man, so orthodox evolution has often insisted, can reason in a sense utterly different from any mental process other animals are capable of; only he can have intentions. To attribute any of these things to any lower animal is to be guilty of "anthropomorphism." But if all higher things have evolved from simpler ones, then how on earth could man have evolved from these lower animals unless they were in some sense anthropomorphic?

"Evolution" and "discontinuity" are antithetical notions and I cannot explain the passion with which they have been simultaneously asserted except on the assumption that some "wishful thinking" is involved. A theory as revolutionary as Darwin's needs, if it is to be accepted, statement in the simplest and most absolute form possible. If the great role played by natural selection was to be recognized, it had to be explained with the fewest possible complications. Admit Purpose at all and the need for any such theory as Darwin's would have been much less obvious. The watch and watchmaker theory would have been much less easy to rout.

But the theory of evolution, in a very broad and very inclusive sense, is no longer in danger of rejection nor is anyone likely to doubt the importance of the role played by natural selection. On the other hand, many of the difficulties that still rise (increasingly, I believe) in the minds of thoughtful people vanish if one admits no more than the, to me, very reasonable supposition that something, no more perhaps than the slight advantage bestowed by purposefulness in the simple sense of effective intention, be admitted, no matter to how slight a degree. Those who reject it categorically are not winning support for what is essential in the theory of evolution but raising doubts about it. If anything could revive the watch and watchmaker analogy, it would be the belief that man is unique in possessing not merely reason but even the ability to intend. If he transcends all other animals, then what can he be except a special creation? If intention is a discontinuous phenomenon, then where does evolution come in? To reject it seems to me to put one right into the hands of the transcendentalist so far as man is concerned.

Much has been made in recent years of abstruse mathematical calculations intended to prove that natural selection will, in the long run, perpetuate a variation that has even a very slight survival value. But surely an equally slight push by an intention would be even more effective and I simply cannot see why, if enormous intelligence is assumed in the case of man descended from the lower animal, it is not reasonable rather than unreasonable to assume the possibility that such a push exists. Evidence against such an assumption is purely negative. "We cannot find it and don't know how we could demonstrate it," reply the mechanists; but that is a practical difficulty not a disproof and I suspect that the real reason for the dogmatic assertion that it does not exist is simply the result of a reluctance to admit that what would be hard to investigate may, nevertheless, be worth considering.

T. H. Huxley himself once wrote: "The materialistic position . . . is as utterly devoid of justification as the most baseless of theological dogmas. . . . But with a view to the progress of science, the materialistic terminology is in every way preferable."

For the time being he was certainly right. But unless you take the position that what is most fruitful pro tem is eternally true this is not conclusive. Newtonian physics was certainly fruitful but the time came when some parts of it had to be abandoned if further truths were to be established. There is no doubt that some of the most remarkable examples of what seemed to our ancestors proof of "design" occur among plants and among the very primitive animal organisms where the push if it existed at all must have been very slight. But there is no conclusive argument against the assumption that it existed from the beginning and increased slowly as time went on rather than that it emerged discontinuously at the moment when a primate became a man.

Two twentieth-century scientists of unquestioned technical competence—Lecomte du Noüy and Teilhard de Chardin

—explicitly reject purely mechanistic interpretations of evolution. If you dismiss them as merely victims of a religious and mystical quirk in their otherwise first-rate scientific minds there are others more cautious who admit doubts or at least confessions of ignorance. Jean Rostand, one of the greatest living French biologists, dismisses Lecomte du Noüy almost contemptuously but he nevertheless says flatly: "In my opinion we know practically nothing about the factors that determine the progressive diversification of living creatures." And that is a long way from the cocksureness of many neo-Darwinians. Sir Julian Huxley, as cautious a scientist as one could find, is orthodox enough when he writes that "natural selection converts accidents into apparent design." On the other hand, he admits in evolution a "desirable trend" toward "the higher" (not merely the more complex) and although he warns that "we have no right to regard this trend as embodying a cosmic purpose or a Divine Intention" he goes on to say that "If we take the monistic or unitary naturalistic view demanded by evolutionary logic, matter and mind cease to appear as separate entities; they are seen as two necessary attributes or aspects of the single universal world stuff." And to me, at least, this seems to suggest that mind might be operable on a very low level. Loren Eiseley goes further: "If 'dead' matter has reared up this curious landscape of fiddling crickets, song sparrows, and wondering men, it must be plain even to the most devoted materialist that the matter of which he speaks contains amazing, if not dreadful powers, and may not impossibly be, as Hardy has suggested, 'but one mask of many worn by the Great Face behind.' "

In quoting from these eminent authorities I do not mean to suggest that they would necessarily be sympathetic to all, or perhaps to any, of the notions I have been trying to put into words. But they do, so it seems to me, suggest that not all competent scientists believe the last word has been said on the question.